# THE KINGS' MISTRESSES

Marie Mancini reading her sister Hortense's fortune,
by Jacob Ferdinand Voet
*The Royal Collection © 2011 Her Majesty Queen Elizabeth II*

The Duchess Mazarin dressed as Diana, by Benedetto Gennari
*Courtesy of Sotheby's Picture Library*

# THE KINGS' MISTRESSES

*The Liberated Lives of*

MARIE MANCINI, PRINCESS COLONNA, AND
HER SISTER HORTENSE, DUCHESS MAZARIN

ELIZABETH C. GOLDSMITH

PUBLICAFFAIRS
NEW YORK

Published in the United States by PublicAffairs™,
a member of the Perseus Books Group

PublicAffairs books are available at special discounts for bulk purchases in the US by corporations, institutions, and other organizations. For more information, please contact the Special Markets Department at the Perseus Books Group, 2300 Chestnut Street, Suite 200, Philadelphia, PA 19103, call (800) 810-4145, ext. 5000, or e-mail special.markets@perseusbooks.com.

Book Design by Pauline Brown
Typeset in 12 point ITC Galliard by the Perseus Books Group

Library of Congress Cataloging-in-Publication Data

Goldsmith, Elizabeth C.
  The kings' mistresses : the liberated lives of Marie Mancini, Princess Colonna, and her sister Hortense, Duchess Mazarin / Elizabeth C. Goldsmith. — 1st ed.
     p. cm.
  Includes bibliographical references and index.
  ISBN 978-1-58648-889-5 (hardcover : alk. paper) — ISBN 978-1-58648-890-1 (e-book) 1. Mancini, Maria, 1639–1715? 2. Mazarin, Hortense Mancini, duchesse de, 1646–1699. 3. Louis XIV, King of France 1638–1715—Relations with women. 4. France—Court and courtiers—Social life and customs. 5. Mistresses—France—Biography 6. Women—Europe—Social life and customs—17th century. I. Title.
  DC130.M3G65 2012
  944'.03309252—dc23

                                                                    2011045731

First Edition

10 9 8 7 6 5 4 3 2 1

# CONTENTS

# AUTHOR'S NOTE

I FIRST ENCOUNTERED Marie and Hortense Mancini through their memoirs, as I was working on a historical study of French women writers. I was interested in how women in the early modern period told the story of their lives and how they thought about themselves as writers at a moment in European history when female writers began to sign their names to printed books. The two sisters were among the first to openly publish their life stories. As I read their narratives, I was amazed by their extraordinary daring—not only in their decision to go public with their private lives, but in the unfolding of the events themselves, which were tales of unbelievable adventure, worthy of a novel. Historians and chroniclers of the age of Louis XIV have tended to refer to Hortense and Marie either as scandalous pleasure-seekers or pathetic victims, usually pleasure-seekers who became pathetic victims. I saw them as bold, energetic, fascinating women who certainly loved pleasure but who also fought for their personal liberty and overcame obstacles so great that in the process they inspired other women of their generation and beyond.

My fascination with them began in 1995 and continued through a series of projects, each one ending with me thinking that I had finally finished my work on Marie and Hortense. But at each "end" of the road I saw another path beckoning. When Patricia Cholakian and I decided to work together on a new edition of Marie's memoirs, I wrote to the Colonna family, Marie's descendants, to see if I could access their family papers. I received no response, and then suddenly, a few months later, I heard that the Prince Colonna had decided to donate all of the family papers to a state library housed in a monastery two hours north of Rome. That news drew me into a series of visits to the Santa Scolastica library in Subiaco, Italy, where I kept searching for the original manuscript of Marie's memoirs, and I kept finding other papers and letters that seemed even more fascinating than the ones I was looking for. I never found the original manuscript but I read hundreds of letters written by Marie, her family and friends, and her obsessed husband. The adventures of Hortense, too, and the amazing travels of both sisters were woven through the accumulated letters that remained mostly unorganized, piled in boxes, but preserved over the centuries by their descendants.

Two biographers of Marie Mancini Colonna had been given access to the Colonna papers before me, both of them while the papers were held in the private family library in Rome. Clara Adèle Luce Herpin, who wrote at the end of the nineteenth century under the male pseudonym Lucien Perey, published a detailed account of Marie's romance with Louis XIV, and she pursued the story in an excellent second volume devoted to Marie's life after her marriage. But the Colonna family had denied her request to read Marie's private correspondence. More recently, Claude Dulong wrote a biography drawing on a broad array of letters and documents that were at the time still housed in the palazzo Colonna. Dulong expresses some exasperation with the character of Marie that she discovered there. At each turn in the complicated route of Marie's life, Dulong admonishes her for her recklessness, her unpredictability, her lack of restraint. This was not my response when I read the letters.

I came to appreciate, making my way through the delicate web of correspondence with the family as Marie and Hortense both tried to negotiate their independence, how "recklessness" and "unpredictability" could be used as strategies, and a viable means of self-protection when one has spies tracking one's every move.

Most biographical studies of Hortense Mancini have focused on her years in London and especially the period when she was mistress to Charles II. Georges Mongrédien (1952) and Toivo David Rosvall (1969) published fuller treatments of her life, but neither of them was able to draw on the Colonna Archive or the many accounts of her travels and escapades recorded in the Roman *avvisi*, the handwritten Italian news gazettes of the period. I was lucky enough to be able to consult this material in the Vatican library just before the archives suddenly closed for a three-year period of restoration and reorganizing in 2007. It was fascinating to see what a media figure she was in these early years of journalism, when reports on her travels and appearances in different cities would be written up next to the latest news on the outcomes of battles and political struggles.

I am deeply grateful to the Benedictine monks, whose task it is to keep the Santa Scolastica archive, for the assistance they have given me on my visits to Subiaco. The librarians Don Romano and Elia Mariano have been particularly solicitous and have alerted me to papers and letters that had gone astray in the depths of the library, manuscripts they thought would be of interest to me, and even, on one blessed occasion, the single letter proving that Marie had mailed her memoir in manuscript form to her family and had arranged for its translation and publication.

There are many other friends and colleagues who have encouraged me on my long and winding route in the company of these intrepid lady travelers. The late Patricia Cholakian first shared my excitement and pleasure in the conversational style and storytelling skills of Hortense and Marie. I miss her generous collegial spirit and I know she would have enjoyed joining me in the adventure of writing this book. I am grateful to Susan Shifrin for her work on the many paintings that were done of Marie and Hortense, and for her constant willingness to share her expertise. My conversations with Valeria De Lucca about Marie's role in the Colonnas' patronage of the arts in Rome have been most valuable, as was her assistance in negotiating the collections of *avvisi* in the Vatican library. Christopher Maurer entered into the excitement of this project and helped guide me at its most crucial, beginning moment. Luisella Brunetti, James Simpson, Harvey Blustain, and Teri Lamitie have all given me the benefit of their readings and thoughts at different stages. Nancy Harrowitz has been able to offer moral support from the point of view of one who knows exactly how far I had to walk each day as I made my way from my hotel in Subiaco down one mountain slope and up another to reach the Santa Scolastica monastery. Erika Storella, of the Gernert literary agency, and my editors, Lindsay Jones and Clive Priddle at PublicAffairs, have been better navigators than I ever could have hoped for. Finally it is to my family, especially my mother, Florence Clark, my sister, Carolyn Clark, my husband, Art Goldsmith, and our daughter, Emily, that I owe the most gratitude. Their enthusiasm for the book and persistent optimism that I would finish it has kept me engaged with the pleasure of its writing.

# HISTORICAL PROLOGUE

LOUIS XIV, THE FRENCH MONARCH who was destined to rule longer and more conspicuously than any other king in Western history, officially assumed the French throne upon the death of his father in 1643. As a child of four, he wore the crown in name only, while his mother, Anne of Austria, served as queen regent. The early years of her regency were difficult. The country was torn by war with foreign states as well as internally by rebellions of nobles and other elites against the authority of the queen and her ministers. But by 1650, France was already beginning to enjoy enhanced power and prosperity with respect to Europe's other sovereign states. Cardinal Mazarin, prime minister to the queen regent, had taken the lead in designing the Peace of Westphalia that put an end to the Thirty Years' War. The long period of religious and dynastic conflict had involved most of the European powers and left vast territories in a state of near-total destruction. But France had come out of the peace negotiations in a strong, unified position. Catholics and Protestants were given equal status by international law. The other great powers found themselves weakened by comparison—territorial claims over German states made by the Holy Roman Emperor were annulled. Rome and the papal states found their influence diminished.

Spain lost territories to the Dutch and to France. France emerged as the leader militarily and in the areas of political governance that would be the most crucial for maintaining power in a community of European states whose common interest it was to resolve its military disputes. Under the leadership of the French, the modern art and practice of international diplomacy was invented. French became the common language for communication between sovereign courts.

After 1661, in the early years of his personal rule, Louis XIV was known as a bringer of peace. He concluded decades of military conflict, consolidated the state's control over warring noble factions, and focused his youthful attentions on enhancing life at court and constructing a palace at Versailles that was destined to become one of the wonders of the world. He turned to Italian Renaissance courts for inspiration, surrounding himself with musicians, painters, sculptors, and poets, and sponsoring lavish court spectacles. Italian artists and statesmen found a welcome place at the court of the young king. During the regency of Anne of Austria, with the encouragement of her Rome-born prime minister, the court had already become a cosmopolitan center, welcoming gifted and ambitious figures, such as the Italian composer Jean-Baptiste Lully, who founded a French academy of music, became the personal ballet master to the young king, and introduced opera to the world.

Throughout the first decade of the French regency, England was engaged in a period of bloody civil strife. While the rest of Europe moved toward a more peaceable end to their conflicts, King Charles I was publicly beheaded in London on January 30, 1649. The event sent shock waves through all of the neighboring royal courts. Louis XIV was just ten years old, but a pamphlet condemning the English for "committing the most barbarous assassination upon his sacred person," their king, was distributed in the name of the king of France.[1] France received and gave protection to the widow of Charles I, Henrietta Maria, who was an aunt of Louis XIV, and her children. The dead king's family would remain in exile for the next eleven years, living at the palace of Saint-Germain-en-Laye. Many English royalists fled to the Continent and lived in France during the commonwealth that had replaced the Stuart monarchy. The diaries and letters of these travelers record their fascination with the glittering sophistication of elite life surrounding the young King Louis XIV and his court. In England, under the Puritan commonwealth, theater and most other forms of public entertainment were forbidden. The French court was a dramatic contrast. During the first phase of the personal reign of the Sun King, spectacle, theater, and art were glorified and supported by the state, especially if made to aggrandize the king. Even the practice of kingship was cultivated by Louis both as his destiny and as an artistic performance. "What other pleasure should we not abandon for it," he remarked. "The calling of a king is grand, noble, and delightful."[2] In the capital city, salons such as those hosted by the famous novelist Madeleine de Scudéry received a diverse company of artists, writers, nobles, and wealthy bourgeois aspiring to the life of the elite. French writers were quickly translated, publications carrying the news of the day were widely disseminated, and these popular publications contributed to the fashionable new image of French styles of living that would be imitated by high society in England, Germany, Italy, and Spain.

By the time Charles II returned the Stuarts to the English throne in 1660, the cultural life of the French elite, as well as the architecture and design of court palaces and grand Paris residences, had become a model to be followed. London was soon after ravaged by an outbreak of plague in 1665, and further decimated by a fire that destroyed most of the city in 1666. Architects and city planners turned to Paris for inspiration as to how to rebuild the city and improve the design of its streets and public spaces. In the first decade of Louis XIV's personal reign, Paris was already being called the City of Light, in reference to a new system of public lighting that had placed uniformed torch- and lantern-bearers on the city's busiest streets. By 1668, thousands of glass lanterns had been permanently installed all over the streets of the capital city, making it possible for merchants to remain open after dark and for Parisians, both men and women, to safely traverse the city as they pleased, day or night. Louis XIV remarked that the city lights "made his reign glitter."[3] The general impression left on foreign visitors to Paris was of a vibrant and exciting modern city, one to be emulated and to which visitors inevitably were drawn to return. In 1665, architect Christopher Wren wrote enthusiastically of his visits to Paris, during which he observed massive building projects including the expansion of the Louvre, where "no less than a thousand hands are constantly employed in the works; some in laying mighty foundations, some in raising the stories, columns, entablements, etc. with vast stones, by great and useful engines; others in carving, inlaying of marbles, plastering, painting, gilding, etc., which altogether make a school of architecture, the best probably, at this day in Europe."[4]

The European states that had for so long been in conflict with the French found themselves in a progressively weakened position. France's political influence expanded and infiltrated other capital cities and foreign courts. In Italy, family dynasties that had held power for centuries were in decline. Florence was no longer the cultural center of the Continent. The Medici rulers had been unable to reverse an impending state bankruptcy. In a desperate attempt to prevent the flight of wealth and population, they passed laws restricting travel and banning the education of citizens outside of Tuscany. Grand Duke Cosimo III's marriage to Marie-Louise d'Orléans, cousin to Louis XIV, was an attempt to buttress the prestige of the declining Medici family. But the marriage had the opposite effect, for the grand duchess found her husband's degenerate and tyrannical behavior to be unbearable. She fled back to France. By the early eighteenth century the Medici family was extinct and Tuscany was ruled by the Franco-Austrian duchy of Lorraine.

Elsewhere in Italy, the popes who governed baroque Rome were politically weakened by the terms of the Treaty of Westphalia, so they focused their attention on redesigning the city. Rome and Paris vied for the services of the great Italian sculptors, architects, and artists of the era: Bernini, Borromini, Pietro da Cortona. The French tightened their links with Rome through political marriages and a carefully chosen succession of ambassadors who established a vital presence for the French community in Rome. Travel between France and Italy was eased by improved roads and strengthened efforts to police them. Soon France was attracting the best of Italy's craftsmen and artists, who were drawn by economic opportunity as well as relative freedom from censorship in the first decades of Louis XIV's reign. Even the republic of Venice, traditionally so protective of its tradesmen and artists, began to lose its monopoly on luxury goods to France. Jean-Baptiste Colbert, the French minister of trade and finance, negotiated a generous agreement with a group of Venetian glassblowers and installed them in the center of Paris. Louis XIV paid them a ceremonial visit and solemnly presented a generous purse to reward them for their defection and to subsidize their training of French craftsmen in the art of glass- and mirror-making. It was a cultural and economic coup on par with a military victory. The Venetian ambassador reported home that the spectacle had reduced him to tears. By the time the new palace of Versailles was under construction in the 1670s, imports of luxury goods from Venice were banned and the newly established glassworks in Paris was producing ornaments and mirrors to decorate the halls of the royal residence and the homes of the wealthy in France and abroad.

The rise of the French in the military, cultural, and political arenas of Europe was accompanied by the demise of the other great nations. By midcentury Spain was no longer the world's foremost power. In 1600, at the height of the age of exploration, Spain had ruled the seas and large parts of Europe, its far-flung empire reaching from the Mediterranean to Africa. By 1659, when the Peace of the Pyrenees finally put an end to the long wars between Spain and France, the Spanish Hapsburg states had been battered by a series of bankruptcies, military defeats, internal rebellions, and epidemics of disease. An outbreak of bubonic plague spread throughout the Spanish Mediterranean encompassing most of southern Italy, killing more than half a million people. There was a shortage of silver, and money to raise armies was not to be had. Even if the funds could have been found, there were no longer enough men available to be conscripted. After Oliver Cromwell, Lord Protector of England, conducted a brief war with Spain that resulted in a treaty ceding the Spanish city of Dunkirk to England, the fearsome privateers and pirates based in that city who had long contracted with Spain to protect Spanish ships were no longer working for the Hapsburgs.

French travelers and diplomats began to take up residence in Madrid following the marriage of Louis XIV to the Spanish infanta and the end of armed conflict between the two countries. But life at the Spanish court held little appeal for them, compared with the courts of Paris and Versailles. Madrid was the capital of the Inquisition. Pierre de Villars, the French ambassador, wrote that the preferred state spectacles were public burnings of heretics on a huge stage erected in the Plaza Major. The English traveler Francis Willoughby wrote home in 1664 that Spain was intellectually backward, and appeared untouched by advances in the sciences and other areas of learning, with universities that resembled English institutions of the previous century. The writer Madame d'Aulnoy published accounts of her voyage to Madrid in which she described the extraordinarily constrained lives of Spanish noblewomen compared with the French. By midcentury, for cultivated young women throughout Europe, it was France—especially Paris—that held a special fascination. Stories of salon gatherings led by ladies presiding over a mixed company of men and women found their way to London and the capitals on the Continent.

Over the decades following the Peace of the Pyrenees, Louis XIV followed the program of consolidating and centralizing authority that had been laid out by Richelieu, prime minister to Louis XIII, and continued under Cardinal Mazarin. The Sun King's overriding ambition, to increase the power and glory of France, led him also to pursue an expansionist military policy that was largely successful. The French army was reorganized and strengthened under the direction of François Michel Le Tellier de Louvois, the minister of war. Modern systems for storing and distributing supplies meant that soldiers on the move no longer depended on foraging and looting for food and ammunition. The efficiency and discipline of the French armies led them to a series of victories that progressively pushed the borders of France farther to the east and southwest. To defend its coastal borders, France bought Dunkirk from Charles II in 1662. Dunkirk was known for its shipbuilders and privateers who sold their services to nations seeking to protect their own merchant fleets on the high seas. This often meant aggressive maneuvers against the ships of competing nation-states. For the next fifty years, mercenary vessels operating from the strategic port city and working for the French attacked Dutch trade ships in the North Sea and the Atlantic.

Within France, Louis XIV worked tirelessly to build a strong centralized state and make the French nation a global cultural center. The French court continued to draw to it the best of Europe's craftsmen, artists, architects, and engineers. Each military victory was followed by days of festivities, fireworks, and elaborate spectacle at the royal residences of Fontainebleau, Saint-Germain-en-Laye, and Versailles. For the French elite, proximity to Versailles and Paris became the only route to prestige and advancement. To be excluded from the king's presence became a nobleman's nightmare. As Stendhal would later observe, "The masterpiece of Louis XIV was his creation of the ennui of exile." But by the end of the seventeenth century exile was a familiar experience for many Frenchmen and women from all walks of life. "Un roi, un loi, une foi"—one king, one law, one faith—became the motto of the reign, and dissenters were not tolerated. After the Edict of Nantes was revoked in 1685, thousands of Protestants fled the country, causing France to lose precious resources and a significant portion of its educated population.

The final decades of Louis XIV's long reign were marked by renewed warring between France and Spain and redoubled efforts by England and the European states to undermine France's dominant position. After England's Catholic King James II was deposed in 1688 and William and Mary took the throne, the English were at war with France both at home and abroad in the North American colonies. It was not until 1713 that a treaty was signed, ending France's battles with the "Grand Alliance" that had been formed to thwart French expansion under Louis XIV. In that year, when the French king was seventy-five years old, the final treaty begun by the Peace of Utrecht was signed. It brought to a close the bloody wars between France and Spain over the Spanish succession, curbed French expansion, and would mark the beginning of the long rise of the British Empire. Now near the end of his reign, with his armies and his population battered, Louis XIV agreed to raze the fortifications of Dunkirk and ceded French claims to the Netherlands, Savoy, Portugal, Prussia, and the Hudson's Bay Company territory in Canada. The royal treasury was almost bankrupt. The wars that had succeeded in expanding the French territories and securing a Bourbon prince as heir to the Spanish throne had been costly. The French armies had successfully fought off a series of European attempts to thwart their king's ambitions, but eventually Spain, England, Holland, and the German states had managed to form an alliance that could contain him. On September 1, 1715, Louis XIV died of a gangrenous infection. It was the end of a fifty-five-year personal reign, the longest in Europe's history at the time.

The lives of Hortense and Marie Mancini spanned seven decades of these volatile changes to Europe's political and cultural territory. The two sisters traversed this landscape with a determination and intrepid spirit that was astonishing to those who followed the complicated route on which their adventures took them. At different points, they lived or moved through all of Europe's principal cultural capitals. They first arrived in Paris from Rome in 1654, as young girls. Their presence soon left an indelible mark on the young king of France, as he approached the age of majority, when he would officially assume personal control of the French state. Their intimacy with him, and their acts of rebellion, inspired the ways in which his own coming to adulthood would be viewed by others as myth, renunciation, and heroic endeavor. Although the Italian sisters ultimately would live most of their lives outside the borders of France, they always viewed themselves as moving in the orbit of the French throne. Like many of their contemporaries, they regarded the French court as the center of the universe. But it was not their fate to remain there for long. ✳

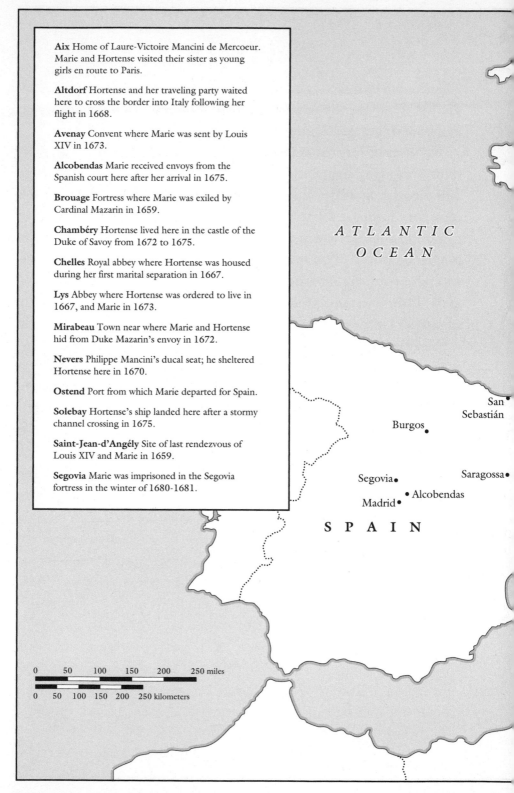

**Aix** Home of Laure-Victoire Mancini de Mercoeur. Marie and Hortense visited their sister as young girls en route to Paris.

**Altdorf** Hortense and her traveling party waited here to cross the border into Italy following her flight in 1668.

**Avenay** Convent where Marie was sent by Louis XIV in 1673.

**Alcobendas** Marie received envoys from the Spanish court here after her arrival in 1675.

**Brouage** Fortress where Marie was exiled by Cardinal Mazarin in 1659.

**Chambéry** Hortense lived here in the castle of the Duke of Savoy from 1672 to 1675.

**Chelles** Royal abbey where Hortense was housed during her first marital separation in 1667.

**Lys** Abbey where Hortense was ordered to live in 1667, and Marie in 1673.

**Mirabeau** Town near where Marie and Hortense hid from Duke Mazarin's envoy in 1672.

**Nevers** Philippe Mancini's ducal seat; he sheltered Hortense here in 1670.

**Ostend** Port from which Marie departed for Spain.

**Solebay** Hortense's ship landed here after a stormy channel crossing in 1675.

**Saint-Jean-d'Angély** Site of last rendezvous of Louis XIV and Marie in 1659.

**Segovia** Marie was imprisoned in the Segovia fortress in the winter of 1680-1681.

*ATLANTIC OCEAN*

San Sebastián

Burgos

Segovia

Saragossa

Alcobendas

Madrid

**S P A I N**

| 0 | 50 | 100 | 150 | 200 | 250 miles |

| 0 | 50 | 100 | 150 | 200 | 250 kilometers |

SEVENTEENTH-CENTURY EUROPE

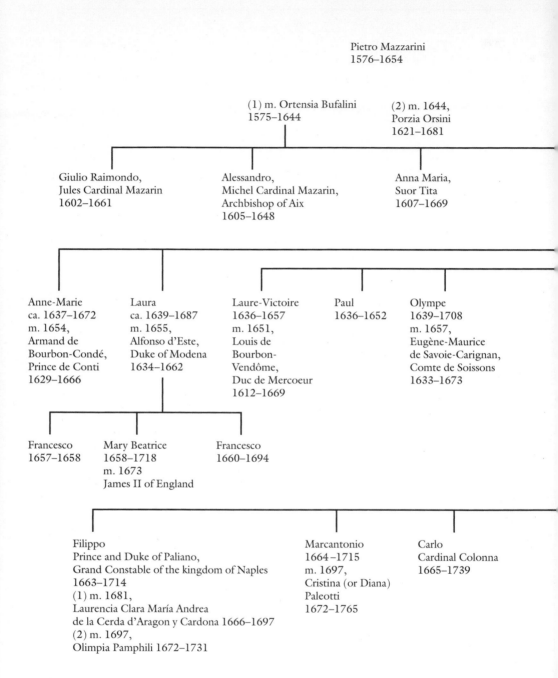

Pietro Mazzarini
1576–1654

(1) m. Ortensia Bufalini
1575–1644

(2) m. 1644,
Porzia Orsini
1621–1681

Giulio Raimondo,
Jules Cardinal Mazarin
1602–1661

Alessandro,
Michel Cardinal Mazarin,
Archbishop of Aix
1605–1648

Anna Maria,
Suor Tita
1607–1669

Anne-Marie
ca. 1637–1672
m. 1654,
Armand de
Bourbon-Condé,
Prince de Conti
1629–1666

Laura
ca. 1639–1687
m. 1655,
Alfonso d'Este,
Duke of Modena
1634–1662

Laure-Victoire
1636–1657
m. 1651,
Louis de
Bourbon-
Vendôme,
Duc de Mercoeur
1612–1669

Paul
1636–1652

Olympe
1639–1708
m. 1657,
Eugène-Maurice
de Savoie-Carignan,
Comte de Soissons
1633–1673

Francesco
1657–1658

Mary Beatrice
1658–1718
m. 1673
James II of England

Francesco
1660–1694

Filippo
Prince and Duke of Paliano,
Grand Constable of the kingdom of Naples
1663–1714
(1) m. 1681,
Laurencia Clara María Andrea
de la Cerda d'Aragon y Cardona 1666–1697
(2) m. 1697,
Olimpia Pamphili 1672–1731

Marcantonio
1664–1715
m. 1697,
Cristina (or Diana)
Paleotti
1672–1765

Carlo
Cardinal Colonna
1665–1739

*Genealogical Chart of the Mazzarini and Mancini Families, Including the Children of Marie Mancini, Hortense Mancini, and Laura Martinozzi (but not those of their siblings and cousins)*

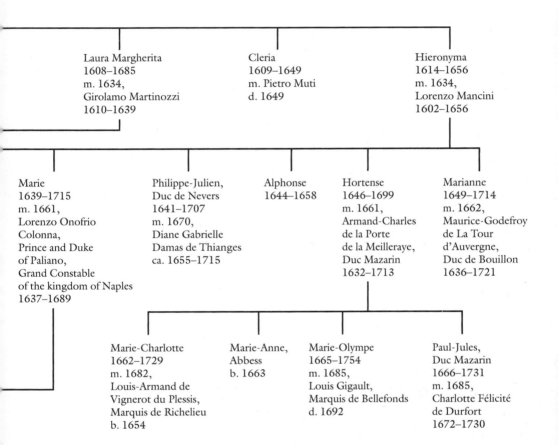

Laura Margherita
1608–1685
m. 1634,
Girolamo Martinozzi
1610–1639

Cleria
1609–1649
m. Pietro Muti
d. 1649

Hieronyma
1614–1656
m. 1634,
Lorenzo Mancini
1602–1656

Marie
1639–1715
m. 1661,
Lorenzo Onofrio
Colonna,
Prince and Duke
of Paliano,
Grand Constable
of the kingdom of Naples
1637–1689

Philippe-Julien,
Duc de Nevers
1641–1707
m. 1670,
Diane Gabrielle
Damas de Thianges
ca. 1655–1715

Alphonse
1644–1658

Hortense
1646–1699
m. 1661,
Armand-Charles
de la Porte
de la Meilleraye,
Duc Mazarin
1632–1713

Marianne
1649–1714
m. 1662,
Maurice-Godefroy
de La Tour
d'Auvergne,
Duc de Bouillon
1636–1721

Marie-Charlotte
1662–1729
m. 1682,
Louis-Armand de
Vignerot du Plessis,
Marquis de Richelieu
b. 1654

Marie-Anne,
Abbess
b. 1663

Marie-Olympe
1665–1754
m. 1685,
Louis Gigault,
Marquis de Bellefonds
d. 1692

Paul-Jules,
Duc Mazarin
1666–1731
m. 1685,
Charlotte Félicité
de Durfort
1672–1730

Marie Mancini Colonna with pearls in her hair
(oil on canvas) by Jacob Ferdinand Voet
*Amsterdam, Rijksmuseum*

Portrait of Contessa Ortensia Ianni Stella, bust
length, in an ivory chemise, with flowers in her
hair (oil on canvas) by Jacob Ferdinand Voet
(1639–1700)

# The CARDINAL'S NIECES at the COURT of FRANCE

*The greatest good fortune which can happen to this person, is my not deferring any longer to regulate matters; and if I cannot make her wise, as I believe is impossible, at least that her follies appear not any more in the view of the world, for otherwise she will run a risk of being torn to pieces.*

—Cardinal Mazarin to Louis XIV, August 28, 1659

*Mazarin was not opposed to this passion as long as he thought it could only serve his own interests.*

—Madame de Lafayette, *History of Henrietta of England*

THE MAZARIN FAMILY did not have noble origins. The rapid rise in their fortunes came from the unprecedented success of one man, Giulio Mazzarini (as he was called in Italy), at the French court. Invited there in 1639 to serve as a diplomat, within two years he was a valued adviser to Louis XIII and his minister Richelieu. In 1641 he was made cardinal, and when Richelieu died later that year, Mazzarini was appointed to the king's council of ministers. After the death of Louis XIII, the queen regent named Mazzarini prime minister, a post he retained through long periods of war, civil strife, and revolts against his personal authority, from 1643 to his death in 1661. Never popular, he was ruthless in his efforts to raise funds for the French wars against the Hapsburgs, the ruling dynasty in Spain, by levying taxes and cutting the salaries of highly placed officials. For himself he loved material wealth, was good at acquiring it, and took pleasure in displaying it. By 1650 he had amassed personal collections of jewels, art, and sculpture that were grander than any in the French royal family. Mazzarini's extraordinary wealth and power and imposing residence near the Louvre palace came to represent all that the French feared in foreign influence. At the height of the Fronde, when French nobles had taken up arms against the powerful prime minister, he took refuge in Germany. Still, by early 1653, he had signed treaties with most of the French princes who had been battling his armies for ten years, and in the spring he returned to Paris. Giulio Mazzarini, now Jules Mazarin, had arrived at the apex of power in France. It remained only for him to embed his family name in the network of royal dynasties that ruled his adopted country. It was only in this way that his personal glory would remain permanently anchored as part of his legacy to France. To that end, he began summoning his family members to Paris. After first importing four of his older nieces and nephews, he wrote to his sisters in Rome asking that they and their remaining children join him at the court of Louis XIV.

On a warm spring day in 1653, two young girls stood on the docks of Civitavecchia, Italy. With them were their twelve-year-old brother, two female cousins, their finely dressed mother and aunt, and a small entourage, preparing to board an elegantly outfitted galley headed for the coast of France. The sight must have caused something of a stir in the busy seaport, where onlookers were more accustomed to seeing fishing boats or larger sailing vessels loaded with silks and other luxury goods. This boat was unusual; it had been commissioned in Genoa and detailed with particular attention to the elegant top deck, which was furnished with tented dining spaces and tapestried furniture. Belowdecks, in the galley, was the more familiar sight of about twenty thin and muscular oarsmen, most of them prisoners or slaves, whose unhappy lot it was to provide the power for the voyage.

The two girls, Marie and Hortense Mancini, were sisters, one a dark-haired and intelligent-looking adolescent of thirteen and the other a mere child of six, with curly black hair and of more fragile appearance than her sister, but striking in her delicate beauty. Marie and Hortense's father, Lorenzo Mancini, was a Roman baron highly respected for his knowledge of astrology and necromancy. When Marie was born on August 28, 1639, his reading of the planets did not augur well. It was said that this child would bring trouble to the family. Lorenzo Mancini would die in 1656, before he could have any idea about the accuracy of the prophecy.

The Mancini children were curious to see for themselves the pleasures of French society that they had heard about in letters and the accounts of travelers. In Rome the girls had received the customary convent education designed to prepare them for either domesticity or a life in religion. Indeed, their mother had urged Marie to think seriously about staying behind in Rome and committing to a religious life. This was never a likely prospect: although the nuns had taught the girls to read, their favorite books were not those kept in convent libraries. Romance novels, plays, and works on astrology and necromancy all were found in the Mancini household. All of the children, especially Marie, had come to love the epic romances of Ariosto and Tasso. She had heard that in France, women were writing novels and tales inspired by these popular Italians. When their mother announced her intention to leave for Paris, taking with her only young Hortense and brother Philippe, Marie had responded deftly that "there were convents everywhere, and that if it should please heaven to inspire such pious impulses in me, it would be as easy to follow them in Paris as in Rome."[1] So both sisters,

Marie and Hortense, were with their mother and brother as the family boarded the galley destined for Marseille.

Twenty years later, Marie would recall her departure from Italy and the marvelous floating home that Genovese boatbuilders had specially prepared for the little group of voyagers:

> So we boarded a galley from Genoa, which that republic had sent to us out of special consideration for Monsieur le Cardinal. I will not stop here to describe that movable house. It would take up too much time to portray all its beauty, its order, its riches, and its magnificence. Suffice it to say that we were treated like queens there and throughout our voyage, and that the tables of sovereigns are not served with more pomp and brilliance than was ours four times a day.[2]

Cardinal Mazarin had arranged for a voyage that was not speedy; he wanted his Italian family to have time to talk about France, practice the language, and become acculturated to French ways en route to Paris, and so the galley slaves were ordered to row slowly, instructions also intended to ensure a comfortable voyage for the passengers above. It took more than a week for the galley to reach the coast of France. After landing in Marseille, the party spent eight months in southern France hosted by their eldest sister, Laure-Victoire Mancini, who had married the French Duke of Mercoeur.

The seventeen-year-old Laure-Victoire was only too happy to be reunited with her sisters and brother, and she delightedly embraced her task of helping her family understand what to expect at the French court. To the mothers' initial dismay but the children's amusement, Laure-Victoire taught them that it was considered gracious to greet a guest with a kiss. They learned the importance of choosing the right visitors with whom to pass the time in salon society, and they watched in astonishment as the regional consuls arrived with delicate and expensive gifts: candied fruits, wines, silver candlesticks. By the time the family left for Paris, they had seen ample evidence of the enormous privilege and power their uncle enjoyed. The days of the Fronde rebellions against him were over. His relatives could bask in the security of the cardinal's prestige in the king's close entourage.

Still, they were stunned by the luxury of the Mazarin palace when they arrived in Paris in February 1654. The cardinal received them in the lavish surroundings that had raised the anger and jealousy of the French aristocracy just ten years earlier. The manner in which Mazarin had acquired his fortune had been the subject of much speculation during his own lifetime, and even today continues to be a matter of historical controversy. He had used his power without compunction, in the tradition set by his compatriots the Medici family of Florence, focusing on exerting control over his potential enemies by using the ruthless financial weapons being perfected in the early capitalist era: speculation, taxation, forced bankruptcy, expropriation, and money loaned at exorbitantly high rates. In the process he had amassed a fortune that had a modern aspect to it, based heavily on material goods and money, not the landed wealth that traditionally had formed a nobleman's net worth. The interior of Mazarin's palace had been covered with frescoes by the best Italian painters and housed the greatest collection of art known in Europe. It was here that the Mancini children received their first visitors from the court, and it was from the Mazarin palace that the family would take the short carriage ride to the Louvre to pay court to the queen regent and her son, Louis.

The newcomers were objects of much curiosity and rumor. Mazarin had already arranged one marriage whose grandeur had secretly enraged many courtiers, and now more nieces were arriving on the scene. Within weeks of their arrival in Paris, young Anne-Marie Martinozzi's wedding to Prince Armand de Conti had taken

place, in a lavish ceremony that publicly displayed Mazarin's reconciliation with a family that had opposed him bitterly during the
Fronde years. The marriage of Anne-Marie to a royal prince was
one of the conditions the cardinal had imposed on this former leader
of rebellions. It was an unbreakable seal of Conti's defeat.

All of Mazarin's relatives were encouraged to spend time in the
salons of the Louvre and the adjacent private residences, where
they were introduced to a life filled with conversation, concerts,
dances, and theater. The Mancini children joined their brother
Alphonse and sister Olympe, who had been brought to Paris a
year earlier. If any of Mazarin's nieces or nephews had aspired to
solitude and shelter from the public view, their arrival in Paris put
an abrupt end to such inclinations. There was no time, and no
place, to be alone.

Nonetheless, the cardinal was concerned that Marie and her
younger sister Hortense were not quite prepared for this new and
intense social milieu. He observed that fourteen-year-old Marie
was particularly awkward, as she later would recall: "The fatigue of
the road, a continual agitation brought on by my cheerful and high-
strung nature, and my poor eating habits—I ate as readily the foods
that disagreed with me as those that might do me good—had reduced me to a pitiful state; for that reason Monsieur le Cardinal
resolved to put me in a convent, to see, as he said, if it would fatten
me up a bit."[3] And so she and little Hortense spent eighteen months
in the Convent of the Visitation in the Faubourg Saint-Jacques,
where they received a more liberal instruction than what had been
prescribed for them in Rome. They studied from a curriculum in
French, literature, religion, and the arts that had made the Visi-
tandine nuns the favorite teachers of young girls of elite society.
When they were finally deemed ready to join the young king and
his court at the end of 1656, seventeen-year-old Marie was prepared
for new friendships and more freedom.

Her mother and uncle were busy trying to ensure Marie's future by planning a good marriage, but she resisted their interference and soon drew the anger of her mother, who insisted on keeping a close watch to limit her from joining the youthful company at court. Madame Mancini enlisted her brother, Cardinal Mazarin, in dominating her rebellious daughter, as Marie would remember: "After my mother's complaints, my uncle reprimanded me in such acid tones and such cutting terms that any other girl than I would have been sick with remorse, but since I did not take things to heart at all, everything he said to me made a clear impression on my memory and made none at all on my spirit."[4]

One reason Hieronyma Mancini could not control her daughters was her own health. Throughout the summer and fall of 1656, she had struggled with a fever. She became consumed with anxiety and fear over her illness, which inexplicably came and went. Overshadowing all attempts to find a cure for her sickness was the knowledge that years before, her husband had predicted that she would die in this, her forty-second year. In October the fever seemed to have gone. But by December Hieronyma lay dying on a bed in her brother's apartment at the Louvre palace. The king's doctors had been summoned but could not reverse the course of her illness. There was nothing left to do but encourage her to receive, as comfortably as possible, the final visits of her family and friends. The king came to pay his respects, as did Cardinal Mazarin, though he would never stay long enough to answer his sister's pressing questions about precisely how he intended to care for her children. Hieronyma knew that her charming young Hortense would inevitably find a good match, but she urged the cardinal to consider consigning her troublesome Marie to a convent life instead of marriage. Mazarin was reluctant, and Marie remained adamantly opposed to any such notion. Marie became so angry with her mother and so unable to exhibit the humility demanded of her that her mother excluded her from her sickroom. When Hieronyma died on December 29, 1656, Marie could feel no grief.

After her mother's death, Marie joined Hortense under the care of Madame de Venelle, a governess appointed by their uncle, who loosened his grip on the daily occupations of his nieces and encouraged their growing acquaintance with the king. At eighteen, Louis was undergoing the finishing touches of a long and careful education to prepare him to officially assume the throne. He was starting to feel irritated by the attentions of his mother and the watchful eye of her prime minister. As he prepared for his first military campaigns, he was trying to form his own opinions about the ever-present intrigues that were the hub of life at court. By the end of 1657, plans for the young king to lead an army into battle against the Spanish in Flanders were completed, and Louis departed amid much fanfare. For the public, his service in battle would be a final requirement before he could officially accede to the throne.

Though he passed this test of his virility and readiness to rule, he returned to court from the battlefield in early 1658 suffering from an illness that quickly spread alarm. The journal of the king's health kept by his physician, Antoine Vallot, details the seriousness of the sickness, describing high fever, difficulty breathing, and skin that was swollen and discolored. Amid the frantic medical consultations, preparations were made to administer last rites. Courtiers held vigil outside the royal chambers and jockeyed for favor, trying to secure protection from powerful patrons in anticipation of the young monarch's death. When suddenly the illness began to dissipate, the printed *Gazette* and the pamphleteers eagerly spread the news across the country.

At court, no one exhibited more relief at the king's convalescence than Marie Mancini. During her mother's illness just one year earlier, she had found it difficult to express grief or concern, but those who knew and watched her during the king's malaise were struck by her distress and genuine sadness. While other courtiers had been caught up by the intrigues and speculation about the political consequences of the king's death, Marie's anxiety seemed to be focused solely on his person. It was a display of affection that made a deep impression on Louis. By the summer of 1658, everyone was saying that the two young people were in love.

Now the court was treated to the spectacle of an ever-so-healthy and virile king, who missed no opportunity to escape with his young love to the gardens of the Louvre and Fontainebleau, where Marie would read to him from her favorite Italian romances. To some it even seemed as though the two were acting out roles from the popular romance epic *Gerusalemme Liberata,* in which the young warrior hero Rinaldo is seduced by the enchantress Armida. Both Louis and Marie had been trained in dance, an art and skill that was obligatory at court and considered central to a worldly education, and they both performed in the court ballets that were commissioned by some of the best musicians and poets of the realm. Marie encouraged the serious attention the king gave to his personal performances, fostering his relationship with the young Italian composer Jean-Baptiste Lully, who was quickly rising to prominence and fame in France for his works of ballet and opera. The popular playwright Molière wrote verses for one of these, the opera-ballet *Alicidiane,* in which Marie danced. The king's cousin Mademoiselle de Montpensier described this cultural education that Marie seemed to be giving the king:

> The King was in a much better humor after he fell in love with mademoiselle de Mancini. He was lively, he chatted with everyone. I think that she had advised him in his readings of novels and poetry. He had a great quantity of them, with poetry collections and theater as well; he seemed to take great pleasure from this and when he offered his opinion, he seemed to have as good judgment

as someone who had studied a great deal and who had a perfect knowledge of literature.[5]

Cardinal Mazarin and Queen Anne were happy enough to encourage Marie's contribution to the cultural education of the young king, but they were caught off-guard by the intensity of the romance. Plans were under way to find a suitable wife for Louis, and even the fiercely ambitious Mazarin could hardly expect to place one of his own family of Italian merchants on the French throne. But this did not prevent public speculation that such a goal was precisely what Mazarin had in mind in bringing his nieces to France in the first place. Madame de Motteville, one of Queen Anne's ladies-in-waiting, reported that Mazarin even tested out the idea of a marriage between Marie and Louis in a conversation with the queen in which he pretended to think the scenario was preposterous:

> The Cardinal could not refuse himself the pleasure of testing so fine an affair, and one day he spoke of it to the Queen, laughing at the folly of his niece, but in a manner so ambiguous and embarrassed that he let the Queen see what he had in his soul clearly enough to make her answer in these very words: "I do not believe, Monsieur le Cardinal, that the king is capable of such baseness, but if it were possible that he should think of it, I warn you that all France would revolt against you and against him; and that I will put myself at the head of the rebels to restrain my son."[6]

In any event, Mazarin never publicly showed any inclination to try to arrange a royal marriage for his niece. But the task of arranging a strong marriage for Louis that would expand France's power in Europe was one that he felt was absolutely his ministerial responsibility, especially because his health had started to fail him. The matter was pressing. Two prominent candidates were under consideration:

Princess Marguerite of Savoy and the Spanish Princess Marie-Thérèse, niece of Queen Anne. The king himself, however, seemed to pay little heed to this strategizing. His attentions were for Marie alone. Even when Louis was sent to Lyon to formally meet Marguerite of Savoy in October 1658, Marie was with him, along with an entourage of one hundred carriages. The slow pace of the voyage offered many opportunities for intimate gatherings and festivities. In Lyon, Marie took part in the balls and lavish ceremonies organized in the king's honor and he continued to pay her court, to the embarrassment of his mother. Louis would escort Marie back to her residence in the Place Bellecour every evening, "first following her carriage, then acting as a coachman, and then finally getting inside."[7]

When he heard this, Mazarin abruptly recalled the party to Paris to pursue marriage discussions with the emissaries recently arrived from Spain. Later, in a letter to Louis XIV, Mazarin would say that he had recognized "since Lyon" the seriousness of the danger Marie posed to plans for a royal marriage.

Negotiations continued nonetheless, through the winter and into the spring of 1659. Though the king made no objection, he also continued to spend most of his time with Marie. "Upon our return to Paris," Marie would later remember, "our sole concern was to amuse ourselves. There was not a single day, or rather a single moment, that was not devoted to pleasure, and I can say that never was time spent more enjoyably than it was by us."[8] Louis seemed eager to assure her that he had no care for his more serious obligations and that he was willing to throw off the weight of his identity as prince and defender of France just to please his young love. Standing out in Marie's memory many years later was one of the more sentimental demonstrations of "how delicately and gallantly the king courted," when he threw away his sword after it had accidentally bruised her as they were walking side by side in the woods of Bois-le-Vicomte.[9] Queen Anne observed these displays with increasing concern. She was not amused when the visiting queen of Sweden, seated at a banquet next to Louis and Marie, openly challenged the young king to defy convention and "marry for someone you love."[10] Queen Anne was even more displeased when Louis made no effort to hide his passion during the diplomatic visits of envoys from the Spanish court. A royal marriage of Louis with the Spanish princess was already a theoretical possibility discussed in diplomatic circles, yet Louis seemed to pay it no heed. Instead he flaunted his growing independence from his mother and the cardinal, refusing to observe the austerity measures she had ordered for the Lenten season and continuing to spend all of his time with Marie in the gardens of the Louvre and on long equestrian outings in the Fontainebleau forest.

It was Queen Anne who decided that the couple had to separate. First she engaged the services of a governess who was instructed to spy on Marie and follow the couple everywhere she could. But soon she decided that the only effective strategy would be to make Louis see for himself that the separation was both necessary and inevitable. Anne's animosity toward Marie was so strong that she had begun to truly see her as an evil enchantress, like the magical Armida in Marie's favorite romance. The queen mother "told the Cardinal, who was preparing to leave, what she felt. She made him see her wish to separate the king her son from one who kept him bound in chains which she thought shameful: she wished to show to the king the mirror that was presented to Rinaldo, not only to draw him from the spell of Armida, but to force him to fly from so fatal a prison."[11]

By the summer of 1659, Mazarin was also scheming to find a way to separate the love-struck couple. A marriage between Louis and Marie-Thérèse of Spain, Mazarin's preferred outcome, would be in effect a treaty between the two countries, and would mark a definitive end to the remnants of French armed resistance to the cardinal that had begun during the Fronde years. The last rebellious French noble army that, supported by the Spanish, had continued its attacks on Mazarin's forces through the 1650s, was defeated at the battle of Dunkirk in June 1658. It was time to seal the peace. After signing an initial preliminary agreement in Paris, Mazarin made plans for a ceremonial meeting with the Spanish emissaries at the border town of Saint-Jean-de-Luz to design a formal treaty and marriage contract.

On June 22, 1659, Louis XIV and Marie Mancini were forced to separate. Marie was ordered to accompany her uncle in the train of carriages heading south toward Spain. At the last minute she was permitted the company of her two younger sisters, Hortense and ten-year-old Marianne, the youngest of the eight Mancini children and the last to join the family in Paris. Mazarin said he would escort his nieces along with their governess to La Rochelle, a city under his personal governorship. The night before the planned departure, the king had met privately, and at length, with both the cardinal and Queen Anne, in interviews during which he had begged, reportedly falling to his knees, to be allowed to marry the cardinal's niece. But the following morning he could accompany Marie only as far as her coach to offer a tearful farewell. The moment was public, and striking to all who saw and heard about it, and the scene would be endlessly replayed in different cultural venues, in politics, and in spectacle. The young king's tearful goodbye as Marie reluctantly boarded the carriage became an emblem in the popular imagination of his coming of age, and a sad acknowledgment of the loss of humanity that necessarily accompanies the assumption of power. It was at this moment, it was thought, that Louis presented Marie with a magnificent strand of pearls she had admired when the queen of England had come to the French court a few months earlier, and which he had since bought. The leave-taking would be, according to legend, the last time the king shed tears. Marie's parting words to him, "Sire, I am leaving and you weep, and yet you are king," would reappear in opera, poetry, and theater for generations to come.

Marie described the parting, and the loneliness that followed, as the most painful period of her life: "I cannot conceal the pain that this separation caused me; nothing has hurt me so deeply in my life. All possible suffering seemed to me as nothing in comparison with this absence. There was not a moment when I did not wish for death, as the only cure for my ills. In short, I was in a state that cannot possibly be expressed either by what I have just said or by any stronger terms."[12]

The cardinal accompanied his niece's carriage as far as Poitiers, then sent her party ahead to La Rochelle while he continued south to devote himself fully to the discussions with the Spanish. In La Rochelle the three girls and their governess, Madame de Venelle, were greeted royally and treated to fireworks, theater, and coastal promenades for several weeks. At first Marie tried to let herself be drawn into the diversions, even organizing a costumed marionette production of Molière's new play, *Les precieuses ridicules,* for her local hosts. But her outings to the city's coastal environs became more frequent, as did her conversations with a recently appointed quartermaster from Paris, a cousin of Mazarin's financial minister, Jean-Baptiste Colbert. Against the specific orders of the cardinal, who had forbidden private correspondence between his niece and the king, the young Colbert de Terron was smuggling a steady stream of secret letters between Louis and Marie. Toward the end of July Marie voluntarily moved from her comfortable quarters in La Rochelle to the austere fortress of nearby Brouage, overlooking the rocky coastline and the Atlantic Ocean, where she devoted herself fully to her solitude, her melancholy, and her correspondence with her lost love.

From his negotiating outpost in Saint-Jean-de-Luz, Mazarin demanded regular reports on the behavior of Louis and Marie. He had a valuable ally in Madame de Venelle, who wrote letters advising him to examine all the mail packets leaving La Rochelle from any of the three girls, as Marie was likely to disguise her letters among those of her sisters. She informed him that Marie was spending long hours in the company of an astrologer from La Rochelle, poring over the celestial indicators of her fate. Madame de Venelle scrutinized the couriers who came and went from her traveling party from the moment they approached La Rochelle. "I'm looking for a secure envoy," she wrote Mazarin, "so that I can write your Eminence to tell you that things seem a bit worse than you feared, and it would serve your Eminence's interests to have the first packets mailed from La Rochelle examined."[13] Marie later remembered that after their separation the king withdrew to his hunting lodge at Chantilly, "where he did nothing but send couriers to me, the first of whom was a musketeer bearing letters of five pages each."[14]

When Mazarin learned of the extent of this continuing contact, he sent blistering reprimands to Jean-Baptiste Colbert for failing to interrupt it. Colbert was doubly mortified by the betrayal of his cousin, who had been instrumental in helping Marie get letters out of Brouage, and he offered Mazarin his resignation. The cardinal turned his attentions to Louis, writing long letters from Saint-Jean-de-Luz imploring the young man to consider the risk he was posing to the state and to his own well-being as king of France, soon to be united through marriage to the Spanish throne. He tried every possible argument, including pleas for the king to have pity on his own vulnerable position. "Pray consider in what condition I am," Mazarin wrote, "and whether there be in the world a man more wretched than myself, who, after applying himself continually with the greatest zeal to raise your reputation, and to procure by all ways the glory of your arms, the ease of your subjects, and the good of your state, has the displeasure to see a person who belongs to me on the very point of overturning all, and causing your ruin, if you go on to give way to your passion for her."[15]

He also sharply attacked Marie's character and motives, declaring that the king was blinded to them:

> I am not surprised at what you write, seeing the passion you have for her . . . hinders you from discerning the truth; and I must answer you, that were it not for this passion you would agree with me; that this Person is not capable of Friendship, that she has an ambition without bounds, a restless and awkward spirit, a contempt for all the world, no prudence in her conduct, and an inclination to all extravagancies, that she is more foolish than ever, since she has had the honor to see you at St. John d'Angely; and that instead of receiving your letters twice a week she now receives them every day.[16]

Louis had even managed to smuggle gifts to his love, including a puppy that he arranged to have delivered in a basket, wearing an embroidered collar that read, "I belong to Marie."

Mazarin insisted to Madame de Venelle that Marie be made to see reason. "I would like to know what Marie thinks," he wrote, "and whether with all the flattery that those readers of horoscopes give her, she does not know that she has taken the road toward being the most unhappy woman of her century."[17] Mazarin discussed the urgency of the situation in letters to the queen as well, even as he publicly behaved as though the Spanish wedding would certainly be concluded. Although the queen thought the king would go through with the ceremony, she and Mazarin both seemed to view his love as an illness that needed to be cured, a spell that needed to be broken, in order for the wedding to be blessed. In this view of passionate love they were perfectly in tune with the culture of the period. Passion was a destructive emotion, while a more controlled love based on tenderness and esteem was the only form of affection that noble souls were to strive for. Although Louis tried to present his liaison as one based on friendship and respectful of authority, his mother and the cardinal insisted that it was a dangerous sickness.

By the end of August Mazarin was on the verge of finalizing the marriage treaty, which included a delay of a few months, to spare the Spanish king the hardship of traveling through the Pyrenees in the winter for the planned ceremony. Both Queen Anne and her prime minister were glad of the postponement, which gave them more time to prepare Louis. In their letters they referred to Louis as "the Confident" and Marie as "the Person." "I believe the Confident," Mazarin informed Anne,

> in the humour wherein he is at present (for I well know he has more passion than ever), will be very glad of this delay: and we shall have more time by this means to tend his cure; for I declare to you, if he marries in that disposition of mind he now is in, he will be miserable, and the Infanta yet more, and you and I beyond all hopes. I have written to him a letter of about sixteen or eighteen pages, and I wish he would let you read it. I am certain 'twill not please him; however, I could not omit it without wronging my own conscience and reputation. . . . I cannot express to you how greatly this afflicts me, the thoughts of it not letting me take a minute's rest, and that which drives me to the greatest despair is that all my misfortune comes from a Person from whom I might otherwise expect to receive comfort.[18]

Eventually both Louis and Marie realized that their liaison could not last. For Louis, the recognition came as he read these relentless missives, along with the reports of Mazarin's superlative powers of political negotiation that were being transmitted to Paris from the party at Saint-Jean-de-Luz. The letters Louis penned have been lost, but we can discern them in the responses he received, and it is apparent that he gradually gave up arguing in favor of Marie and instead simply continued his secret correspondence with her. Madame de Venelle was trying to play an effective role as Mazarin's spy, but she only managed to enrage him with her reports of the

large packets being delivered regularly to Marie's room, where
Marie refused to allow entry to anyone but her sister Hortense.
What angered Mazarin even more was that, given the reported size
of the bundles, it was clear that not only was Louis writing his own
letters to Marie, but he was also sending her copies of the letters
he had received from others, including Mazarin himself.

At the beginning of August 1659, the full court made a formal
voyage to join the marriage negotiations in Saint-Jean-de-Luz, and
Louis somehow managed to persuade his mother to permit him to
visit Marie en route. Mazarin was in Paris, and the queen had been
unhappy with the miserable state to which her relations with her
son had fallen since she had demanded that he end his affair with
Marie. She blamed the cardinal for having allowed the liaison to
flourish in the first place. Persuaded that the king would not break
his promise to spend just one day in the company of Marie and her
sisters, she indulged him. Madame de Venelle received a letter from
Queen Anne summoning the girls to a rendezvous in the town of
Saint-Jean-d'Angély, halfway between La Rochelle and the Spanish
frontier. Despite frantic letters from Madame de Venelle asking for
guidance, the cardinal found himself powerless to prevent the meeting. There, during a daylong series of private conversations, the
king reaffirmed his feelings for Marie. The thirteen-year-old Hortense
was witness to many of these interviews, and she would later recall
that "nothing could equal the passion that the king showed and
the tenderness with which he asked Marie's pardon for all that he
had made her suffer because of him."[19]

But sometime between this meeting and the king's return voyage
from the Spanish border in October, Louis accepted his fate. Was
his rendezvous with Marie a bargain struck with his mother, in exchange for a promise to go through with the planned marriage?
Madame de Motteville wrote that after sacrificing Marie, the king
seemed to become even closer to his mother. "The king and queen

were both deserving of praise for having on this occasion preserved their union uninjured, he bearing generously the hard effects of her perfect affection, and she feeling the hurt that she did with her own hand to the son she loved so dearly."[20] At Saint-Jean-de-Luz, the king gave his personal approval to the progress of the Spanish treaty negotiations and the impending marriage, which would take place the following summer.

After the king returned to Paris, Queen Anne encouraged him to appear in public with other young women. She made sure that reports of his activities and apparent gaiety were transmitted to Marie in Brouage. The cardinal's agents took an even more targeted approach, one that was sure to arouse Marie's jealousy and disappointment. They pressured Marie's older sister Olympe, who had remained at court and enjoyed a close relationship with the royal family, to cultivate an intimacy with Louis, bribing her with the offer of a lucrative position as lady-in-waiting to the future queen. "I have urged Madame the Countess to spend more time with the king and lavish more attention on him," wrote Mazarin's informant Bartet. "The Queen will be even more pleased by this if news of it is sent to Brouage."[21]

In Brouage, Marie read with dismay reports of the king's high spirits and his outings with her sister, some of which Olympe herself had written, with the queen's encouragement. Isolated and unable to investigate the rumors for herself, and fully aware that in any case she had lost Louis to the Spanish marriage, Marie did not take long to understand what her own role had to be. She wrote a pleading and submissive letter to her uncle. "I beseech you to grant me two requests: the first, to keep people from mocking me, and the second, to save me from their cruel laughter by arranging a marriage for me, quickly."[22]

By September Mazarin was writing letters to Marie congratulating her on having come to her senses, and strongly assuring her that he would reward her for her obedience: "You will not be the worse for this, because, continuing to conduct yourself in this manner, you will receive marks of my tenderness on all occasions relating to you and you will see, with satisfaction, that you have not only a good uncle in me, but also a father who loves you with all his heart."[23] Madame de Venelle sent reports that Marie was no longer responding to the king's letters, which were arriving with decreasing frequency. Marie had seen that she depended on her uncle's good-will. Her letters to him expressed only submission:

> I never tire of reading the letters you write me and I have the greatest pleasure and joy in the world in seeing the satisfaction I have given you and the friendship that you now show me. I promise you, again, that I will give you reason to continue it forever. Today I received a little letter from the king. There are only a few words, in which he expresses his joy in seeing that Your Eminence is so satisfied with me. I did not answer and I think that soon he too will stop writing me. I admit that it causes me no small pain to keep from writing him. What gives me the strength to do it is my duty and my wish to satisfy Your Eminence. I want thus to show you that I am the most devoted of nieces.[24]

Was Marie secretly holding on to the hope that the situation would reverse itself? She insisted on remaining at the fortress of Brouage, close to Bordeaux, rather than returning to Paris. Madame de Venelle noted in a letter to Mazarin that although Marie was obeying his orders to cease writing letters to Louis, she was nevertheless sending word to him, via messenger, that she could not respond only because she was obeying orders. "I think that Mademoiselle's intentions are good," Venelle wrote, "but I fear that fire is smoldering under those ashes, and if the two were to see each other, I doubt that their generosity would last."[25]

Mazarin did not let this worry him. He returned his attention to the details of the treaty with Spain, which in his declining state of health, he had come to view as his most important, and final, legacy. At her uncle's insistence, Marie left Brouage to return to Paris on December 30, 1659, but by this time Louis and most of the French court had moved to Provence to await the finalization of the treaty, which was ratified on January 23, 1660. Preparations for the marriage ceremony itself were initiated immediately, and Marie heard constant talk of them during the weeks and months that followed. The marriage of Louis XIV to Marie-Thérèse of Spain was finally celebrated on June 9, 1660, in the royal chapel of Fontarabie near Saint-Jean-de-Luz, on the Spanish border. The following day the kings of France and Spain knelt together and placed their hands on a Bible in a promise of peace and eternal friendship. It was a glorious moment for Mazarin, who personally orchestrated the ritual by giving signals from his seat on a balcony overlooking the ceremony, to indicate precisely when the two kings were to enter and leave the room together. Six days later the newlywed couple and their train of more than a hundred members of the French court left for the long trek back to Paris. The route took them near La Rochelle. There the king, suddenly instructing his wife and all but a few cavaliers to wait for him, made a solitary detour to the fortress of Brouage. He knew that he would not find Marie there, but it was where she had been living when they had last seen each other.

News of this sentimental pilgrimage alarmed Mazarin, who had turned his attentions to the need to quickly find a suitable husband for his niece. He had heard that Marie, in Paris, was receiving the attentions of the young Prince Charles de Lorraine, and Mazarin was inclined to consider him as a possible candidate, except that a French marriage meant that Marie would remain at court. An Italian marriage was favored by Queen Anne, who seemed to want Marie as far away from Louis as possible. And there was a good candidate, the Grand Constable Lorenzo Onofrio Colonna, a Roman prince, who had been proposed once to Marie before the king's marriage and who did not seem discouraged by her initial refusal. Meanwhile, Mazarin worked to destroy the affection and nostalgia that still seemed to consume the newly married king. He made sure Louis received reports that Marie had been welcoming possible suitors in Paris and was not conducting herself like a person stricken with grief.

Marie was not unrealistic. She had been grateful to be permitted to return to Paris, where, she wrote, "Prince Charles (of Lorraine) began to show me attentions which were not disagreeable to me."[26] A marriage arranged by her uncle, she knew, was inevitable, and at this point desirable. She wanted to have some influence in the matter. Still, she did not intend to consent to any marriage until after she had seen the king in person. The requisite meeting, where she would be introduced to the new French queen, took place in August, immediately after Marie-Thérèse was installed at Fontaine-bleau at the end of the long voyage to her new home. Marie had dreaded the moment, and her fears were even more justified than she had anticipated, for not only the new queen but even the king received her with a studied coldness. Her detractors had done their job well:

> The Cardinal sent for us in Paris to come and curtsey before the queen. Because of a presentiment that this honor would cost me dear, I cannot deny that I was prepared to receive it with consid-erable displeasure. I saw only too well that the presence of the king was going to reopen a wound that was not yet fully healed, and that his absence would have been better suited to curing me. And since I had not counted on the coldness and indifference with which His Majesty treated me, I confess that it caused me such surprise and grief that it made me wish the whole time that I could return to Paris.[27]

Marie turned her efforts to regaining some control over her feelings and also to the marriage plans that were being made for her with frightening speed. Charles de Lorraine was suddenly withdrawn from consideration as a result of the scheming of his uncle, who was worried that his nephew would gain too much personal power by a marriage into Mazarin's family, and he proposed himself in his nephew's place. Marie refused the old man's attentions, scoffing at his arrogance: "he took the nephew's place, without considering that at his age he could not play the role fittingly, and that his efforts to pursue me at the Cours and the Tuileries could not meet with the same success as the attentions of his nephew."[28] For advice and assistance, she trusted almost no one. Only the writings of her favorite authors gave her comfort, and she also turned to them for strategic counsel. "I needed a cure for my pain," she wrote, "and so I put all my efforts toward finding one." Marie enlisted her sister Hortense in helping her follow the advice to the lovesick found in Ovid's *Remedies to Love*. "Thus I practiced a part of what Ovid teaches for countering love. I removed from my sight all the objects that might keep my passion alive, and in search of a specious pretext for banishing it from my heart, I beseeched my sister, in whom I had the greatest confidence, to speak ill of the king to me."[29]

Meanwhile, Cardinal Mazarin's health was rapidly declining. The parade of doctors he summoned to his rooms in the Louvre could no longer give him relief from the pain of gout and kidney disease. He knew his life was nearing an end. A marriage for Marie, one he hoped would keep her at a distance from the French court, and also for fourteen-year-old Hortense, were among his most compelling remaining projects. He turned to the Italian prince Lorenzo Onofrio Colonna, and Marie finally gave her consent. Mazarin signed the marriage contract on February 21, 1661.

## ( 2 )

## *The*
# DUCHESS MAZARIN

*You will doubtless find it hard to believe that at that age, when philosophical reasoning is usually the last thing on a person's mind, I had such serious thoughts as I had, about every aspect of life. And yet it is true that my greatest pleasure at that time was to shut myself up alone and write down everything that came into my head. Not long ago I came across some of these writings again; and I confess to you that I was tremendously surprised to find in them ideas far beyond the capacities of a little girl. They were filled with doubts and questions which I posed to myself about all of the things I found hard to understand. I never resolved them to my satisfaction, but I kept doggedly seeking the answers that I could not find; and if my conduct since then has not shown great judgment, at least I have the consolation of knowing that I once wanted very much to acquire it.*

—Hortense Mancini, *Memoirs*

ROM THE MOMENT that Marie stepped onto the galley ship taking her to France, her most loyal friend had been her young sister Hortense, living with her in the Mazarin palace, accompanying her on outings with the court at the Louvre and Fontainebleau palaces, and finally serving as her only confidant in exile in Brouage.

Although Marie's relations with her mother and uncle had always been strained, Hortense and her older sister Olympe enjoyed their favor. Even as a child of seven, the pretty Hortense was admired at court for her engaging ways. Cardinal Mazarin, it seemed, was immediately smitten with her. Olympe, for her part, had no trouble learning the arts of dissemblance and manipulation that were so crucial to social survival at court. She readily accepted the marriage that Mazarin arranged for her in 1659, to the Count of Soissons, and her new husband seemed not to object to her own flirtation with Louis XIV, which Mazarin encouraged to arouse Marie's jealousy.

Hortense watched all of this through the eyes of a child, and she took her own lessons from it. "I have told you," she later wrote, "that my sister always wanted me to be in love."[1] But Hortense found that, unlike Marie, she was not romantically inclined. Her uncle, "who was very afraid that I might commit myself to someone out of love," was reassured when even the spying and encouragement of their governess, Madame de Venelle, could not produce any evidence of romantic sentiment in his favorite niece, who flatly said of herself, "I had nothing in my heart." She watched, perplexed, as Marie begged Hortense to help cure her of her love for the king, even as "my age did not allow me to really understand what she desired of me. All I could do to help her, since I could see she was miserable and I loved her dearly, was to weep with her over her misfortune, until such time as she could weep with me over mine."[2] Her uncle kept a sharp eye on Hortense's reactions to the drama and expressed some concern that her sympathy for Marie would exert too strong an influence on her. "I observe with great displeasure that she is dragging Hortense into her way of thinking," he wrote Madame de Venelle.[3] But nine-year-old Marianne, the youngest of the five Mancini sisters, had joined the little group in Brouage by late summer, and she sent more reassuring messages to their uncle. Hortense, she reported, "thinks only of her pleasure, and loves you very much," while Marie was often alone, "reading astrology, Plutarch, Seneca, and philosophy."[4]

Although romance was not to Hortense's liking, she had embraced the many pleasures of life at court and did not shun the ample attention she received there. Even as a girl, she was beautiful, with a sensuality in her features that drew men to her. Cardinal Mazarin had high marital ambitions for Hortense, first turning his eye to the young Charles Stuart. Heir to the throne of England, Charles had lived in France since Oliver Cromwell seized power and had Charles's father, King Charles I, executed in 1649. Charles Stuart himself had been the first to broach the idea of marrying Hortense, though Mazarin harbored some reservations about the young royal exile's future. In the end, after several discussions with English emissaries, Mazarin withdrew his niece from consideration. "The King of England has offered to marry my niece Hortense," he told Mademoiselle de Montpensier, cousin of Louis XIV, "but I replied that he was paying me too great an honor."[5]

Other candidates for Hortense's hand included the Duke of Savoy, who had proposed the idea to Mazarin when the court traveled to Lyon to explore a possible marriage between Louis XIV and the duke's sister Marguerite. This option dissolved when it became clear that Mazarin's principal motive for publicly considering a royal betrothal to Marguerite was to prod the king of Spain into making a counterproposal for his daughter, Marie-Thérèse, to marry the French king. And although Mazarin had put off the overturned English king's overtures toward Hortense while he was in exile, after Charles II returned to London, the cardinal's interest had been piqued once again. But with the reversal of Charles's fortunes, the opportunity had been lost. His English ministers persuaded him to turn his back on Mazarin and focus on the prospect of a more ambitious marriage with the princess of

Portugal. He would have to wait to meet Hortense again in another chapter of her life.

After the king's marriage, Mazarin's degenerating health probably played a role in the choice he finally made for Hortense. Rushing to put his family affairs in order and to select a trustworthy nobleman who would not dissipate the inheritance he intended to provide Hortense and her future husband, he turned his attention to a supplicant who had long been pressing to marry this particular niece. Armand-Charles de la Porte de la Meilleraye, in line to acquire from his father the distinguished title of grand master of the artillery and marshal of France, had been obsessed with Hortense since she was a child of nine or ten. Now he was twenty-nine and she fourteen. Armand-Charles cut an odd, awkward figure at court and as an outsider could only observe the lively social circles of which Hortense often found herself at the center. He was devout and becoming increasingly fanatical in his religious habits, as intensely attracted to the more extreme forms of Catholic devotion as he was to this girl who was regularly scolded by her uncle for her lack of piety. In his declining physical state Mazarin may not have been thinking clearly, but he also may have seen in Armand-Charles a dim reflection of his own stubborn rise from modest origins. Armand-Charles's family had originally been small merchants and apothecaries but over three generations had managed to claw their way to noble rank. To Hortense's uncle, ever watchful over the wayward tendencies of his nieces and sharply aware of the temptations of the court, Armand-Charles's austere incorruptibility might have seemed just what the young bride needed to keep her pleasure-loving personality in check. Sobriety and discipline surely had positive advantages when it came to managing the fortune the cardinal intended to bestow on the couple.

In late 1660, Mazarin's doctors had given him two months to live. He suffered from a painful array of ailments, all of them seemingly converging to crush him. The doctors who surrounded him argued over what course to take. Among others watching the spectacle there were mixed emotions, for the cardinal had more enemies than friends. In letters to a colleague, the celebrated physician Guy Patin described in excruciating detail the final weeks of Mazarin's life:

> As for Mazarin, he is languishing. . . . He is asthmatic, . . . he has coughing fits at night, so that his windows have to be opened to allow him to breathe, for fear that he may choke; he is swollen, distended, exhausted, discolored; in short he is no longer that ruddy Mazarin who was such a fine man. His nights are very bad and only opium can barely let him sleep. Judge for yourself how long this can last.[6]

While he could still walk, the cardinal remained in the Mazarin palace at the center of Paris, close to the magnificent art collection lining the walls of his gallery, where he would wander at night, murmuring to himself, "I must leave all of this." He was a rich man, perhaps the richest in all of Europe, and he had spent a lifetime building and defending the colossal reputation that came to be associated with his family name. Giulio Mazzarini, son of a Sicilian small landowner who had moved his family to Rome so the father could work as a household servant to the Colonnas, had become Jules Mazarin, a towering figure in French statesmanship, whose niece Marie would marry a Colonna prince. Mazarin wanted his name to bear a noble title and become part of his legacy.

When the cardinal contemplated which of his relatives could inherit his fortune and his name, the only surviving nephew, Philippe Mancini, did not seem to be a good candidate. His brother Alphonse had died in a schoolyard accident in 1658. In 1657, Mazarin had reestablished the military unit known as the king's musketeers and made sixteen-year-old Philippe its captain. But Philippe had little inclination for combat and he let his senior comrade, the Count d'Artagnan, assume the role of captain. Philippe was a hedonist. He frequented the circles of the king's younger brother, and some said the two had an amorous relationship. The young Mancini quickly became notorious for his escapades, the most scandalous of which would be a wild three days of debauchery in 1659 at a country chateau, beginning on Good Friday. During this weekend, some of the invited guests composed an obscene series of verses parodying the "hallelujahs" that were part of the Easter liturgy. The verses and the story of the weekend orgy circulated in Paris not long afterward, and Philippe was abruptly shipped off to a military fortress in Brisach on the German border, where Mazarin left him for several months to reflect on his folly.

On his deathbed, Cardinal Mazarin turned to the most appealing solution: marry young Hortense to a religious nobleman with impeccable family credentials, and bestow on both of them the title of Duke and Duchess Mazarin. Others, including the father of the potential groom, had found Armand-Charles's unwavering fascination with the girl to be somewhat troubling and advised against the marriage, but the cardinal was determined to make the choice for his niece before he died, and in his moribund state he believed he was choosing an heir who would safeguard his fortune as well as his family honor. Armand-Charles, the Marquis de la Meilleraye, had been a faithful postulant for Hortense's hand and even seemed to bear no grudge after her uncle withdrew his approval for the union when it seemed for a time that a better match might be made with the future king of England.

And so the fourteen-year-old Hortense learned of her uncle's final choice for her in late February 1661. When she accepted, the cardinal gave her a gift to indicate his gratitude. "As soon as the marriage negotiations were concluded," she later wrote, "he sent me a large cabinet in which, among other objects of value, there were ten thousand pistoles in gold. I shared them liberally with my brother and my sisters, to console them for my opulence, which my sisters could not look upon without envy, no matter how they hid it."[7] Ten thousand pistoles in Spanish gold coin were a sum equivalent to $1 million today.[8] The marriage was celebrated on March 1, and in the evening the king joined the bridal party at the Mazarin palace. Over the next few days the cardinal occupied himself with finalizing his will, leaving most of his material possessions to Hortense and her husband, the newly named Duke and Duchess Mazarin, and making his favorite niece, in her own words, "the richest heiress and the unhappiest woman in Christendom." When the cardinal died on March 9, 1661, he left no genuine mourners among his family. "When we first heard the news," Hortense wrote, "all that my brother and my sister did by way of grieving was to say to each other, 'Thank God he's croaked!' To tell the truth, I was hardly any more afflicted."[9]

From the start, the Mazarin couple was positioned squarely at the center of the most favored social circles in the city and at court, where Hortense had already made her mark. Her youthful and fun-loving presence at the Louvre and especially at Fontainebleau, where with her sister she had been permitted to roam freely on horseback and on foot in the woods and gardens, had been noticed and admired. She had been at Queen Anne's regular gatherings and listened to her sister recite from memory her favorite speeches from Pierre Corneille's play *Le Cid*. She had learned to sing, play guitar, and speak French fluently, retaining only a slight accent that was thought to add to her charm. At the age of twelve, with Marie she had danced in the court ballet *Alcidiane,* which Molière had written to showcase the young king's dancing skills. Armand-Charles had married a young woman who was utterly comfortable with, and excelled at, a public life.

Their residence was the cardinal's sumptuous Mazarin palace, not far from the Louvre. As a showcase for the material wealth they had inherited, the place featured the magnificent gallery where the

cardinal had loved to pace in front of his grand collection of paintings. Now the palace was filled with young friends of Hortense and
her lively brother Philippe. Armand-Charles watched this regular
stream of fashionable visitors with some dismay, but at first he tolerated it. One wing of the palace had been left to the wayward
Philippe, who would frequently join the gatherings his sister Hortense arranged. It was at these concerts and banquets that many of
their friends first saw at close range just how astounding Mazarin's
art collection was. It included nearly nine hundred paintings, many
of them by Italian masters: Raphael, Caravaggio, Carracci, Giorgione, Mantegna, Titian, da Vinci. Even more impressive were the
hundreds of statues from Roman antiquity lining the halls and filling
the courtyard.

But the new Duke Mazarin did not like all this company, and in
social gatherings at court, he had never felt at ease. He had seen
the eleven-year-old Hortense dance with the king's brother at a
ball during carnival, he had watched her practice perfect curtsies
for the queen, and he had read the praises of the loveliest Mazarin
niece in the gazettes following her first public appearances: "the
adorable Hortense, that eastern star." Cardinal Mazarin had first
suggested to him that Marie, and then Olympe, might be suited to
be his wife, but Armand-Charles had let it be known that he was
in love with the child Hortense from the beginning. Now that he
finally had the prize he had longed for, he could not bear watching
others admire her. He began to restrict her comings and goings,
forbidding the staging of plays and concerts in their residence and
banning all the friends whose company his wife seemed to enjoy
the most. Within a few months of their marriage, he insisted that
she accompany him on long trips away from the capital to tour the
most remote of the couple's provincial holdings. In the summer of
1661 the couple set out for Alsace, not to return until winter. When
Hortense found that she could actually enjoy herself at a stop on

their journeys, her husband immediately made plans to leave. "As soon as he knew I was happy in some place," she would later recall, "he would make me leave it, no matter what reasons there might be to keep me there."[10] She became pregnant while they were in Alsace, and he waited until she was close to full term before bringing her back to Paris, making sure she remained strictly confined until well after their first child, Marie-Charlotte, was born in early 1662.

Louis XIV had given Duke Mazarin the title of governor of Alsace and royal administrator of extensive lands in Brittany. The duke embraced his responsibilities with an enthusiasm and sobriety that at first gratified, then alarmed the king. Armand-Charles's religious fanaticism was beginning to appear mad; he claimed the Angel Gabriel spoke to him in dreams. He obsessively interfered with the smallest details in his peasants' lives, claiming to want to help them walk the road to salvation. He objected to female domestics in the households of priests and warned poor farm families not to let brothers and sisters sleep in the same bed. He was troubled by the physicality of agricultural life, warning milkmaids against spending too long milking cows and suggesting that they practice more modest postures when tending to tasks such as churning milk. In his own household, he imposed rigid rules requiring that everyone go to bed early, discouraged conversation and laughter, and promptly dismissed any servant unfortunate enough to receive an expression of affection from his wife. Hortense later wrote:

> Just imagine an implacable hatred for everyone who loved me and whom I loved; an avid effort to set before me all the people I could not abide, and to bribe those whom I trusted the most in order to discover my secrets, if I had had any; a tireless diligence in disparaging me to everyone and in putting a shameful cast on all my actions; in short, everything that the malice of a sanctimonious cabal can dream up and implement in a household where it holds tyrannical sway.[11]

Meanwhile, Hortense gave birth to two more daughters, Marie-Anne and Marie-Olympe, in 1663 and 1665. Three weeks after Marie-Olympe was born, the duke took his wife to family lands in Brittany, where he could more easily keep her away from society, and where she stayed until she became pregnant again. Once again, as late as possible in her pregnancy he brought her back to Paris, where finally she gave birth to a son, Paul-Jules, in 1666.

The arrival of a son and heir to the Duke and Duchess Mazarin was occasion for much public congratulation. Hortense's brother and sister Marianne, Duchess of Bouillon, were hopeful that the event would mark a more relaxed regimen in the Mazarin household. The poet Isaac de Benserade wrote a celebratory verse wishing the couple happiness:

*This son is your support*
*and he will be your sweet helper,*
*if he has the beauty of his mother*
*and the heart of his father,*
*he will never fear anything but God.*[12]

However, the marriage was not improved by the arrival of little Paul-Jules. Having produced the requisite male heir and survived four pregnancies in five years, Hortense was eager to spend as little time with her husband as possible. But the duke was more possessive than ever. He became obsessed with the fear that his wife would leave him and determined to remove any possible means for her to do so. He demanded that she give him her jewels and had them removed from their residence so she would have no access to funds other than the modest allowance she had been allotted in her marriage contract. She later wrote:

Every day I saw immense sums of money, priceless furniture, offices, governorships, and all the rich remains of my uncle's fortune disappear. I saw more than three millions' worth of it sold before I made any public protest; and there was almost nothing of value left to me but my jewels when Monsieur Mazarin took it into his head to seize them from me. He took advantage of his opportunity to lay hold of them one evening when I came home very late from the city. When I desired to know the reason before going to bed, he told me *that he feared I would give some of them away, liberal as I was, and that he had taken them only in order to add more to them.* I replied to him *that one could only wish that his liberality were as well ordered as mine, that I was satisfied with my jewels as they were and that I would not go to bed until he returned them to me,* but seeing that no matter what I said he replied only with bad jokes, spoken with a malicious smile and in a tone which seemed serene but was actually very bitter, finally in desperation I left the room and went off to my brother's wing, in tears and not knowing what to do. We sent straightaway for [my sister] Madame de Bouillon, and when she had heard about my new cause for complaint, she told me that I deserved it since I had borne all the others in silence.[13]

Philippe and Marianne were becoming exasperated with their sister's reluctance to openly oppose her husband. Once she had produced a son, like many other women of her station, she might at least have been allowed to move into separate living quarters. But Armand-Charles wanted his wife closer to him than ever, and at first Hortense complied. Within a few months of their son's birth, the duke was pressing his wife to accompany him on one of the provincial voyages she so detested, this time to Brittany where he had volunteered to serve Finance Minister Colbert in the royal project to examine the financial affairs of all the cities in the realm. After a boring summer in Nantes, Hortense was dragged off to keep her husband company as he sought a cure for his permanently tormented mental state at the hot-water spas of Bourbon l'Archambault, where much to his consternation she encountered Philippe, himself enjoying a brief respite from his own pleasure travels. Though Hortense was delighted to see Philippe, he was sorry to see her depressed. He and his sister had long conversations about the duke's erratic behavior, demanding ways, and apparent mismanagement of the couple's wealth.

Unlike Cardinal Mazarin, who had built a fortune based on material goods and moveable wealth, Armand-Charles was interested only in landed property. When the colossal Mazarin fortune became his, he threw himself into what he viewed as the most aristocratic of spending habits: making charitable donations to the church, and purchasing and managing land. The former, of course, was an investment without financial return, and he was taken advantage of at every turn. "Monks and holy men profited from his weaknesses and drew freely on his millions," wrote Saint-Simon.[14] Immediately following his marriage, the duke had started to give away his money, often in the form of pensions guaranteed for life, to a seemingly haphazard array of individuals with whom he came into contact, from old family servants to doctors at the Sorbonne to aspiring nuns and priests in far-flung dioceses. Furthermore, in the late seventeenth century, real estate in the French provinces, the duke's only other financial interest, was not a good investment.

Hortense and her brother discussed the dwindling Mazarin fortune during their long evenings in Bourbon. Philippe admonished his sister for her tolerance. He warned her that she would forever be traveling to destinations not of her own choosing, perpetually getting pregnant, spending time in the most tiresome company, and being allowed none of the pleasures that her inheritance should have brought her. He urged her to appeal to the sympathy of both the king and Colbert to request a *séparation de biens,* or legal division of property, to safeguard at least her portion of the Mazarin legacy.

Such a request was not unprecedented, but the peculiar status of the Mazarin marriage contract made this move even more complicated than it would have been had Hortense been wed under more conventional terms. Her uncle, obsessed with keeping his fortune intact and perhaps foreseeing a possible separation, had designed a marriage contract that gave the couple a common share of the inheritance but did not specifically protect Hortense's portion. Only her jewels were clearly hers and not her husband's, in the eyes of the law. All other property was subject to dispute. The terms of the inheritance had been kept deliberately vague, ensuring that Hortense would have to make an exceptionally strong legal case if she ever attempted an official *séparation de biens*.

And so when Hortense took the first step, immediately after returning to Paris in late 1666, toward a legal separation, she knew she was making a move that carried high risks. She knew her husband, and knew that she would not be dealing with a gracious nobleman like the Count of Lafayette, who, once he had acquired one or two sons, had been quite content to let his writer wife keep her own house in Paris where she could compose her novels and receive her friends while he remained on their provincial estates. Not only was Hortense's husband fanatically devout, but he also was obsessively jealous, a most ungenerous and unaristocratic combination of personality traits. "Jealousy," wrote François de La Rochefoucauld, "is the greatest of all evils, and the one which excites the least pity in those who occasion it."[15] Hortense certainly was beyond feeling any pity for her husband.

Being all too familiar with Armand-Charles's obsessions, she was prepared for the devastating consequences that her formal request to separate their common property had for her already fragile relations with him. Before her husband had heard of the measures she had taken, she left the Mazarin palace to take shelter at her sister Olympe's residence, where she remained while Jean-Baptiste Colbert considered how to deny her request and mediate a reconciliation. After two months she was ordered to return to her husband, while Armand-Charles was told to allow his wife to select her own servants and to stop forcing her to employ maids of his choosing, whom he had enlisted as spies. But this truce was broken almost immediately. The duke refused to allow his wife to leave, screaming at his servants to lock all the doors whenever she tried to venture out, even on foot (he had already locked up her carriage). When the terrified servants moved out of her way he tried to physically restrain her himself, though, she reported, unsuccessfully: "Monsieur Mazarin . . . threw himself in front of me and pushed me very roughly, in order to block my way; but my grief and vexation gave me extraordinary strength, and I broke through even though he was strong, too."[16]

It was clear that the household was irreconcilable. Armand-Charles resorted to his habitual demand that she leave the capital with him for an extended stay in Alsace. This time Hortense's friends were more blunt than usual in their warnings to her. "After what has happened, you would be a fool to expect to come back from there," they told her, "where his actions would not be open to public scrutiny as they are in Paris, and where we would no longer be able to do anything for you but send useless wishes."[17] Hortense once again took refuge with Olympe, and when Armand-Charles arrived to take her with him, she refused to leave. The duke responded by giving her two choices of places where he would permit her to reside in his absence: the Notre-Dame-des-Chelles convent, about ten miles outside of Paris, where one of his relatives was the abbess, or the residence of Hortense's older cousin Anne-Marie, married to the Prince of Conti, a close friend of the duke and, like him, a convert to Catholic extremism. Forced to choose between what she called "two equally odious propositions," Hortense chose the convent. She stayed at Chelles through the summer of 1667, when once again the duke demanded that she accompany him on a voyage, this time to his ancestral village in Brittany. Once again his wife refused, and this time the duke appealed to the king for support. Louis XIV partially acceded to the duke's wishes and ordered Hortense to move to another convent, this one of the Order of the Visitation on the rue Saint-Antoine, where the duke believed she would be under closer supervision.

The duchess was infuriated by this royal order, which came shortly after she had made it known to both Louis XIV and Colbert that she was preparing a legal case to recover control of the wealth she had inherited. Believing that her maniacal husband was squandering the fortune to which she and her four children were entitled, the Duchess Mazarin found herself escorted by royal armed guard to be incarcerated in a Parisian convent that also served as a prison for wayward noblewomen. Her situation was desperate.

One of the other unfortunate women being kept under lock and key at the Convent of the Visitation was Marie-Sidonie de Courcelles, a seventeen-year-old whose husband had brought a legal suit against her for adultery. The Marquise de Courcelles was a stubborn and resilient young woman who knew something about how to navigate the labyrinth of courts and patrons that constituted the legal system. She was building a case in her own defense, drawing upon personal contacts while also negotiating for her cause to be heard by sympathetic judges. The marquise would later write her own memoirs, in which she expressed her anger at the legal predicament faced by wayward wives who were imprisoned for adultery while noblemen were simply exiled from the court for far more serious offenses. Hortense was consoled and delighted to find herself in the marquise's company. Not only did the young marquise, who had some powerful friends at court, offer to assist the duchess in her legal challenge to her husband, but she also was, Hortense observed admiringly, "very attractive and very amusing."[18] For these two, finding themselves together in a convent was a predicament to resist through mockery. They flaunted their youth and energy before the elderly nuns who had been assigned to watch them. "Under the pretext of keeping us company, the sisters were keeping us under surveillance," Hortense wrote. "We soon exhausted them all one after another, until two or three of them sprained their ankles striving to keep up with us."[19] Stories of their pranks and their resilience made the rounds of the Paris salons and the court, garnering the women sympathy. An anonymous poet circulated a popular verse declaring that until the two were liberated, there would be no laughter among the ladies of Paris.[20] It was not long before the nuns tired of their roles as jail keepers and were only too happy to see the two friends win a formal request to be transferred together to Chelles.

Governed by an aunt of Duke Mazarin, Chelles was already familiar to Hortense, who earlier had chosen to stay there rather than be confined in the household of the Prince de Conti. To her surprise, during her first stay she had found her husband's aunt to be sympathetic to her. The Chelles abbey, Hortense learned, had a long history of powerful women who had governed both the abbey and the community surrounding it. Residents of the convent traditionally had been permitted to own and manage properties, and the abbess had complete autonomy in governing the community. In its nearly thousand-year history, many generations of royal women had chosen to "retire" there. Armand-Charles was not particularly pleased to learn of the decision to send his wife back to Chelles, but when he demanded that the abbess return his wife to him, he was refused.

This was a show worth watching. It must have been especially gratifying to female observers, for whom the threat of being locked up in a convent was routinely held over them from childhood anytime they dared to go against the wishes of father or husband. Hortense and Marie-Sidonie were both in desperate situations with little hope of resolution based on legal precedent. But they flaunted their gaiety and their ability to escape the grasp of their persecutors. They certainly feared what would happen to them if they managed to return to the outside world without permission, but they were determined to let the world know they could escape. They received visitors, with whom they chatted through the metal grille separating the nuns from the convent parlor. One day, hearing a commotion outside and fearing that the Duke Mazarin had arrived with an armed guard to move Hortense to a more secure prison, they managed to actually squeeze their thin bodies between the bars of the grille. Hortense later remembered the pleasure the two of them took in imagining this adventure as a rehearsal for their eventual escape: "In the grille of our parlor there was a hole big enough for a large tray, through which we had never imagined before then that a person might be able to pass. And yet we both got through it, but it was such a tight fit that Monsieur Mazarin himself, if he had been in the convent, would never have suspected it and would have looked for us everywhere but in that parlor."[21]

News of the convent escapades of the marquise and the duchess made the rounds in Paris, providing not only a source of entertainment but also fodder for public discussions concerning the legal rights of husbands over their wives. In the eyes of the law and of marriage contracts, women were regarded as their husbands' property. But challenges to this status were being vigorously argued in many forms, from popular fiction to legal dossiers. For decades the writer and philosopher Madeleine de Scudéry had been arguing against marriage and its power to enslave women. "Those whom Nature or custom gave as our masters want us to extinguish in our souls the lights Heaven put there and to live in the deepest shadows of ignorance," she had written in 1653.[22] Legal debates over the status of married women as property were quickly absorbed in public conversations. In 1667, when Hortense and Marie-Sidonie were in the Convent of the Visitation in Paris, everyone was following the efforts of another particularly prominent unhappy wife, Marie de Savoie Nemours, to extricate herself from a miserable marriage. Her drunken and violent husband was Alphonse VI, king of Portugal. Marie had fled less than a year after her marriage, taking refuge in a convent. By early 1668 she was negotiating for a papal dispensation to have her marriage annulled. She was successful, and in April she married Dom Pedro of Portugal, her former brother-in-law, who overthrew Alphonse and had himself declared regent.

The contemporary legal struggles of rebellious women were on the mind of the feminist writer Poullain de la Barre when he condemned lawyers who "place women under the tutelage of their husbands, like children vis-à-vis their fathers, and say that it is nature that has assigned them the basest occupations in society and has placed public positions out of their reach."[23]

Marie-Sidonie and Hortense both threw themselves into the task of appealing to the courts for legal separations that would provide them with income to live independently. Legal opinion was as divided as the public on these issues. With the marquise's encouragement, Hortense submitted her first appeal to the Court of Requests in Paris, and the young judges who constituted this judicial body handed down an encouraging decision, authorizing the duchess to return to the Mazarin palace and ordering her husband to take up residence, for the time being, in the Arsenal of Paris (he was, after all, grand master of the artillery), provide his wife with a pension of 20,000 livres per annum, and produce the documents she had requested showing how he was disposing of their fortune.

For a brief moment, Hortense felt triumphant. "The Chamber was composed almost entirely of very reasonable young men," she declared, "and there was not a single one of them who did not strive to serve me."[24] But she knew that Armand-Charles would not simply settle for the decision and would instead launch himself into the battle even more energetically in public than he had in private.

The duke appealed the lower court's decision to the more senior Grand Chamber of judges, hoping for an outcome that would be more favorable to him. And he waited, furious, as Hortense returned to public life, to court festivities, and to company that included Marie-Sidonie, who had won temporary permission to move from the convent to the Mazarin palace. When Hortense resumed hosting productions in a small theater she had constructed in her wing of the palace, Armand-Charles could no longer contain himself. One day when his wife was absent, he had the theater demolished.

It was clear that the duke had no intention of respecting the terms of the couple's authorized separation. The king, who did not relish intervening in marital quarrels, was nevertheless persuaded that the duke's official exclusion from his own residence was too harsh, and while everyone was waiting for the final judgment of the Grand Chamber, he overrode that particular provision of the Court of Request's decision. Hortense was further dismayed by Marie-Sidonie's apparent reconciliation with her own husband. This was bad timing; it seemed to hold out a model for the Mazarin couple, one that the duchess was determined not to follow. The two friends quarreled, and Hortense committed a serious indiscretion by informing the Marquis de Courcelles that his wife was receiving secret visits from the young Marquis de Cavoye. Courcelles decided to avenge himself and the result was a predawn duel between the two men in the Marais district, not far from the Mazarin palace. Both Courcelles and his opponent, though uninjured, were thrown into the Conciergerie prison for such a blatant violation, in the heart of the city, of the royal interdiction against dueling, and Cavoye would remain in prison for two full years. Meanwhile, public opinion toward the young duchess started to cool.

Hortense was mortified. Making matters worse, at around the same time, one of her pages was seriously wounded in a street brawl, and it was whispered that somehow the duchess had arranged the incident to prevent the young man from giving up a secret that would have damaged her reputation and her legal case. In the public eye, she realized, she was losing her innocence. "Everyone at court called me a troublemaker and accused me of brutality toward this worthy subject," she wrote, "saying 'that I would do my best to get plenty of others slaughtered too.'"[25] In a somewhat desperate move, she decided that the best course of action would be to appeal directly to the king for solidarity and sympathy. She made an appearance at court accompanied by Olympe, who immediately attempted to make light of their visit by saying to the king, "I am bringing you that criminal, that wicked woman, of whom so much ill is being said." Louis promptly replied, "I never believed a word of it." "But," Hortense later noted, "he said it so succinctly, and in a manner so different from the openness with which he was in the habit of treating me, that anyone other than I would have seen cause to doubt whether he was telling the truth."[26]

It was early May 1668, only five months after the Court of Requests had awarded the Duchess Mazarin a favorable decision. But this judgment that she had hoped would provide her with protection from her husband was fragile. The Court of Requests was only one of several judicial chambers, or parlements, that might hear her case, and she knew that Armand-Charles would pursue his suit against her with another chamber. She also needed public opinion on her side, and in particular the support of the royal court. Although she did not lack confidence, and though she did have many supporters, her position was now uncomfortably reminiscent of the one in which she and Marie-Sidonie had pushed and pulled each other through the grille of the convent to escape the unwelcome arrival of Duke Mazarin: she was managing, but it was a tight squeeze. In the middle of May, Hortense received a visit from a highly placed friend who gave her sobering news about her husband's countersuit: "The Duke controls the Grand Chamber, his cabal is all-powerful there, he will obtain whatever ruling he desires, and even if you were awarded the separation of property you are requesting, they will surely revoke the physical separation that you have won."[27] Of the two types of legal separation that were possible, *séparation de corps* (physical separation) and *séparation de biens* (separation of assets), it was the former that Hortense was determined to retain at all cost. "Just imagine," she thought, "what treatment I could expect from Monsieur Mazarin, if I returned to him under the force of a legal ruling, with the court and the Parlement against me."[28]

By the end of May, Hortense had made her decision. The plan was hatched in the greatest secrecy, with only a handful of people who were close to her. She contacted her sister Marie in Rome and asked that she rendezvous with her in Milan. With their brother, Philippe, their loyal friend the Chevalier de Rohan, and Hortense's servant Nanon, she plotted a risky escape to Italy, outside the jurisdiction of husband, court, and king. She informed none of her other siblings, even Olympe, the Countess of Soissons, who had been sheltering her and helping to build her legal case. Hortense's children were to be left behind. In her memoirs, Hortense says she was persuaded that if she could manage to negotiate with her husband from outside the reach of the French legal system, he would be forced to give her a more favorable settlement.

Philippe encouraged this plan. But most of her other allies, including Olympe, would have opposed it. In the last days of May, the countess had become alarmed by her sister's distracted demeanor. She scolded Hortense for not focusing on her lawsuit and was angry when she one day arrived in Hortense's rooms to find her still lounging about in her dishabille, strumming on her guitar, when she should have been busy consulting with her lawyers. Hortense would later remember her own behavior then as a strategy, and a fragile one at that:

Once I had made my decision, I was so neglectful of my lawsuit that a hundred times I marveled that those who took an interest in it did not guess my plan. Madame la Comtesse, with whom I was more on my guard than with any other, was the only one who had any suspicion of it, but she did not believe it. She came from time to time to my brother's house, where we pretended to think of nothing but amusing ourselves, the better to fool people, and she wore herself out harping at us *that we were not attending to my case, and that it was a disgrace.*[29]

Was she secretly hoping that someone would prevent her from taking this rash step? The possible consequences could not have been more uncertain. Writing her memoirs seven years later, she remembered every detail of the preparations she was making in those last days before fleeing. The date of her departure is the only one in her life that she specifies in the memoirs. It was a fateful day for her, and one that would send her down a path that had not, she knew well, been explored by other women before her. She knew, too, that the king, the one person who had the power to either force her to remain with her husband or allow her to leave, had committed to stay out of her affairs, and in doing so had essentially left her to assume, on her own, whatever risks she chose to take. When, at three A.M. on June 14, 1668, Monsieur Mazarin rushed to the Louvre to have the king awakened, Louis XIV already knew she had left. His response to the duke was clear and, for Hortense, "generous": "The king had the generosity to reply to him *that he wanted to keep the promise he had made to no longer involve himself in our affairs . . . and that it did not seem likely that I could be caught, given the head start I had and the advance preparations I had made.*"[30]
The Duchess Mazarin's adventures on the road had begun.

## ( 3 )

# MARIE'S ROME

*In winter, there are no grand social events in Rome. Women
can find no more amusement than at any other time there,
they are only permitted to go to plays. Balls and smaller
social gatherings are held only by the Constabless Colonna,
who has determined to live as one does in France and to
introduce complete freedom in her house. This at first caused
much murmuring against her, especially by husbands, but
now everyone has grown accustomed to it.*

—Jacques de Belbeuf, *Travel Journal*

WHILE HER SISTER IN PARIS was arriving at the decision to flee both the capital and her husband, Marie Mancini Colonna had become well established in her native Rome as a member of one of that city's most prominent families. In June 1668, while Hortense was preparing her escape, Marie was helping her own husband prepare for an annual social ritual that preoccupied him obsessively: the *chinea*, a ceremonial cavalcade of Roman noblemen. Every June on the feast of Saint Peter, Lorenzo Onofrio Colonna, Grand Constable of the Kingdom of Naples, Prince and Duke of Paliano, Prince of Castiglione, Duke of Taglia-cozzo and of Marino, would gallop on horseback from the Corso to the Vatican, where he and the other Roman princes would present a tribute of gold coins from the Kingdom of Naples to the pope. In June 1661, when Marie, newly wed, had lain gravely ill on a bed in Bologna, Lorenzo had insisted that she be carried by carriage to Rome rather than wait for her recovery, so that he would not miss this yearly opportunity to put his power and prestige on display.

Since her marriage by proxy, in the king's chapel in the Louvre, to Lorenzo Colonna in April 1661, Marie Mancini's life had been radically transformed. For her, the move to Rome was clearly an exile, from her family, her happy youth at the court of France, and from her fairy-tale romance with the young king that had so abruptly ended. In the months leading up to her wedding, as she waited for letters from Rome confirming the marriage contract, she had occasion to regret having agreed to it so quickly. She wrote to Cardinal Mazarin, "I am obliged to tell you that I will not possibly be happy in Rome, and I may even make unhappy the man who would marry me, for it would be impossible for me to become accustomed to the way of life in that country."[1] This was a notion she might easily have developed from talking to French travelers returning from that city, who reported that Italian women were expected to stay in their houses and go about in public only in the company of brothers, fathers, or husbands. In his treatise on the equality of the sexes, François Poullain de la Barre had described France as a country where women were far better off than in most parts of the world. "There are even some places," he wrote, "where women are treated like slaves. In China their feet are bound during childhood to stop them leaving the house, where they see virtually only their husbands and their children. They are also shut in in Turkey. They are not much better off in Italy."[2]

In August 1660 one of Lorenzo Colonna's emissaries in Paris wrote to him that Marie was finally getting over the idea that "women are like slaves" in Rome. When she finally left for Italy, her voyage was made more difficult by an illness she contracted en

route, and by her new husband's impatience to consummate the
marriage immediately after meeting her for the first time at their
rendezvous point in Turin, without regard for her physical and
emotional exhaustion. She arrived in Rome seriously ill but managed
to survive the elaborate formal presentations arranged for her there.
For the rest of her life she frequently would associate Rome with
illness, complaining of the bad air and poor sanitation compared
with Paris.

Rome in 1661 was a city in the throes of architectural and urban
development. As Marie traversed the city from the north, she reflected on how much it had changed since her departure just seven
years earlier. The new pope, Fabio Chigi, who had assumed the
name Alexander VII, had ambitious plans to redesign the city, build
new churches, and impose a more modern urban landscape onto a
city whose people had suffered from malaria and economic decline
since the beginning of the century. In 1656, with a new outbreak
of bubonic plague in Rome, the pope had instituted sanitation measures to contain the spread of the disease. Almost as soon as Alexander's pontificate began, it was clear that he intended to spend a
considerable portion of the Catholic Church's resources on roads,
waterworks, buildings, and architectural projects. He was helped
in the latter two goals by the incomparable genius of Gian Lorenzo
Bernini, whose many commissions of monuments, fountains,
churches, and sculpture would continue to transform the city until
the latter's death in 1680.

Marie had married into a family whose noble credentials extended
back before the year 1000. The family even claimed ancestry dating
to the era of Julius Caesar. Their prominence was anchored, as was
that of all Roman nobility, in military exploits and in the Church—
five popes had been Colonnas. Lorenzo's great-great-grandfather
Marcantonio Colonna was the most famous Roman military hero
since antiquity, having led a coalition of Christian states against the

Turks in the 1571 Battle of Lepanto, which decisively halted the expansion of the Ottoman Empire into Europe. The city of Rome was dotted with statues and monuments commemorating this achievement, reminding anyone who walked through its streets of the debt Rome owed to the Colonna dynasty. One of them, a statue of Marcantonio Colonna in antique garb, continues to preside over the garden behind the family palazzo today. The ceiling of the Grand Gallery of the Palazzo is still covered with frescoes commemorating the great battle, and numerous giant seascape oil paintings depict the historic victory. Lorenzo Colonna's rank as constable designated him as a military commander in the family tradition.

On June 30, 1661, Marie, weak from her illness, was carried into her new home, where she was placed in her room on the ground floor, cooled by a small fountain and darkened to keep out the summer heat. There she prepared to meet the flood of curious visitors who would come to pay their respects to the newlyweds. If she had doubted it before, she could have no more uncertainties about the prestige of the family she had married into. Lorenzo's uncle the Cardinal Colonna was one of the first to arrive, bearing expensive gifts of jewels and money. Marie observed this parade with her characteristic curiosity, remarking on the styles of dress of the Roman women and the particular protocols surrounding any interaction with the pope and his relatives. Letters from the Italian abbé Elpidio Benedetti, formerly an agent of Cardinal Mazarin and whom Louis XIV had engaged to report on Marie's trip to Rome and her reception there, describe the lavish entertainments designed to amuse her because, he wrote, "we were trying to make Madame forget the gallant fetes at Fontainebleau and the pleasures of her beloved country."[3] As she recovered, she soon appreciated the efforts her husband was making to ease her entry into Roman society:

> After a few days, when my health was a bit restored despite the meager diet I had kept, I began to go out on promenades and anywhere

else where there was some entertainment. I went there in proper dress, that is dressed in the Italian style, having wanted to adopt that fashion because of its novelty for me. . . . Although the customs of Italy scarcely agreed with my temperament, the liking that I was beginning to feel for the constable made them easier for me to bear, for indeed, he did everything he could to please me in any way.[4]

Lorenzo Colonna was extremely pleased with his young wife. She was a showpiece for him, a new and exotic conquest, very gratifying for a man famous for the obsessive pride with which he held his family name. Visitors who came to the palazzo to call on the new Constabless Colonna were also expected to make obsequious demonstrations of loyalty and respect to the family patriarch. Lorenzo was known for insisting on such displays. Just before Marie's voyage to Rome he had challenged a minor nobleman to a duel for not having addressed him as "your excellency." Marie represented, too, a strengthening of Colonna's links to the French throne. Once she had arrived safely, Colonna wrote to Louis XIV, taking care to express his generous feelings toward the king's past "friendship" with Marie. Louis made a polite response, addressing Lorenzo as his "cousin" (Louis had often referred to Mazarin as his uncle), and expressing his own good wishes for the couple. It was a message in which much was left unsaid but also much was understood, in which Marie's recovering body seemed to have become the sign of a strengthened tie that would hold the two men together in the future.

FONTAINEBLEAU, 6 AUGUST 1661

Cousin, after the trials of a great journey and a dangerous illness, it is no small thing that my cousin, your wife, is finally arrived in Rome and convalescing. I was very pleased to learn this good news in your letter and hope that rest and the satisfaction of being with you will

soon bring her back to perfect health, I wish it with all my heart. I
also saw with great pleasure the feelings that you tell me she still has
for me, and your own sharing of those feelings. Be assured that mine
will also always be as you desire for you and for her, and that I will
joyfully embrace all occasions to prove this to you with my actions.[5]

Immediately upon their arrival in Rome, Lorenzo made it clear
that he would not keep his new wife, or his own admiration for her,
to himself. Proud of his family status and eager to display his wealth
and power, he reveled in the public celebrations that normally accompanied the marriage of a great nobleman. He delighted, too,
in impressing his French wife with the grandeur of her new residence, which in fact was unmatched by any private residence of the
time in Paris, save perhaps the Mazarin palace. And he wanted to
impress Marie, familiar with the court spectacles of Fontainebleau
and the Louvre, with the wonders that could be orchestrated in the
grand squares of Rome. As a surprise for her and a public display
for the Romans, he commissioned Bernini to design an elaborate
nighttime seascape in the Piazza Navona, which was flooded so that
pleasure boats could float across the square, perfectly outlined by
grand building facades. On this night, their windows were hung
with richly brocaded banners with the initials "MMC" embroidered
in gold. Stepping into a boat decked with flowers, Marie was surrounded by musicians. The concert that followed was punctuated
by fireworks that lit up the night sky. Benedetti wrote to Paris describing the event, adding that "she seems to take pleasure in [the
fetes], but she says that to enjoy them she must forget what is in
her heart! Her gracious manner leads her to courteously receive all
of these diversions, but she is much more gay when she has received
letters from France."[6]

Lorenzo was not discouraged. He continued his lavish attentions
to his new bride, attentions that were usually closely connected to

the ostentatious display of his own prestige. At the end of August he paraded Marie, seated in an elegant carriage, across the city accompanied by a cavalcade of twenty horsemen. On August 29 and again on September 13, he organized an evening concert and serenade for his wife, with more than thirty instruments playing in the courtyard of their palazzo.

Later that year, in November 1661, Queen Marie-Thérèse of France gave birth to a son, and the Colonnas were among those invited to watch the lavish celebrations produced for the French community in Rome. Marie herself was acutely aware that she was expected to produce a strong Colonna succession, and she had rewarded the family's hopes by becoming pregnant almost immediately but had miscarried in the second month, "which made people all over Rome say that the constable had married an incurable woman and that I would have greater need of doctors than of midwives."[7] By the summer of 1662 she was pregnant again. This time her husband forbade her to ride on horseback, which he believed had precipitated the miscarriage. Marie reluctantly agreed to go about only by sedan chair or carriage.

This did not mean, however, that she would agree to miss her favorite outings, which in those early years in Rome often meant going on a hunt for the boar and deer that proliferated in the countryside and were protected for the amusement of noble hunting parties. Opportunities for some of the diversions familiar to Parisians—theater, dance, music—were scarce under the rule of Pope Alexander VII, who was a lover of monumental art and architecture but had banned all public theater. On his desk he kept a marble skull, designed by Bernini, as a reminder of the inevitable futility of human endeavor. When Marie's brother, Philippe, arrived in Rome, he was immediately treated to a hunting outing in the country with his new brother-in-law. Marie insisted on joining the party: "Even though my pregnancy did not permit me to ride a horse, I still was able to enjoy all the entertainment, because the hunters make the hunt pass fairly often by some covered wagons of a sort which they make for such purposes. I was safe there, since even the most furious boars could not tip them over."[8] As a girl in France, Marie, along with her sisters, had learned to ride. Though not as important for ladies as for gentlemen, equestrianism was part of a young noblewoman's education, particularly in France, where girls learned to ride both sidesaddle and astride, and where the ladies often accompanied the men on hunting expeditions. Even sidesaddle, a good rider could keep up with the hunting party, thanks to the horned sidesaddle, designed by Catherine de Medici to permit the rider to lock her leg firmly around a saddle horn while still keeping both legs to one side. Marie was adept at riding both ways, and she loved the speed of the hunt. This was a pleasure that she shared with Lorenzo, himself a renowned equestrian who was proud of his stables and owned a large stud farm outside of Rome that he visited frequently. So he indulged his young wife's passion for hunting, except during pregnancies.

Marie's first child, Filippo Colonna, was born on April 7, 1663, to the great joy of the family. After the requisite forty-day confinement, Marie was put on display in a magnificent bed that Lorenzo had commissioned on the occasion of her first pregnancy. It was a wonder of baroque art, designed by Paul Schor, who in collaboration with his mentor, Bernini, had been producing elaborate decorative and monumental objects for the churches, squares, and palazzi of Rome in response to the huge demand created by the city's prosperity and the festivals and renovations that had come in its wake. In November 1661, just after Marie's miscarriage, Schor and Bernini had created a stunning spectacle of decorations and fireworks in front of the French church of Saint Trinita dei Monti in Rome, commissioned to celebrate the birth of a son to Louis XIV and Marie-Thérèse. But the bed created for Marie Mancini

Colonna was a more durable artifact and quickly became one of the sights that visitors to the city wanted to view. Marie took great care to describe the bed in her memoirs. It was a vision out of a fairy tale, in the shape of a giant gilded seashell floating on waves and drawn by four seahorses mounted by mermaids. The bed was framed by a giant canopy of gold brocade held up at the ceiling by an array of cherubs carved of wood and gilded. Marie lay as resplendent as Venus on this marvelous creation. Benedetti's letters to France describing the spectacle were gushing: "If Venus had been a dark haired goddess one would have thought that it was she herself in her seashell. It is certain that neither the bed of Cleopatra and Antony nor that of Venus and Adonis were equal to this one."[9] In the Parisian salons that Marie had left behind, hostesses typically would receive their guests while lying on a bed. Marie's was over the top. Visitors coming to pay their respects to the new mother and her son marveled at this vision of the goddess on her seashell-turned-chariot. The bed would become an emblem of Marie's triumph as mother, patron of the arts, and host to the elite of Roman society. Later generations of the Colonna family would invite visitors to Rome to view the bed, which became one of the sights highlighted in early guidebooks written for young English travelers on the grand tour of the Continent.

Despite her persistent view of Rome as a second-rate urban center, the new Princess Colonna soon began to devote her attention to enhancing the city's cultural life. She also entered into the political as well as the artistic interests of her family. This meant that in her new role she would not always be viewed as supporting the interests of France and King Louis. In fact, though Lorenzo was cordial with the French king, in Rome the Colonnas had closer ties to the Spanish faction, while the rival Orsini family was more closely allied with the French. Marie's position at times was delicate: On the one hand, she made no secret of her French disdain for some of the more repressive Roman customs, particularly regarding limitations on the freedom of women. She dismissed those who criticized the liberties of her French lifestyle and encouraged other Roman noblewomen to join her in "considering Rome as Paris," urging them to come out from "behind the windows and blinds that limit a woman's pleasure." On the other hand, as the Constabless Colonna, she was often in direct competition with the French in Rome. In alliance with her husband, she quickly became a fierce defender of the family's high status, sensitive to the slightest social misstep made by diplomatic envoys from France. Before undertaking their missions in Rome, emissaries from the French court had to be briefed on dealing with her.

In the cultural arena, the Colonnas' tastes were decidedly French. By 1660 Lorenzo had already established a reputation as a collector and patron of art. Once Marie arrived in Rome, the two of them worked together to build a collection that would become one of the most famous in Europe. Their favorite painters were from the community of French artists residing in Rome and led by the celebrated Claude Lorrain, already a mature artist in 1660 and known for his particular mastery of the relatively new genre of landscape painting. A few months after the marriage, Lorenzo commissioned a painting from Claude depicting the story of Cupid and Psyche, a popular tale that was often used as a wedding theme, telling as it does the story of the god of love arranging to have his beloved wafted to a dream castle for their married life together. The story had a particular resonance for the Colonna couple. Marie was like Psyche, taken from her home to join a husband she had never seen. Claude chose as his subject an early moment in the story, when Psyche, overwhelmed by the long aerial voyage that has transported her to the land of her new husband, is resting by a stream and staring into the distance. Behind and above her, like a vision she is not yet aware of, looms the magnificent palace that is her new home. Its architecture is a composite of the facade of the Colonna residence in Rome and the walls of their country estate in Nemi. Claude worked on the drawings for the painting for two years, finally completing it in 1664, just after the birth of the Colonnas' second child, named Marcantonio after his illustrious ancestor. Two years later, Claude produced a companion piece, a painting depicting a later moment in the Cupid and Psyche romance, when Psyche, exiled from the enchanted castle for having disobeyed her husband and wandering in the wilderness, is saved from drowning by sympathetic gods of nature. In the myth, Psyche learns to obey her husband and joins him in eternal happiness. Was this painting intended as an admonishment to Marie?

By 1666, the harmony that the Colonna couple had found in the first years of their marriage was already weakening. Lorenzo had mistresses, which in itself was not a transgression that would have seriously damaged most aristocratic marriages. But one of his affairs was with a prominent noblewoman, his wife's social equal, and this Marie found particularly humiliating. In 1665 Christina Paleotti, daughter of one of the wealthiest families in Rome, gave birth to a girl whom, everyone knew, Lorenzo had fathered. In November of that same year Marie delivered their third son, Carlo. Soon after, Marie told her husband that she wanted to break off conjugal relations for good and establish a *separazione di letto,* or separation of beds. In her memoirs, she wrote only that she feared the health risks of another pregnancy, and having produced three sons, her husband had no cause to be concerned for the family succession. Her third delivery had been a difficult one. Though later she would remember that her husband had rushed to be with her for it, as he had promised her he would, she also recalled that the experience had frightened her and made her decide that she had given him enough:

> The very evening he arrived, I gave him a third successor, but since this gift cost me much dearer than the first two, and even threatened

my life, I took the view that I should give him no more of these gifts which might expose me to such perils. However, it was not enough for me to have made this resolution, if he did not confirm it with his consent. It was toward that goal that I worked, and I was quite successful, as he has since kept his word to me very scrupulously in all the time that we have been together.[10]

Marie's views on this subject were decidedly foreign to Lorenzo. They were influenced by the aspects of her French upbringing that he found most annoying: the feminist streak in those salon conversations of which she was so fond, and that inspired her to exhort Roman women to a greater degree of independence from their husbands. Her ideas on pregnancy and motherhood were influenced, too, by the readings and storytelling of her youth that remained popular among female readers long into adulthood, fairy tales and legends that relentlessly focused on fertility, pregnancy, and the power and danger that came to women through their capacity to bear children. Like the husbands in these tales, Lorenzo had indulged his pregnant wife, sometimes to his regret (as when he allowed her to go riding), other times to his satisfaction (as when he rushed to be with her for the birth of a son). Marie understood the importance of fertility in a noble marriage and the control this could give her over her husband. She also was apprehensive about the loss of power that their *separazione di letto* would generate for her. But in this era when one out of ten women could expect to die in childbirth, she also believed strongly in her own right to a long life after becoming a mother. Her older sister Laure-Victoire, who had been so welcoming to her younger siblings when they first arrived in France, had died at twenty-two after the birth of her third child. Marie was determined not to let this be her own fate.

Later, in her memoirs, Marie lucidly acknowledged the consequences she faced as a result of this decision. She wrote that others

were quick to profit from her new "political sterility" with respect
to Lorenzo and his family. While she was pregnant with her own
third child, she had learned of Lorenzo's illegitimate daughter.
And so, jealousy reared its ugly head in this marriage that had enjoyed a period of conjugal peace and collaboration. Lorenzo would
quickly prove himself to be even more prone to that passion than
his wife was.

Still, the public face of the Colonna couple continued to be a
fairly harmonious one, particularly in the cultural sphere where
they had enjoyed their most spectacular mutual successes. From
1663 to 1667 Marie and Lorenzo spent every carnival season, run-
ning from the day after Christmas to the beginning of Lent, in
Venice, where they were deeply involved in promoting theater and
spectacle. Beginning in 1667 they turned their attention to producing theatrical performances in the palazzo, which became the
centerpiece of the dramatic arts in Rome. During the reign of the
severe Pope Alexander, theater was banned in the holy city, but
when Clement IX succeeded him in 1667, a new era of public art
and spectacle was initiated. Not only did Clement permit plays to
be produced, but he also wrote them himself and was often in the
audience. The exiled Queen Christina of Sweden, who had made her
principal residence in Rome since dramatically renouncing the
throne and converting to Catholicism, presided over a second theater and hosted intellectual discussions among (mostly male) scientists and philosophers at her residence close to the Vatican. Queen
Christina's gatherings provided lively competition for Marie's salon-
style conversations grouping men and women, artists, writers,
and travelers.

Their long seasons in Venice had established both Marie and
Lorenzo as important patrons of theater, with six operas over three
seasons dedicated to them. The couple personally supported the
most famous opera singers of the day, one of whom, Antonia Coresi,

was close to Marie personally, serving as her maid for ten years. The young singer was brought with her husband, the musician Nicolo Coresi, to live in the Colonna household and remained there until Marie herself left. Marie referred to her proudly in describing the operas in which she sang, singling out Cesti's opera *Titus,* which was dedicated to Marie. The theme of the opera, which tells the story of the Emperor Titus, who must give up his true love to make a royal marriage, had a special resonance for Marie. In France, Jean Racine would write the play *Berenice* on the subject in which Marie's famous words addressed to Louis XIV would be echoed by the rejected title character: "Sire, you are emperor, and yet you weep?" She later wrote, "They put on wonderful operas in Venice, among them the *Titus,* to which I went often. I was no less attracted by the sweetness of the voices and by the acting of the players—particularly that of a musician of His Royal Highness called Cavagnino, and of one of my maids who performed admirably—than by the beauty of the work, which earned the applause of everyone and which was assuredly among the most beautiful that have ever been seen."[11]

It was not difficult, for either Marie or her husband, to see themselves in the grand characters from history and legend who were familiar to the baroque stage. The theaters of Italy and France in the seventeenth century did not produce plays about the real world around them. Instead, spectators were treated to dramatic enactments of familiar stories from myth and history that sought to strike their audiences with wonder, admiration, sadness, and joy. In Marie's day the staging of an opera often would include marvelous and complex machines to enable actors to fly across the stage or rise to the rafters, special effects to simulate cataclysmic events such as earthquake or fire, and elaborate sets evoking exotic and imaginary locales.

In Rome as in Venice, the carnival season gave rise to numerous masquerades and public parades, with noble families competing to produce the most luxurious and imaginative float, and with members of these families participating in costume. After 1667, when the new pope lifted restrictions on carnival masquerade, Marie and Lorenzo stopped spending their winters in Venice and instead focused on the cultural entertainments being generated in Rome. When Rome seemed to offer little of interest to travelers from France seeking the sort of artistic and social entertainments they could find in Paris, the Colonna couple hosted balls, gambling parties, concerts, and generally open-ended visiting hours. "Without this house foreigners and especially Frenchmen would have difficulty passing the time," wrote one traveler. One could enter and exit "when one wants; there one dances, gambles, has conversation and passes the evening very nicely."[12]

In 1664 the Colonnas began renovating their palace to install a theater. The work continued even during their long absences in Venice, and productions started in 1666. By 1668 the theater was staging large-scale affairs with more than thirty actors and dancers. The Colonnas employed their own impresario, the playwright and director Filippo Accaioli, who also tutored their sons. Beginning in 1668, the dramatic productions alternated with parades during carnival. The floats Marie designed created a huge sensation. In 1665, after the birth of their second child, Lorenzo had designed a float on which he and Marie's brother had stood dressed as the twin celestial gods Castor and Pollux. The float in which Marie was featured for the 1668 carnival took the planetary metaphor to a more elaborate level. Constructed in the shape of a giant cloud rising some thirty feet into the air, drawn by four horses and escorted by a dozen more, along with numerous foot soldiers bedecked with feathers and Roman armor, the float was topped by a man dressed as Saturn, and below him appeared the figures of Mars and Jupiter. In the central position was Apollo as the sun, and to his left just below him were Venus, Diana, and Juno. Marie was Venus and her

close friend and lady-in-waiting, Countess Ortensia Stella, was Diana.
Spectators could not have failed to recall that the sun-god figure
was the favorite emblem and masquerade of Louis XIV, and they
certainly were astonished by the daring of these noblewomen, whose
participation in the Roman carnival parade was "a completely new
thing, never seen before."[13] For a woman to appear masked in public
was a violation of a long-standing ban in the holy city. Marie's planetary carnival machine engaged more than one prominent aristocrat
in violating that ban, a collective rebellion of noblewomen that had
the effect of doing away with the restriction for good.

For the 1669 carnival season Marie undertook projects that were
even more provocative. She was tired of the constant criticism of
her French-style "liberty" and her refusal to conform to Roman
norms that kept women and men from socializing openly together.
By this time her sister Hortense, the Duchess Mazarin, had joined
Marie in Rome and they both took pleasure in challenging the city's
conservative customs. It was in this spirit, and to assert her innocence and fortitude, that Marie decided to disguise herself as the
warrior maiden Clorinda from her favorite work, Tasso's *Gerusalemme liberata*. "Thus," she wrote,

> in order to pass the time less gloomily, and to silence those who
> were grumbling about the liberties they saw me taking, I conceived
> of a masquerade in which I played Clorinda. Followed by thirty or
> forty horsemen dressed as soldiers, I went around tossing a madrigal
> about in the way that maskers do; my brother and a friend of his, a
> gentleman called Marescoti, had composed it based on that idea,
> and here are the words:
>
> > *Do not suspect this warrior lover*
> > *Of any lapse in decorum,*
> > *For even if I've a virile air,*
> > *I keep intact the treasure of my honor.*

*How many women in the world*
*Are Penelope outwardly, but at heart, Phryne!*[14]

The madrigal playfully yet boldly asserted four identities—warrior, maid, faithful wife, courtesan—for the disguised Marie. And why would Marie think that such flaunting of her liberty would silence those who criticized her for it? Marie embraced the "warrior lover" identity that Clorinda represented: Clorinda, the foreign princess knight who was beloved of her enemy, Prince Tancredi, and whom Tancredi would tragically and unknowingly kill in a nighttime battle. Describing her own personality, Marie would later write that she "loved vivacity and novelty, and talk of arms and soldierly subjects, rather than a peaceful place and a pacific government."[15] Her choice of theatrical disguises certainly helped keep this combative spirit alive. Lorenzo at first went along with even the most outrageous of Marie's masquerade schemes. He had his own reasons for encouraging the curiosity of Roman onlookers, even for offering fodder to the scandal-hungry gazettes. His approach to publicity was decidedly modern—whether the media coverage was positive or negative, Prince Colonna seemed to think that being in the public eye was almost always good. Enhancing his public profile by sponsoring spectacles that were both magnificent and titillating became a project he embraced, and one he viewed as comparable to the strategic use of spectacle that his "cousin" Louis XIV was famously achieving at his new palace of Versailles.

During the 1669 carnival season, the lively competition between Marie and the expatriate Queen Christina of Sweden was played out in masquerades the two women sponsored as part of an equestrian tournament held on the Piazza di San Marco. Six cavaliers, including Lorenzo Colonna and Philippe Mancini, competed to catch a ring on the point of their lances and strike a dark-skinned figure symbolizing the Saracens, ancient adversaries of the Crusaders.

Queen Christina presided over the event, watching from her box overlooking the piazza, surrounded by twenty-four cardinals. Marie's contribution to the spectacle was daring and provocative: in keeping with the theme of the Crusades, but drawing on the more fanciful legendary characters from her favorite work of literature by Tasso, Marie entered the parade on horseback, dressed as Armida, the sorceress who seduces the crusading hero Rinaldo, and followed by twenty-four cavaliers dressed as Turks. "It was hard to tell," wrote one amused and bedazzled chronicler, "which of the two had a more impressive following, Princess Maria Mancini with 24 Turks or Queen Christina with 24 Cardinals."[16]

If anyone doubted Prince Colonna's approval of his wife's designs for carnival, the final masquerade in which he and Marie collaborated for the 1669 festivities laid those doubts to rest. It was unlike anything seen before. Seated on top of a huge rolling cage filled with animals, Marie presided, dressed as the sorceress Circe from Homer's *Odyssey*, who had famously transformed Ulysses's men into beasts. Lorenzo, masked as Ulysses, was among the gentlemen seated at her feet, holding dogs on leashes to represent the lovers Circe had transformed into animals. Drawings by the artist Pierre Perrin documenting the occasion illustrated Marie's elaborate use of costumes, animals, and human actors. Circe, everyone knew, ultimately would be vanquished by the clever Ulysses, but his encounter with her was a familiar parable of male power vanquished by female seduction. Resplendent in her crown and holding a golden scepter on that February day in 1669, Marie was triumphant.

The association of Marie Mancini with legendary enchantresses had begun with her liaison with Louis XIV ten years earlier. In choosing to represent Armida, Marie may have been remembering the whispers of those in France who thought she had "bewitched" the king. Anne of Austria's lady-in-waiting Madame de Motteville had described Marie as Armida, and young Louis as the enchanted

Rinaldo, who had to be brought to his senses. As a young bride in Rome, Marie was compared in less ambiguous terms to the goddess of love, and her residence to the palace of Armida. At the palazzo Colonna, the art collections being amassed by Lorenzo and his wife included a painting depicting the legendary judgment of Paris, commissioned from the landscape artist Gaspard Dughet. Lorenzo posed as Paris, gazing in pride and adoration at the lovely Marie, who was Venus. Sometime in the year following the 1669 cavalcade, the Colonnas commissioned another painting of Marie by the portraitist Voet. This one, however, was much larger in scale and was a full-body portrait of the subject, dressed as an oriental queen in exotic furs and jewels. Everyone thought it was Armida.

But the lavish celebrations at the palazzo Colonna and the public displays by a couple who collaborated in their patronage of the arts could not disguise the fact that their marriage was disintegrating. Foreign correspondents operating in Rome for the European gazettes sent reports of the breakdown in relations between the constable and his wife.[17] Marie began to spend more time in retreat in her library, poring over her collection of books on astrology. Predicting the future based on the alignment of the stars and planets had always fascinated her, and she had considerable expertise in the practice. During a difficult series of months in 1670, she wrote and published an astrological almanac. During the same period she felt her health declining, and by the late winter of 1671 she was seriously ill.

Lorenzo was indifferent to her health. Even when she was crying out in pain for several nights, convulsed with stomach cramps, he exhibited no emotion. Though she recovered from this particular crisis, his indifference left her with dark suspicions that she could barely bring herself to share with those close to her. The Roman gazettes, though, did not hesitate to insinuate that Marie Colonna's ailments might have been caused by poison. And some of Marie's closest associates, including her longtime maidservant Morena, brought her "evidence" of what they thought was a plot, hatched by Lorenzo, to do away with his wife. An anonymous letter addressed to the constable was intercepted and shown to Marie. In it the writer assured Colonna that his wife's malady was incurable and urged him to find a new wife without delay.[18]

Meanwhile, as her estrangement from Lorenzo grew more marked, Marie had been able to renew her intimacy with Hortense as she watched her younger sister embark on what would be a long and adventurous life as a fugitive from her husband.

# ( 4 )

## *A*
## RUNAWAY DUCHESS

*I see wives do not love devout husbands, which reason this
woman had, besides many more, as I hear, to be rid of her
husband upon any terms—and so I wish her a good journey.*

—Charles II of England to his sister the Duchess of Orleans, June 1668

O N THE NIGHT OF JUNE 13, 1668, Hortense ran away from
her husband, leaving her four young children behind.
Philippe provided a carriage but remained behind to deflect
suspicion for as long as possible. Hortense was accompanied by
Philippe's manservant, Narcisse, and her own maidservant, Nanon.
Both women were disguised in men's clothing. The group escaped
Paris by the closest city gate, the Porte Saint-Antoine, next to the
Bastille. At the gate the duchess was met by the Chevalier de Rohan,
who had volunteered his squire Courbeville to join Narcisse as an
escort. She had decided to take an eastern route rather than the
southern one, which would have been a more obvious choice for
a flight toward Italy but would have required her to pass through
more of the city of Paris and to traverse the Left Bank to leave by
the Porte Saint-Victor. So she and her little party left just before
midnight in a six-horse coach. Her flight would be only the first in

a long series of trips across Europe in search of a court to provide her with protection.

It was a momentous decision, but not one that she had made impulsively. Philippe and the Chevalier de Rohan had worked closely with her in the preceding weeks to ensure her safe and fast transport out of the city and toward the eastern frontier of France, where she would be sheltered by the Duke of Lorraine as she waited to leave the country. In the many voyages her husband had forced her to take with him during their marriage, Hortense would have noticed that new roads were being cut and old ones improved as the state-run postal service expanded. Travelers to France frequently remarked on the good quality of the roads, which often were paved in stone, compared with the bumpy dirt roads of their homelands. Postal relay stations also provided some reliability for travelers. Fresh horses could be rented for private coaches, or passengers could ride in the mail-carrying stagecoaches that followed regular schedules.

But long-distance travel was still slow, uncomfortable, and risky. One of Philippe's squires had been sent ahead to confirm where the carriage transporting the runaways could stop to find quick changes of horses. In the month leading up to the planned escape, Hortense was so nervous that she became sick and unable to eat, causing her sister Olympe some concern, but the secret was carefully kept from her. Philippe and Hortense did not trust their sister; although she supported Hortense in her legal battle with the duke, she would never recommend such a risky move. Olympe was a seasoned courtier, adept at intrigue, but always wanting a clear picture of the likely outcome of her actions. Hortense was hurling herself into a void, with uncertain consequences.

The route was a difficult one, with little rest. Heading for the city of Nancy, capital of the independent duchy of Lorraine, Hortense traveled by private carriage, postal coach, open buggy, and then horseback, covering nearly 250 miles in less than two days. In

Nancy she was welcomed by the Duke of Lorraine at his ancestral palace, from which he governed. Hortense and Philippe had chosen this destination carefully; it was a border territory that still enjoyed political autonomy from France and for the time being was not challenged by Louis XIV's expansionist policies. Hortense's host was the elder Charles de Lorraine, who along with his nephew had unsuccessfully tried to betroth himself to Marie some eight years earlier. He was only too happy to provide shelter for Hortense, on the way to join her sister. There Hortense and Nanon were able to rest for several days, enjoying the long summer evenings in the duke's gardens. En route to Nancy they had maintained their disguises, dressed as men, like heroines of a romance novel, even in the inn where they had spent the night. To their dismay and amusement, the women had found that such disguises worked better in fiction than in reality, as Hortense wrote:

> We had been recognized as women almost everywhere. Nanon was always slipping up and calling me Madame; and either for that reason or because my face gave away some hint of my sex, people watched us through the keyhole after we shut the door to our room, and they saw our long hair, which we let down as soon as we were alone, because we were very uncomfortable with it up under our men's wigs. Nanon was extremely small, and she looked so unnatural dressed in that way that I could not look at her without laughing.[1]

In Nancy, Charles de Lorraine dismissed the anxious warnings of the local representative of the French court, who argued that the runaways should be returned promptly to France. Instead the duke provided the party with twenty armed guards for their continued safety through Switzerland and the Alps. Proceeding on their way southeast toward Italy, they stopped only one night at an inn in Neuchâtel, then circled the edge of Lake Lucerne and arrived in the town of Altdorf, high in the mountains at the opening of Saint Gotthard Pass. There they learned that travelers leaving Switzerland headed for the state of Milan were being quarantined, owing to the threat of plague. Hortense and her entourage settled in for what looked to be a long respite.

The group soon received word that Duke Mazarin was busy plotting to have his wife kidnapped and brought back to Paris. But Hortense was not convinced that such threats could be carried out, and in any case she was determined to continue on her path. Already, she knew, her decision meant she was even less likely to receive a favorable hearing from the Grand Chamber of judges, and the king appeared to be keeping his promise not to intervene. Besides, the farther she traveled, the more she felt free of her former identity, and was even attracted by the riskiness of her venture. She laughed off the fact that her disguise had fooled no one. On the other hand, in Neuchâtel she enjoyed the incongruous experience of being mistaken for Madame de Longueville, Duchess of Nemours. The Longueville family did in fact govern the city of Neuchâtel, but few of its citizens had ever seen the duchess. Hearing that a French duchess was in their city, they rushed to see her. "You would not believe the joy that these people showed me," Hortense later wrote. "As they were not accustomed to seeing women of quality from France pass through their land, they could not understand how anyone other than Madame de Longueville might have business there."[2]

In the beginning, at least, the traveling party's forced layover in Altdorf may have provided welcome rest for Hortense. She was in pain from a leg wound she had suffered in a fall in the Lorraine palace gardens and that had been aggravated by the voyage. Doctors were called and she was bled in an attempt to relieve the swelling, but to little avail. She worried that the infection would become gangrenous without constant care. And the care she was receiving in "this barbarous country" was not what she could have counted on in Paris—earlier, when the group had asked for a surgeon to attend an ailing Narcisse, they were sent a farrier, who was accustomed to working with animals and "who set to work to draw blood with a veterinary lancet but missed," causing poor Narcisse to bleed profusely from a large vein. The surgeon sent to treat Hortense was more competent, but after his visits she shut herself up in her small room and would not allow anyone but Nanon and Courbeville near her. The young squire was tireless in his attentions to her needs, spending long hours with her even after Nanon became fatigued. "I am still persuaded," she later wrote, "that my leg would have had to be amputated without him." The leg healed, and Courbeville was henceforth Hortense's favorite, to the consternation of her other servants. It soon became clear that his nights in Hortense's room had a new purpose. When Philippe set out to join the travelers, he became furious upon learning that his sister and Courbeville had become lovers.

Within a few days of arriving in Altdorf, the group had received an unwelcome visitor. Acting on counsel from Finance Minister Colbert, the Duke Mazarin had sent his own emissary, Monsieur de Louvière, in pursuit of his wife. Louvière informed Hortense that her husband was prepared to negotiate with her, provided that she would willingly return to him. Failing her agreement, he said, she faced forced repatriation. Hortense received him coldly and dismissed her husband's threats, stating that she would not answer until she had completed her voyage to Milan and could take counsel with her sister. She paid no attention to Louvière's lengthy questioning of her servants. In his report to the duke, he spared none of the details from these interviews and included two letters he had found in the Neuchâtel inn where she had stayed. Written by Hortense to her brother and to the Chevalier de Rohan, the letters left no doubt that Hortense had been plotting her escape for some time, against the directives of both the king and the courts. The jealous duke further concluded that Rohan had been in love with his wife, and he declared publicly that his suspicions extended even to her brother, accusing them of incest.

Such a shocking accusation, had it come from the fanatical husband a few months earlier, would not have endeared him to the judges reviewing his legal dispute with his wife. Even immediately following her disappearance, public sympathy was more with the wife than with the husband. But before long, Duke Mazarin's diligence began to pay off, especially when Olympe, feeling betrayed by her sister's secret escape, agreed to lend her support to forcing Hortense's return. No one but the duke would repeat or support the incest accusation, but the king took a first step against Hortense by punishing Rohan, stripping him of his offices and thus plunging him into debt. Hortense could only express outrage, from a distance, at the turn of events and especially the "foul accusation" that her husband brought before the courts along with his "evidence," consisting of poetry that Philippe had written in praise of his beautiful sister. Hortense later wrote:

> There is nothing so innocent that it cannot be poisoned in support of such a foul accusation. They stooped to producing letters in verse, for lack of any better evidence. Posterity will find it hard to believe, if knowledge of our affairs reaches it, that a man of my brother's quality could have been questioned in a court of law about trifles of that nature; that they could have been held up as serious evidence by judges; that such odious use could have been made of the exchange of thoughts and feelings between people who are so closely related, finally, that my esteem and friendship for a brother whose merit was as well known as his, and who loved me more than his own life, could have served as a pretext for the most unjust and the cruelest of all defamations.[3]

But at this moment there was not much hope of finding a remedy favorable to the duchess. Her husband certainly was not disposed to negotiation, and Louis XIV showed no inclination to indulge his runaway subjects. Hortense turned her attention to pressing for a quick end to the quarantine that was keeping her from continuing to Milan. She soon received that permission. The little group set out for Italy, undaunted by the rigors of an Alpine crossing.

In the seventeenth century, the Saint Gotthard Pass was a busy trade route linking the Rhine Valley in the north, in what is now Germany, to the valleys and the Po River basin of northern Italy. But the pass was not much more than a long mountain path, winding between rocks, over rushing water, and along the edge of cliffs. It could accommodate foot travelers, horseback riders, and donkey carts, but not carriages. Stone bridges built in the sixteenth century enabled travelers to avoid the lethal rushing waters of the Reuss River, but accidents were frequent. The pass took a heavy toll on those who were brave enough or simply obliged to climb it as they crossed the Alps. But somehow Hortense and her party made it through without injury.

Marie later recalled the reunion with her sister, in a country house outside of Milan, after her own exhausting six-day voyage by postal chaise from Rome, in the company of her close friend Ortensia Stella and a grumbling Lorenzo Colonna, who had opposed making the trip. She was astonished by her sister's beauty and somewhat embarrassed by her own outmoded attire compared with Hortense's Parisian stylishness. Even in her exhausted and weakened state, Hortense managed to seem fashionable, dressed in the loose summer fashion that was just appearing in Paris. Roman women did not yet wear lace or ribbons in the casual abundance that was becoming so popular in France. In Italy women's clothing was cut more modestly, and lace was typically seen only in the collars that covered low necklines. In Milan, as Marie later wrote, her "French" sister was greeted with great curiosity and enthusiasm: "People's eagerness to see Madame Mazarin was incredible. Most things do not really live up to one's expectations of them, or else when one gets in the habit of seeing them, their luster tends to wear off. This was not the case with my sister's beauty. It seemed even greater than people had imagined it to be, and they discovered new charms each time they saw her, which did not happen as often as they wished."[4]

Lorenzo, however, was not thrilled by his sister-in-law's arrival. He had received letters from France warning him against receiving the fugitive duchess. And his wife, delighted by the excuse to leave Rome, a city she had always found stultifying compared with the northern city-states of Venice and Milan, not to mention Paris, was only too happy to prolong the Italian "reception" of Hortense for as long as possible. Philippe had joined his sisters, after having briefly left the traveling party when he discovered Hortense's relationship with Courbeville. When Lorenzo pressed for a quick return to Rome, Marie, Hortense, and Philippe—reunited for the first time in eight years—countered that a side trip to Venice was far preferable. Together they managed to persuade Lorenzo to accompany them for an extended stay in Venice, where they enjoyed theater, opera, and more social introductions for Hortense. When Lorenzo's insistence on departure finally won out, it was to go only as far as Sienna, where the travelers settled in for a fortnight, at the country estate of the Roman Cardinal Flavio Chigi, nephew of the pope. There, the women accompanied the men on hunting outings. Hortense had impressive success: Hortense was used to being flattered with comparisons of her beauty and power to Diana, goddess of the hunt. Both sisters were excellent riders and loved hunting. Even in Italy, where girls were kept more sequestered from young men, highly placed women were permitted to ride and hunt, and were often portrayed in official portraits wearing hunting attire, surrounded by their dogs, and holding guns.

By the time the traveling party resumed the return voyage to Rome, more than four months had passed since Hortense's initial departure from Paris. Tensions in the family group were growing, for several reasons. Lorenzo was not eager to continue to shelter the wayward Hortense in the Colonna palazzo. Pressure from French emissaries was increasing. The Duke Mazarin saw to it that his brother-in-law received copies of a steady stream of reports from informants in Rome regarding Hortense's behavior. To complicate matters, Hortense's intimacy with the young squire Courbeville was by now quite open, angering both Marie and Philippe, who demanded upon arriving in Rome that Courbeville be sent back to France. In her memoirs Hortense is frank about the confrontations that ensued. Her attachment to Courbeville had been born with her newfound freedom and she resisted the pressure to break off the affair, which she knew full well could only severely damage her chances of a favorable settlement in the legal dispute with her husband. But in the end Courbeville himself may have made it easier for her, for he behaved so outrageously toward his former employer the Chevalier of Rohan, accusing him, along with Hortense's brother, of attempting to poison him (which may have been true), that she ultimately had to agree to send him away. "The bad behavior of Courbeville," she wrote, "the unpleasant sensation which this affair was causing in society, and my desire to be at peace finally made me resolve to part with him, not doubting that he would willingly release me from the promise that I had made him."[5]

Nevertheless, the parting was not easy. In the courtyard of the palazzo Colonna, Courbeville refused to leave unless Hortense herself gave the order. Marie taunted him, daring him to try swaying Hortense again as he had in the past. Hortense recalled later that he declared that he respected no one but her, but in despair, and with Marie threatening that if he stayed in the courtyard any longer he would "find someone who wanted a word with him," Courbeville left the palazzo grounds. Distraught, the Duchess Mazarin followed, and fearing for his life she accompanied him to the house of her uncle Cardinal Francesco Maria Mancini, where he obtained temporary shelter. Hortense herself went to the home of an aunt who reluctantly took her in but kept her securely behind locked doors.

Within weeks, the family arranged for her to move permanently to the convent in the Campo Marzio, where Hortense's aunt Anna Maria Mazzarini, sister of the Cardinal Mazarin, was the abbess, presiding over a community of nuns who, in the Benedictine tradition, were educated, and proud of their learning. This was a place that was familiar to Marie and Hortense from their childhood. Like many Roman noblewomen, their mother had chosen the convent as the best place for schooling her older daughters, and Marie had lived there among the nuns just before leaving Rome. Now, receiving the wayward Hortense into their midst, the abbess was concerned for both her family and her community, but she accepted the task with her usual sobriety and prepared to keep her young niece close to her for a long time. Hortense herself agreed, entering the convent accompanied by Nanon, but only because she was told that the move would be temporary. No sooner was she out of the way than her uncle withdrew his protection of Courbeville and sent him fifty miles outside the city to be incarcerated in a papal fortress in the Mediterranean city of Civitavecchia.

A report of the duchess's seclusion was dispatched to the duke in Paris, where it was also publicized in one of the popular news gazettes. Marie seemed to enter into the spirit of independence her sister had begun to represent. She threw her sympathies with Hortense and first demanded permission from her aunt for her sister's release, and when told that such permission would have to come from the Duke Mazarin, Marie helped her escape (much to the consternation of the elderly abbess, who died just weeks later). Philippe was dispatched to Paris to help spin the story in Hortense's favor, and Marie addressed a letter of appeal to Colbert:

I would be very annoyed, sir, if you were to learn from another what has happened here regarding Madame Mazarin. The bad air in the convent was making her ill and she requested permission to leave from my aunts and Monsieur the Cardinal Mancini, which they denied her. In view of the fact that her willingness to enter the convent gained her nothing from Monsieur Mazarin, who continued to press his case against her more strongly than ever, she and I thought that it would not be bad to remove her from a place where she had voluntarily entered. She did this in agreement with me, without communicating anything of our intentions to anyone else, for fear that we would be impeded. . . . I urge you, sir, to make every effort to obtain for her the pension that I mentioned in my last letter, for the time that she is obliged to stay here. My brother left the day before yesterday in the evening and will tell you more that is too long to write.[6]

And so the two sisters resumed a shared life in the Colonna household, without, however, the presence of the unhappy Courbeville. Hortense wrote a letter to Flavio Chigi, the nephew of the pope who had received her with Courbeville during her voyage through Tuscany, pleading for his release from the Civitavecchia fortress. Chigi managed to obtain permission for the release, but subsequently Courbeville disappeared without a trace. There is no further mention of him in any of the family memoirs or letters, though rumors persisted about the reasons for his imprisonment and disappearance.[7]

The sisters turned their attentions to drawing as many visitors as possible to their social gatherings and jointly sponsored theatrical productions, on which they collaborated and in which they sometimes acted or danced. Hortense's presence fueled Marie's fondness for flouting the restrictive conventions of Roman society. The two sisters regularly moved around the city on their own, in open carriages or even on foot. The gazettes reported on their sightings, and not always favorably: "The constabless and her sister, sumptuously dressed, were mistaken by some Spanish gentlemen for nymphs of the bordello."[8] With Hortense's legal dispute hanging in the balance, there was nothing for the sisters to do but wait, enjoy their own celebrity, and work to make the most of the family allegiances that remained strong, as well as cultivating new ones. The exiled Queen Christina of Sweden declared that she would welcome Hortense as a resident in her palazzo (though she quickly gave in to friends who advised her against such a risky alliance). While she waited for the judges' decision, Hortense often sat for artists who delighted in painting portraits of her, many of them in miniature so they could be easily mailed home to other parts of Europe along with letters describing the pleasures of her company. According to the Amsterdam gazette, her portraits were so coveted that two gentlemen had nearly fought a duel over one of them, until the Prince Colonna intervened. Portraits of the Duchess Mazarin were quickly copied as engravings and sold as prints. In a short time her image became the face of beauty in European painting, "an iconographic success without precedent," in the words of one art historian.[9]

Rome was a city that drew artists from all over Europe, and the Colonnas received many of them in the French-style salon gatherings and theatrical productions they hosted. The Colonna palazzo, from the time of Hortense's arrival in 1668, saw even more artists than usual, as the Duchess Mazarin's beauty, and her willingness to sit for portraits, was legendary. Numerous portraits of each sister were produced in the short time—less than four years—that Hortense lived in Rome. Their portraits were hung in private collections known as "beauties series," which displayed paintings of prominent women alongside mythological ones. Often the two types of image were blended, with the real-life subject dressed as a legendary or mythical woman. The Dutch painter Jacob-Ferdinand Voet produced portraits of Hortense dressed as Cleopatra; one of these depicts Hortense holding a chalice and a large pearl, evoking a story in which the Egyptian queen dissolves the jewel in a cup of wine to show her disdainful mastery over her great wealth. Hortense was also painted as Aphrodite, an Amazon, an oriental queen, and the goddess Diana. Her face appeared in allegorical portraits of nature, such as the much-copied *Fruit Gatherer* by the French painter Jacques Courtois, known as il Borgognone. Owning one of the "beauties series" quickly became a mark of power and prestige for noblemen at the end of the seventeenth century, and in this way portraits of Hortense and Marie were shipped throughout Europe and England for display in the palaces of powerful families. Lorenzo Colonna was one of the first to commission a series, which he purchased from Voet in 1673, as did the heads of the rival Italian families of Chigi, Altieri, Durini, and Odescalchi. A few years later, similar series were commissioned by nobility outside of Italy. The Duke of Savoy purchased a series of mainly French "beauties," and the English royal family one of English, but they both included a portrait of Hortense.

The portraits of Hortense in Voet's and in many other "beauties series" stand out in one dramatic respect: she is always painted against a sky, in a natural, unenclosed background, unlike the others, where the subjects are placed against an indoor wall. The representations of Hortense in these paintings contributed to the public image of the Duchess Mazarin as a free spirit, a defier of convention, and a woman whom walls simply could not contain. Her public quickly came to think of her as an escape artist of sorts. In the span of just a few years she had conducted an impressive series of breakouts from the familiar spaces used in those days to incarcerate women: family fortresses and convents. In her memoirs she was precise about the moments when she had to be physically prevented from leaving these places, just as she took care to explain exactly how she managed to escape them. In Rome, where for a time she was "locked up as if I were in prison" at her aunt's home, she refused to stay away from the windows until dragged away by her aunt's confessor, who "performed the errand so insolently that tears came to my eyes."[10]

As Hortense's escapades became popular fodder for conversations, letter correspondences, and news gazettes, her itinerary seemed exhilarating, even when it was told as a kind of warning to young women of the many forces that were firmly in place to contain a woman's liberty. Every attempt to arrive at a compromise with her husband created new suspense. Would he send her money? Would he permit her to find shelter with new protectors? Could he even prevent her escape if he wanted to? Throughout her stay in Rome, her money problems progressively worsened. She consulted alternately with Marie and with Philippe, who had settled in for what he hoped would be an extended visit to Rome at his own residence on the grand Roman avenue called the Corso. Both were forbidden by directives from France to house Hortense.

While Hortense's activities were causing tongues to wag, Marie was attracting attention by taking the lead in the palazzo's cultural offerings. After the death of the liberal Pope Clement IX in December 1669, theater and spectacle were once again discouraged in Rome, and public masking was forbidden. But in the Colonna household, newsletters claimed, "the French liberty" continued.[11] Although concerts and public performances had to be held indoors, Marie rose to the occasion, and during the 1670 carnival season she personally arranged a theatrical production that included a ballet in her private theater, and in which both she and her sister danced. During the preparations for this production, Marie was reported to be almost frenzied in her energy and enthusiasm. Both sisters were competitive, argued frequently, and once even came to blows over the organization of the spectacle. The end result, however, was greatly admired and received much attention in part because of the novelty, in Rome, of the participation of women in the dance. A newsletter reported the event: "This play came out quite delightfully, and even more because it was adorned by three beautiful ballets, in one of which Madam Colonna danced, together with the Duchess Mazarin, another lady, and cavaliers, all in very gallant costumes; and it is a very unusual thing to see women on the stage in Rome."[12]

The event would be the apex of Marie's cultural career in Rome, though she continued to sponsor musical and theatrical performances that received considerable attention, including, much later, a public serenade outside Queen Christina's home in 1671. But relations with her family were strained. Hortense was renting living quarters but her financial situation was worsening. So when Philippe suddenly received word that King Louis had arranged a marriage for him and was ordering him to return to court, Hortense decided to accompany him to face her husband directly in an attempt to arrive at a financial settlement and a separation supported by a contractual agreement.

Of course, returning to Paris would also allow her to see her children. None of her many contemporary observers left the slightest suggestion that she had been judged badly for abandoning her four young children when she fled Paris. Leaving her husband was thought to be the serious transgression, and more broadly, so was leaving her "house," which included children and extended family, each of them tightly embedded in a web of mutual dependency. She had tarnished her name, and by extension that of her children, by disrupting that network. But she was not expected to feel a strong emotional attachment to her children, nor they to her. This does not mean that she felt none, and certainly some women of her milieu—including Marie, as we shall see—did express strong emotions for their children. But on this point, in her memoirs, Hortense was almost silent, though she always claimed that her principal motivation for bringing suit against her husband was to preserve the Mazarin fortune for the sake of her children.

So we cannot know with certainty her feelings as she set out on the road once again with her brother, this time bound for Paris. She may have been thinking of her children, who in 1670 were ages eight, seven, five, and four, and wondering about how they may have changed in her absence. She certainly was thinking of her husband and wondering how he might be persuaded to receive her with some favor, although on this point she was not optimistic. He had welcomed the news of her return to Paris with a relish that was not reassuring. Her best hope was to win the king's sympathy, if not that of the legal courts, where her case was still being reviewed.

But the trip would not be a speedy one. Philippe was not particularly eager to meet his bride-to-be, for he was entering into this arranged marriage with little enthusiasm, and he recognized that in the king's mind the union was a way to rein him in, to introduce some moderation and order in his life. The two travelers took their time, so much so that the extraordinary length of the voyage (which ultimately took six months) itself became a subject of public gossip and seemed to be an act of defiance. They eventually arrived in Nevers (Philippe held the title of Duke of Nevers), a small but ancient stronghold in the Loire Valley in the center of France, on the main route north from Lyon to Paris. There, brother and sister settled in to enjoy the hospitality that was their due. This was too much for Duke Mazarin. Their delay, in the ducal castle perched over the crossroads of France, where the travelers could contemplate at their leisure the different routes that lay before them, seemed to taunt him. He heard reports of late-night banquets, and dancing, and theater. Summoning his lawyers, he obtained a warrant from the Grand Chamber of Paris for the forcible arrest and return of his wayward wife. The document was delivered to the City Council of Nevers by Duke Mazarin's captain of the guards, escorted by a band of armed soldiers. The city fathers, offended by this show of force, promptly refused. Their defiance was endorsed by the king, who sent his own orders that the Duchess Mazarin was not to be molested.

Hortense's husband was stunned. From the fortress of Vincennes on the edge of Paris, where as grand master of the artillery he had spent much of his time since his wife's flight from their home, Armand-Charles considered his options with growing rage. Early one morning he set out for the Mazarin palace, carrying a hammer, a knife, and a bucket of black paint. Upon entering the palace, he went directly to the long galleries on the second floor, which housed the magnificent collection of paintings and sculpture that Cardinal Mazarin had left to the couple as part of their inheritance. There he had to wait for the sleepy curator to unlock the giant doors. What happened next sent shock waves far beyond the confines of the palace, where distraught servants tried in vain to calm their master's fury as he mutilated the prize art collection that was the envy of Europe. Hortense's friend later in life, the writer Charles de Saint-Evremond, described the frenzy: "He chose to focus his attack on this sex that he desired but sought to escape, threw himself on the most prominent parts and was so carried away that one saw, in the fury of his blows, that those cold and insensible marbles had at some point inflamed him, and that his repentance was perhaps taking revenge upon the errors of his imagination."[13]

The Duke Mazarin had made sure to target certain objects that reminded him the most of his estranged wife: an antique statue of a wounded Amazon, a painting of Diana and her nymphs by Francesco Albani, and another of the sleeping lovers Mars and Venus. Hortense would also later reflect that the public perceived her husband's attack as a jealous rage. "People jeered that he was even in love with the beautiful statues of the Palais Mazarin; and the love of that man truly must have brought bad luck, since those poor statues have been so cruelly punished for it, just as I have, although they were no guiltier than I."[14] Dismembering the "nude" ancient statues with his hammer, throwing black paint over the naked flesh in paintings by the likes of Raphael, Correggio, Titian, da Vinci, and Giorgione, and slashing the giant tapestries with his knife, Armand-Charles worked tirelessly for an entire day. After supper he enlisted help from his servants and stopped only when exhaustion forced him to rest. The next day, a courier arrived from court carrying a royal order to desist, but the destruction had already been done. The king sent guards to the Mazarin palace. There was nothing left to do but survey, aghast, the damage wrought on what had been the greatest collection of art ever assembled in Europe. News of the crime quickly circulated and even took on lyrical form as artists and writers lamented the event in poems and pamphlets, imagining the statues imploring Louis XIV to "save the living marbles" and "tame the violence of an excessive zeal."[15] At his estate in Burgundy, the writer Roger de Rabutin, the Count of Bussy, received letters from his friends describing the excitement caused by the Paris events. Madame de Scudéry wrote him that the duke had been placed under house arrest: "Monsieur de Mazarin is imprisoned in his house for having broken or burned more than four hundred thousand francs worth of statues and paintings because they were nude. Monsieur Colbert, having discovered this fine intention before it was executed, had sent an order from the king to prevent it."[16]

But it was too late.

Before leaving Italy, Hortense had written to Finance Minister Colbert expressing the terms she was hoping for in a settlement with her husband: she would be willing, she wrote, to live in a convent of her choice in Paris, where she could receive visitors at will; she wanted to be free to remain in Paris when her husband made his numerous official trips to the provinces; and she wished to choose her own servants. At the time, neither Colbert nor the king had replied to her overtures, but now, as she learned of her husband's violent attack on the collection that the king considered a legacy to the nation, she realized that her own position might be viewed more sympathetically. The incident had certainly gained her allies and cemented the solidarity that many already felt for her rebellious choices. "The world has never seen a more deserving cuckold than the Duke Mazarin," wrote the Count of Bussy, "and every day of his life adds new esteem to that which I had for his wife when she preferred to stay out in the street rather than see him any more."[17]

As she was en route from Nevers, Hortense received the order to go to the Cistercian abbey Notre Dame du Lys, some forty miles southeast of Paris. This was a good sign. The place was a school and residence for young noblewomen under the protection of the Crown, and arrangements for her to reside there had been made personally by Colbert, whom she thanked profusely: "Truly, Sir, nothing is so obliging as what you have done for me. And I will behave in a manner such that my conduct will always be worthy of the grace you have shown me, as that is the only way I have to thank you."[18]

The abbess of Lys was less enthusiastic about the arrangement. She discussed her concerns with the archbishop of Sens, recalling with alarm the stories they had heard about Hortense's escapades with her friend Marie-Sidonie de Courcelles when they both had been confined to a convent. So the two decided to spell out the conditions under which they would accept this new pensioner. The Duke Mazarin had rushed to send his own demands, which they also were trying to satisfy without offending Colbert or the king, as the prelate wrote in a letter to Colbert:

I have thought it necessary to take somewhat severe precautions regarding visits, because I learned about everything that happened in the Convent of the Daughters of Saint Mary in Paris when Madame Mazarin was there. The charges that were made against persons of quality (Nevers and Rohan) when she fled the country are widely known and it would be very bad if all sorts of people went to visit her in a monastery surrounded by country fields and whose walls are very low and in poor condition, . . . I beg you, sir, to be very careful that the abbey of Lys does not suffer the prejudice that other religious houses have feared when it was proposed to them to receive Madame Mazarin.[19]

But their concerns proved unfounded once Hortense was established in her new surroundings. "We are most surprised to observe the conduct of Madame the Duchess Mazarin, after the impressions we had been given," they wrote. "She must be extremely changed or else others serve her very ill, for one could not act better than she in all things. One hears no more noise than if she were not even in the house and she works and reads the books of piety that we give her, which she seems to enjoy."[20]

During those cold winter months in the country abbey, the duchess was on good behavior. Meanwhile, she was being pressed by the duke, "who presented me with several proposals for accommodation, but all by miserable monks or other persons of similar substance, and all without any guarantees."[21] Philippe, newly married, sent petitions to the king on his sister's behalf. After two months of this the king decided to attempt his own intervention and summoned Hortense for an audience in the presence of Madame de Montespan, the king's mistress and aunt of Philippe's new wife. All of these comings and goings were watched with great interest. A carriage was sent to fetch the duchess and she was brought to court accompanied by a chaperone the king had chosen who was thought to be incorruptible, and eight armed guards. In her audience with Louis XIV, Hortense felt she received a respectful and sympathetic hearing. Still, the king directed her to tell him exactly what she wanted: If it was to return to Italy, he promised to provide her with some support in the form of a pension of 24,000 francs. But he advised against it and urged her, as Hortense later reported, to stay with her husband. If she would stay, he promised to "make my agreement as advantageous as I desired, that I would not be compelled to follow Monsieur Mazarin on any journey, that he would have no say over my servants, even that if his caresses were odious to me, I would immediately be relieved of any obligation to suffer them, and that he was giving me until the next day to think it over."[22]

Hortense's friends and acquaintances advised her to accept this offer of a mediated reconciliation, even as she contemplated another quick getaway. "What do you hope to do with your twenty-thousand francs?" one asked, while another commented that her perpetual need to flee her husband at any cost illustrated what happened when "we women have our brains fall to pieces."[23] But the thought of returning to a life in the company of the duke, even in separate wings of their residence, was unbearable to her. She did not believe that Armand-Charles could be contained. She wrote a letter to the king saying as much: "I replied the following day, . . . that I could not resolve myself to return to him, that no matter what precautions might be taken against his moody temperament, I would have to face twenty small acts of cruelty every day, about which it would not be fitting to trouble His Majesty."[24] As for her friend's skepticism regarding Hortense's ability to survive on the pension the king had offered, she reflected that in the three years since she had first left Paris, she had learned more than her friends there could understand. "But he did not know that I had learned to use money wisely. It is not that I was blind to the fact that I could not possibly live decently for very long with that sum; but . . . I calculated that it would at least give me the time to take other measures."[25]

And so on February 24 the Duchess Mazarin once again left Paris, accompanied by her designated chaperone, Madame Bellinzani, who was to ensure that her charge be suitably restricted during the voyage and upon her arrival in Rome. As ever, Hortense's movements were observed, debated, and circulated for the entertainment of all those who were missing the news as it broke in Paris. Madame de Sévigné wrote delightedly to her daughter in Provence that Hortense left the capital echoing the voices of the Fronde rebels who had risen against her uncle the cardinal thirty years earlier, shouting, "No more Mazarin! No more Mazarin!" Madame de Scudéry wrote to the Count of Bussy in Burgundy describing the duchess as a madwoman, to which he replied, "Madame Mazarin is quite mad, I admit, but you must confess that Monsieur Mazarin is an idiot."[26]

It would be the last time Hortense saw Paris. But she was optimistic and managed to direct the traveling party on an itinerary that took her through cities where she knew she had friends ready to receive and entertain her. The return trip to Rome took three months, including a long layover in Turin, where she was well received by the Duke of Savoy. Unlike her first trip to Rome three years earlier, she did not rush, she suffered no injuries, and when she finally reached her destination, at the end of May 1671, at the peak of the Roman springtime, her sister found her to be "more beautiful than ever." Roman society had missed Hortense's presence. The *avvisi*, or handwritten newsletters, had reported that in her absence, social gatherings did not attract as many interesting people, and they lacked "that liberty that was only found in the company of the Constabless and the Duchess Mazarin, . . . that wit and graceful skill that reigns in the French ladies."[27] In March the newsletters were triumphant: "The Duke is greatly troubled by His Majesty having given permission to his Duchess to return and continually live in Rome. . . . Madame Colonna is hoping that she will bring back some unusual new fashion, . . . and with her company give Rome the pleasure of that amusement that can only be found in their conversations."[28] Marie celebrated Hortense's arrival by resuming her "conversations" and salon gatherings at the Colonna palace.

While Hortense had been gone, in 1670 and 1671, the work on enlarging the art collection, decorating the palazzo, and supporting theatrical productions there moved ahead at an accelerated pace. When Hortense returned to Rome in 1671, Marie embraced every opportunity to leave the palazzo Colonna with her sister and move freely about the city. The Roman gazettes recorded the public fascination with these two sisters, who had introduced a "French liberty" to the lives of Roman women. The Duchess Mazarin's presence added to the animation of the Colonna palace as well as providing fodder for the ever-curious readers of the gazettes. Finishing touches were made to the trompe l'oeil frescoes covering the walls in Marie's salon, depicting a rural landscape that looked so real that one was tempted to walk through the wall and into the open countryside beyond the confines of the city. In the grand gallery linking the two main wings of the palace, the walls were covered with maps of the world in fresco, and the ceiling represented the star-filled skies so familiar to Marie from her studies of astrology. Voet continued his project of producing more portraits of both sisters, including one of the two together that shows Hortense holding out her palm to Marie, who points her finger toward the sky as if in warning as she reads her younger sister's fortune.

In the hot summer of 1671, Hortense joined Marie in swimming in the Tiber, scandalizing the Romans. Marie had started her swimming outings the year before, accompanied by an entourage of ladies, gentlemen, and servants who more than once had scooped her out of the strong currents to avert disaster. Philippe de Lorraine, a longtime friend of the Mancinis, was in Italy in that year with his brother the Chevalier de Marsan. The Chevalier de Lorraine was a notorious bisexual whose intimacy with the king's brother was causing tensions in the royal family, and he had in effect been exiled to Rome. He and Marsan were quite happy to keep company with Hortense and Marie. Rumors abounded; it was said that Marsan became a lover of Hortense and Lorraine of Marie, who wrote:

> [The] city pleased the chevalier immensely; however, what impelled him even more to remain there during the space of two years that his exile lasted was the throng of elegant society who frequented our house, which teemed with delights as if it were the very center of pleasure. For indeed, I can say without exceeding the truth in the least that the plays, the conversation, the brilliant gaming, the music, the magnificent meals—in short all the entertainments that one can imagine—followed one after another, without anyone's ever tiring of them, since their variety always served as a seasoning.[29]

Lorenzo Colonna, though, had become less inclined to enter into the risky spirit of his wife's cultural projects, and he was angered by some of her escapades with her sister. Their lives had become quite separate. Even conversation between them was stiff and distant, as Marie would later reflect, though they continued to attend public events together. He "barely even spoke to me, and if he did, it was in such a way as to make me prefer his silence to his words," she wrote.[30]

By the time Philippe Mancini returned to Rome after a few months' absence, the tension between the Colonna couple was becoming alarming to Marie's friends, and she seemed afraid of her husband. During her illness in 1671 she had even become morbidly afraid that her husband wanted to do away with her. Philippe discussed with her Lorenzo's reputation for violence. He urged her to leave, warning that she might soon lose the liberty that was so precious to her. Marie's excursions with the Chevalier de Lorraine had aroused her husband's jealousy, but his coldness left her uncertain about what measures he might have been contemplating. And Lorraine left Rome suddenly in January 1672, just when Marie was coming to rely on him for support and after she herself, as Hortense put it, "had quarreled with all of Rome for his sake."[31] Before leaving, Lorraine had presented Marie with a gift from the king's brother Philippe d'Orleans, a present that must have reminded her of the independent spirit she had long cherished in herself. It was a magnificent hunting outfit, "a hunting equipage worth a thousand pistoles, trimmed with loads of the richest and most beautiful ribbons from Paris."[32] Sitting in her salon, Marie contemplated the paths lacing the painted countryside covering the walls that enclosed her. She thought of the road her sister had chosen. She obsessively studied her astrological charts and confided her fears in Hortense, who could not help but feel a sense of alarm as she observed that "the same star that drew me to Italy was drawing her to France."[33]

*On the*
# ROAD

*Most Christian Majesty,*
*In this most strange adventure that is the departure of my*
*wife, . . . I appeal to Your Majesty's royal and powerful*
*protection so that, in your sympathy for my disgrace, you*
*may impress upon Madame just how disruptive a flight of*
*this kind has been, both for herself and for the honor of my*
*house, and order her to return to Rome and not add a cul-*
*pable resistance to the fault she has already committed. . . .*
*I hope that your Majesty will consider that my marriage*
*originated in your royal counsel, and will deign to employ*
*your wisdom to cut the thread of greater scandals than those*
*that have already been caused by this flight.*

—Lorenzo Onofrio Colonna to Louis XIV, June 21, 1672

*If we grant women who flee their husbands the freedom to*
*decide for themselves what will become of them, these cases*
*will not be rare in the world!*

—Cardinal Altieri to the papal envoy in Paris, August 20, 1672

THE PRECISE REASONS for Marie's decision to flee Rome on May 29, 1672, will never be completely understood. In her memoirs and letters she alludes to fears for her health, her liberty, and her life. Her brother, Philippe, had been more blunt, warning her that "one day when I least expected it I would find myself locked up in Paliano, which is a fortress belonging to the constable."[1] Marie knew that her husband wanted her out of the way. He barely spoke to her and openly kept mistresses. In her final years in Rome, Marie was deeply preoccupied with astrology and even composed two astrological almanacs for the years 1670 and 1671, which she published under her own name. In letters to her friend the Countess Ortensia Stella, she alluded to "the fear that you know," and in a letter to her husband after her departure she made similarly mysterious statements about a "suspicion" that made her leave and that had turned the talk in Rome against him.[2] It seems clear that she feared for her life. Friends thought she was afraid her husband would try to poison her. Her sister Hortense wrote Lorenzo denying any involvement in pushing Marie to make the same risky choice she had made, and in that letter she, too, alluded to a dark fear that spurred her sister on, though she tried to make light of it: "Please believe that I would never forgive myself if by caprice or by carelessness I had cleared the path for my sister to distance herself from you. Terror, or what I think was panic, based on counsel indiscreetly given and repeated many times, were the only counselors of this disappearance."[3]

It would not have been the first time in Marie's world that a jealous nobleman killed his wife and got away with it. In 1667 the young Diane-Elisabeth de Rossan, Marquise de Ganges, had been murdered on orders of her husband, and although the assassins had been convicted of the crime, the marquis himself had gone unpunished. The victim had frequented Roman society and was a favorite of Queen Christina of Sweden; by 1670, the case was already a cause célèbre. And Lorenzo Colonna was known to have a violent temperament. He was famous for flying into rages when he felt slighted. He was thought to have been responsible for "a few assassinations," as the French ambassador wrote of him when he died.

Marie and Hortense had become very close in the year since the duchess had returned to Rome. Marie envied her sister's courage and confided her own fears about what Lorenzo's coldness toward her, and jealousy, might lead him to do. Noting Hortense's sympathy, Marie later wrote that she "implored her not to return to France without bringing me."[4] Hortense acknowledged her sister's anxieties but tried unsuccessfully to dissuade her from taking the same steps she had taken. Marie pointed to Lorenzo's rages. She assured her sister that she could not know the dangerous extent to which jealousy and hatred between Roman families could lead, and she feared what might become of both of them if they became isolated in Rome, "where dissimulation and hatred among the families reign more supreme than among other courts."[5]

But Hortense saw that in Marie's heart the choice had already been made. "And so," Marie recounted, "I set out on the twenty-ninth of May, carrying no more on my person than 700 pistoles, my pearls, and some diamond pendants, and Madame Mazarin having lost all her clothes and effects by leaving them in Rome."[6] Pretending to set out on a day outing to the country, the two sisters fled the city for good. On that day Lorenzo was in Frattocchie, south of the city, visiting one of his stud farms and surveying the horses that he would use in the upcoming *chinea* ceremony, in which a cavalcade of noblemen rode through the streets of Rome to the Vatican, where they offered homage and gold coins to the pope. Not wanting to attract attention, Marie and Hortense set off in a small coach accompanied by only their maidservants Nanon and Morena, a valet, and almost no luggage. The jewels that Marie carried with her represented the parts of her identity that were most precious to her. The pearls that Louis XIV had given her had stayed with Marie throughout her years in Rome. She had worn them as she sat for portraits done by the celebrated artists who found patronage from the Colonna family. Her diamonds had been given by her husband on the occasion of their marriage. Having the jewels in their possession as she and Hortense became fugitives caused her servants much anxiety, but for Marie they had a magical and protective effect.

Under their dresses, all four women wore men's clothes. It was a warm day and Marie cried out loudly to the carriage driver, "To Frascati!" thereby indicating to anyone who happened to be listening that they were headed southeast to a country villa just outside the city. But at the first corner, the valet, a German who worked for the Duchess Mazarin and had secretly arranged for a small boat to be readied for them, ordered the coachman to head northwest toward Civitavecchia on the Mediterranean instead. They were headed for the same port from which they had first embarked for France with their mother nineteen years earlier.

The two sisters had made secret and precise, if risky, arrangements. They hoped that they would not be missed for at least a day or so, but they were also very aware of the likelihood of being recognized or of drawing suspicion to themselves. It was not a common sight for two wealthy ladies to be traveling alone far outside of the city. Nor was it safe—their serving women, Nanon and Morena, were petrified and quite astonished at the ladies' calm when they decided to pull off the main road and wait to hear from the boatman some five miles from the port. Such was their fatigue that they even managed to sleep for two hours. They were exhilarated and tired but not frightened, though Marie began to despair of their escape as the hours flew by and no boatman appeared:

> The heat of the sun, which had been pounding down on my head for five hours and which was then at high noon, a forced fast of twenty-four hours, and my worry over our lack of news about the boat all threw me into a despair which made me say to my sister that I wanted to turn back, and that I might just as well lose my life in

Rome, in whatever way, as die of hunger where we were. But my
sister, who is in all the world the most patient woman with the best
temperament, bucked me up with her reassurances, adding in the
end that if we did not have some favorable news within the half hour,
we could always turn back then.[7]

Just a few minutes later, they heard a horse approaching and
waited anxiously, Hortense holding two pistols, until they recognized the rider as a valet who had been sent ahead to scout out the
boat that had been arranged for them. He told them that the boat
had been found. Despite their best efforts, the little party that strag-
gled into the port must have drawn considerable attention. By this
time the women had thrown off their outer layer of petticoats and
were dressed in men's riding attire, but their disguises did not seem
any more effective than the ones Hortense and Nanon had donned
four years earlier on her flight from Paris. Even before they boarded
the felucca that was waiting for them, the captain was demanding
more money, and once they were on board he continued to raise
his price, saying that he clearly was taking a great risk by agreeing
to transport them. Hortense's valet, Pelletier, tried to argue, but
Marie paid the man what he asked.

Travel by boat in the seventeenth century was a risky business.
Not only might one encounter the usual array of storms and rough
seas, but there was also the more serious danger of attack by pirates
or capture by merchant ships of any number of countries that might
not be on good terms with one's own. For an Italian vessel, the
possibility of kidnapping was very real, and everyone was familiar
with tales of capture by Turks or North Africans. An encounter
with an unfriendly vessel could easily result in prolonged captivity,
until family members or a religious order dedicated to the ransom
of Christian captives might manage to negotiate a release. The
felucca that the runaway sisters had boarded had the advantage of

speed—it was the narrowest and most nimble of sailing ships—but it was not well equipped for defense in the event of direct attack. And so Marie and Hortense did not doubt the danger ahead of them when after a few hours of sailing the captain spotted a brig and immediately steered their boat to the rocky coastline until he could determine that it was Genovese and not Turk. Their ship resumed its course that night, only to confront another hazard, a storm that produced waters so rough that everyone felt ill, especially Hortense, who told Marie she thought she would die. Marie was more worried about a shipwreck, as well as the honesty of the ship's crew. Both women were grateful to have found a captain who proved himself "honorable," as Hortense later wrote: "Our greatest stroke of luck was to have fallen into the hands of a captain who was as skillful as he was honorable. Any other would have thrown us into the sea after having robbed us, for he could see from the first glance that we were no beggars. He said to himself, and his crew asked us 'if we had killed the pope?' As for skill, suffice it to say that they sailed in a straight line one hundred miles off Genoa."[8]

It took the ship eight days to reach Monaco, where the traveling party obtained counterfeit bills of health declaring them free of plague so that they could be permitted to enter French territory, and from there on to La Ciotat, a port city at the mouth of the Rhone River. There the four women and Hortense's valet were left to proceed by land.

The fugitives had been lucky in that Lorenzo had stayed at his stud farm for three days before returning to Rome. But upon his return he immediately knew what had happened. And he did not hesitate to take steps to retrieve the runaways. First he sent a dozen horsemen in pursuit, then a galley boat. So as Hortense and Marie made their way with Nanon and Morena over land, a galley filled with Lorenzo's men awaited them in Marseille, which seemed the most likely harbor to which they would head.

Lorenzo had no doubt that his wife was headed to France. Indeed, as his informants must have told him, Marie had obtained a letter from Louis XIV guaranteeing her safe passage into the country. She had written the Chevalier de Lorraine declaring her intention to leave Rome, and Lorraine had obtained this favor for her through his liaison with the king's brother. That Louis XIV had produced the letter, thus risking a break in his relations with Lorenzo and his faction in Rome, indicated that he believed Marie's fears about what might happen to her if she remained there. Armed with this royal passport, the Princess Colonna and the Duchess Mazarin approached Marseille. For his part, the Prince Colonna did not hesitate to appeal directly to the French ambassador in Rome and the ambassador's brother the Cardinal d'Estrées, who dispatched a letter to the bishop of Marseille:

> Monsieur the Constable Colonna just left here after recounting a story that will no doubt be no less troubling and surprising to you than it was to me. Madame his wife and Madame Mazarin left on Sunday afternoon . . . and as he assumes that Madame his wife can only have decided to withdraw to France and that she apparently will have landed in Marseille, he has asked me to write to someone who can speak to her . . . and make her wait for more specific news from him about a person he intends to send to her to make her understand his position and his feelings.[9]

The person in question, a Captain Manechini, in fact did arrive promptly and delivered Lorenzo's message to Marie as she waited in an auberge near the home of Monsieur Arnoux, the superintendent of the galleys in Marseille. Arnoux had previously delivered two letters to Marie, one for her from King Louis and one from his secretary of state for foreign affairs, Arnauld de Pomponne, directing the bearer to offer hospitality to the runaways. Following instructions from Lorenzo, Captain Manechini attempted to persuade them to return to Rome, whereupon Marie refused, noting that Lorenzo was offering no real assurances for her safety and seemed concerned only that she not embarrass the family: "the messenger . . . came with nothing more to propose to me than that I return to the constable, or at the least that I wait until he could send me a train more in keeping with my quality, and all that was needed to continue my journey with greater splendor and decorum." Manechini also attempted to appeal to her motherly instincts, but although she was touched by his invocation of the children she had left behind, she could not overcome her suspicions: "Although I loved them tremendously, I feared peril even more, and having no doubt that there was some scheme hidden beneath his charming words, I told him succinctly that I had no intention of returning."[10]

While Captain Manechini returned to Rome with this refusal, Marie and Hortense were visited by the lieutenant general of Provence, the Count of Grignan, who offered his hospitality and protection. The Countess of Grignan sent the women fresh clothing, remarking that they were traveling "like two heroines out of a novel, with plenty of jewels but no clean linen."[11] She reported her observations in letters to her mother, Marie de Sévigné, and the comparison captured the imagination of other men and women who were waiting to see what the two fugitives would do next. The flow of letters sending news of the escapade to more distant places accelerated. Though some onlookers seemed to just lean back and prepare to enjoy the show, others were more judgmental and took sides with either the women or their husbands. Rumors quickly spread that the women, like the character of Angelica in the popular romance *Orlando Furioso,* were roaming the countryside in pursuit of wandering lovers. In her reports to the Count of Bussy, Madame de Scudéry was quick to accept this version of events and condemn the errant ladies (though neither of the men she mentioned were in fact in Provence at the time): "Mme Colonna and Mme Mazarin have entered Aix; the word is that they were disguised as men come to see the two brothers the Chevalier de Lorraine and the Count of Marsan. . . . To tell you the truth I can imagine that one can love, but I cannot understand how a lady of quality can bring herself to renounce all manner of honor, proper deportment, and reputation. I declare, there should be a corporal punishment for such uncontrolled ladies."[12]

Although corporal punishment was not an option he was yet prepared to exercise, Lorenzo wasted no time in trying to bring his wife back to Rome. Although the Roman gazettes portrayed him as morose, inconsolable, and locked in his palazzo, in fact he was busy in his retreat, orchestrating a massive effort to force his wife's return. He directed his energy to fully exploiting his vast network of contacts. And he continued to send a steady stream of messengers to try to negotiate with Marie in person, each one bringing increasing pressure on her as she began to recognize how difficult it would be for her to find protection from people who had any reason to fear her husband's influence. After Captain Manechini's failure, Lorenzo sent another emissary, Jean-Baptiste de Saint-Simon, first to talk with Marie in Aix and then to continue north to Paris and Versailles and attempt to receive assurances in advance that neither the French king nor any of his subjects would offer his wife protection.

Saint-Simon was an eager agent. He had served as squire to the recently deceased Cardinal Antonio Barberini, who had close ties to France and had valued his French entourage. Now he was working for the opposite faction, as an agent of Cardinal Altieri, the most powerful statesman of Pope Clement X. Saint-Simon welcomed the opportunity to prove himself to Lorenzo Colonna by exploiting his contacts with both factions, and Lorenzo engaged his services, knowing that he could use him to argue for his interests at the court of France. Saint-Simon's first assignment, though, was to persuade Marie to return to Rome, while also investigating all the circumstances surrounding her flight. He did not disappoint his new patron, sending Lorenzo frequent, detailed written reports on his inquiries regarding Marie's flight, spelling out exactly what he said in each conversation with her and what was said to him in reply. In a long letter describing his first encounter with Marie in Aix, dated June 10, 1672, he even seemed to relish the drama of the situation. Noting that the Count of Grignan had sent two armed guards to watch over the runaway sisters, he described to Lorenzo how he managed to gain an audience with his wife:

> In the room I found two of M. de Grignan's guards with their uniforms and carabines. . . . Shortly after that I was admitted to their room where I found them both in bed. Madame said to me as I entered, "Well, Saint-Simon, what have you come here for? . . . I think that you never thought on Sunday morning when I spoke to you in Rome that you would be coming to see me here! . . . What are people saying about us in Rome?"

> He replied to her that all conversations in Rome "are to your extreme disadvantage, for no one understands what your reasons are," "all appearances are against you, no lady was ever treated as you were, if you want to know the truth you had no reason to take this resolution, believe me Madam do not push this further for the more these things are in the open the worse it is, what on earth did he want to do to you?"

> He knows my reason! He knows what made me take the resolution
>    that I did in order to preserve my life!
> What, Madam, to preserve your life? You do a great injustice to Monsieur the Constable and to his reputation.[13]

This report and others similar to it quickly persuaded Lorenzo that getting his wife to return home voluntarily was not going to be easy. So he turned to an alternative strategy, which was to effectively limit Marie's options if she failed to return to Rome. Instructions sent to his agents in all the cities where he thought she might stop made it clear that he would fight any effort to help her live independently of him. He was particularly concerned that she not be able to reside in France, even in a convent: "If she wants to go to Genova or Torino, I will agree to it, if she is in a convent in Italy, but I will never allow her to be in liberty except with me."[14]

Marie quickly realized that she would need to negotiate directly with her husband to achieve the independence she was seeking. Almost immediately after leaving Rome she began to write to Lorenzo, urging him to understand the seriousness of her decision. Unwilling to rely on her husband's emissaries to communicate her point of view, she argued with him in her own words, never quite abandoning a polite tone but always utterly clear in describing her own intentions. The tone she took in her first letter to her husband following Saint-Simon's visit was one she would continue to assume throughout her correspondence with Lorenzo for many years to come:

As concerns what you have conveyed to me, I can tell you that I do not reject the offers you have made me; on the contrary, it will be a pleasure for me to let it be known that you still have regard for me. As for the decision I took to withdraw to France, it was prompted only by the worries I had about my health; and as well, by what my brother said several times to me and to others about the designs someone had against me. (I could say more but will keep silent, for you would not want such things to be common knowledge.) Yet I will accept whatever you are kindly disposed to do for me, and you must never doubt that, wherever I am, I will give you a full account of myself. And I will make you understand that this decision of mine was not a whim, but rather that it was an attempt on my part to ease my spirit and live out my days in peace. This is all I can say to you, with the assurance that you will always find in me the cordial feelings and affection I have always had for you. I send my love to the boys with all my heart. And assure them that I will never forget them.[15]

Hers was a delicate balancing act. She had left her husband but hoped to retain some measure of his support. She had fled his home in secrecy and brought shame upon his family, but she wanted to negotiate her independence. She knew her husband's public image was everything to him. Although this meant that her actions had enraged him to distraction, it also meant that he would be unwilling to let her bring even more embarrassment to the family by roaming around the country without suitable escort or financial support. What else did she hold over him? The threat in her letter ("I could say more but will keep silent") was indirect, but crystal clear.

From the moment of her departure, both Marie and her husband had been posting letters to the king of France petitioning for his support. Marie had entrusted Hortense's valet, Pelletier, with delivering her letters in person, and he had set out from Marseille. Lorenzo sent letters using multiple contacts, from the French ambassador to his personal agent Saint-Simon. It was Marie's misfortune that her own letters did not reach the king quickly. During the summer of 1672, Louis was in Holland with his armies and had entrusted Queen Marie-Thérèse with a nominal authority in his absence. And Pelletier had bad luck in his role of courier. He had been successful, after a long time, in obtaining letters for Marie from Louis XIV and his representatives. But he had also been robbed and beaten by bandits en route. Some of the letters he was carrying were lost. Lorenzo's couriers had better protection, and better luck, so by the time Louis XIV replied to Marie, he had already been amply briefed by the emissaries her husband had sent.

After Saint-Simon left Marseille, Hortense and Marie did not wish to linger there to wait for official authorization to continue north toward Paris. Marie's memoirs describe her travel strategy and how she managed to pursue her itinerary while also evading the agents of both the Duke Mazarin and the Prince Colonna who the sisters knew had been dispatched to intercept them. The women stopped first at the medieval town of Mirabeau, where the local lord gave them shelter for a few days but could do nothing to turn back the Duke Mazarin's agent, who arrived with orders to kidnap his wife. Just in time, Hortense fled to a wooded area outside the chateau and Marie was able to convince the agent, Polastron, that she had already taken the road back to Italy. This made Hortense decide that she would have to take a different route from Marie's:

> And that very night Madame Mazarin set out for Savoy, accompanied by the aforementioned knight (Mirabeau), by Nanon, and by half of the guards, the other half having stayed with me. This separation from my sister was very painful for me, and in return for the promise she made me to stay in Chambéry, where she was headed, until the king permitted her to live in France, I promised her not to go further than Grenoble, in order to be nearer to her and to have news of her more often.[16]

Marie arrived outside of Grenoble in early July. She was pleased to have made it there without drawing great attention to herself and her party en route, and though it was quickly apparent that her presence in the city was known to some, including the local Duke of Lesdiguières, who sent his greetings, most people did not recognize her. She decided to stay in an inn outside the city walls rather than ask for the duke's hospitality, and there she awaited news from her sister and from the king. She was not aware of the unfortunate adventures of Pelletier, nor did she know whether the king, in Holland, had received the letter she had sent him more than a month earlier. The first letter she received was from Queen Marie-Thérèse:

> There finally arrived a gentleman sent by the queen, to whom the king had left the government of his realm while he was at war in Holland. He handed over to me a letter from Her Majesty in which she commanded me, but in the most obliging manner in the world, to remain wherever this gentleman who gave me the letter found me, adding that she had no doubt that such would be the intention of the king. I replied to this gentleman that I did not plan to go further and that I would obey Her Majesty's orders most scrupulously.[17]

This was discouraging. Marie remained convinced that if she could gain an audience with the king he would support her, but she had lost precious time and did not understand what had happened to her messages. She also learned that Lorenzo was orchestrating his own lobbying interests at the French court. But she had no choice but to remain in Grenoble, as ordered, and try to gather as much information of her own as she could. She had written letters to her brother and to Ortensia Stella, explaining her decision and asking that they work on her behalf to help people understand the choice she had made and to soften the constable's attitude toward her. To Philippe she stressed the role he could play by assuring Lorenzo that she would do nothing further to damage the family name:

> I beg you in the name of God to soften things with the Constable . . . for if I did not feel safe in his presence before, you can imagine that I would be even less secure now. Be assured, moreover, that I will not cause others to talk about me and I will do him no wrong, and also I ask nothing from him. You are clever, and if I have also the

fortune of your friendship toward me I will have no complaints about anything, and I will be obliged to you as the most grateful and tender of all sisters, who loves you with all her heart.[18]

Marie's letters to the Countess Stella were more openly affectionate and trusting, and also apologetic, for she had offended her friend by not confiding in her from the beginning. Ortensia had originally come to Rome with Marie in 1661, to be Marie's principal lady-in-waiting. She had married the Count Stella in Rome and had been widowed before Marie fled. After her mistress's departure, Ortensia remained as a dependent living in the Colonna household. Marie had intended to leave a letter explaining herself at her departure but had been persuaded by others to tear it up. From Grenoble she wrote to Ortensia asking that she try to have one or two serving women from her household sent to join her, along with some fresh clothes:

> My poor Countess, I have always loved you and I promise you that it was to save you from trouble that I did not confide in you, not that I doubted you, as I know well that you can keep secrets. . . . Send me Nene and you will give me great pleasure, and send some of my girls to me, those who will be happy to come join me. If they are permitted, have them bring me some clothes, I am in great need of them . . . you can manage my affairs now in Rome. I will be here for a long time, I am waiting for my brother. Madame Mazarin is in Savoy, I am very solitary and completely yours, Contessa.[19]

In the first days of August, Marie finally received her response from Louis XIV. Along with this message, which has since been lost, was a cover letter from Charles de Créquy, first gentleman of the court and former ambassador to Rome, spelling out the king's wishes. Despite strong urgings from Lorenzo and his supporters, including Cardinal Altieri and the pope himself, Louis stopped short of ordering Marie to return to her husband. But neither did he grant her permission to come to court, or even to Paris. Créquy opened his letter with reassurances of the king's goodwill and affection: "I assure you that he has for you every possible tenderness and in the midst of his prosperity it pains him to see that you are not happy." But the king was trying to effect a reconciliation, and to achieve that objective he could not permit her to return to France other than to briefly visit her family. Failing that, she could remain in France only if she agreed to retire to a convent, preferably "one as far as possible from Paris, in order to prove that your motives for doing what you have done were not those which people have imagined." As to the fears that Marie had expressed in her own letters, the king would be satisfied with a personal assurance from Lorenzo that his wife had nothing to fear from him: "I well understand that you may have fears, but I can also see that it is possible to receive assurances such that you will have no more reason to be afraid. And once word has been given to the master that I serve this will be, madam, a good guarantee of the promises made to you."[20]

This domestic rift was rapidly becoming an international affair of state. Louis XIV returned earlier than planned to Versailles and the court, where he found waiting for him additional letters from Lorenzo, Altieri, and the pope. Colbert was waiting to brief him on other petitions that had been submitted on behalf of Lorenzo's interests. Queen Marie-Thérèse wrote a letter to the queen of Spain, and another to Lorenzo confiding that she had done all she could to personally sway the king: "Cousin, I have contributed as much as I could with the king, my lord, to your wish that you expressed to me that the ladies be sent to a convent to await measures that could be taken to your satisfaction."[21]

Marie's reaction to the messages Pelletier finally delivered to her was rebellious. She did not accept the notion that a promise made to Louis XIV would suffice to protect her from her husband, and she was unimpressed by his arguments for her withdrawal to a convent. The king "advised me to enter a convent in order to stop the malicious gossip which was producing unsavory interpretations of my departure from Rome," she wrote, but as "I was not entirely satisfied with this letter, I resolved to go to Paris unannounced to throw myself at the feet of the king."[22] Indeed, had she been able to read the secret missives sent by Cardinal Altieri to the papal envoy in Paris, she would have found support for her skepticism. "Only much later," the cardinal confided, "after Madame has decided to return and has done so, will we talk here about the actions that will be taken after that return, that is incarceration in Rome or perhaps in Italy as the easiest to execute; but for the moment, only insist on the first point, that is, that she return to the palace."[23]

Consulting only with Hortense, who had rejoined her in Grenoble, Marie left the city for Paris. For this stage of her voyage, mindful of the possibility of interception, she embarked on a less predictable itinerary. Not wanting to draw attention to herself by traveling in an easily recognizable private carriage, she opted to use the postal coaches, where passengers could travel anonymously, and to travel alternately by river and by road. Later, she would reflect with some pride at how she had outwitted her pursuers. The gazettes and public letters followed her adventures, but in the memoirs she wrote four years later she would describe exactly how she managed to get from place to place. The sisters chose a private courier they had known in Rome to escort them, setting out modestly and slowly at first, by litter (a covered and curtained chair carried on the shoulders of servants). Once out of the city, they continued more quickly in a small post chaise pulled by a single horse, with Morena and the courier following on horseback. As they approached Lyon, hoping to move more comfortably and quickly, they moved to a boat,

but the water was so low and that vehicle was so ill suited to my impatience that I got out at the first village, where, finding no postal horses, I was obliged to use those that some peasants lent us. As luck would have it, not one was fit to pull the hackney, so a man had to lead by hand the one to which it was hitched, which caused me to despair, seeing that by some twist of fate I could never go fast, either by post or by relay, and that some obstacle always kept me from making haste.[24]

This particular impediment, it turned out, would not be the worst they encountered, for as the two women approached a post station outside of Saint-Eloy, they learned that a royal messenger, Monsieur de la Gibertière, had arrived ahead of them and left orders at all the postal stations not to provide them with horses. Undaunted, Marie bribed the keeper of the stable ("whatever the cost, we needed to gain the cooperation of the people at the post station"),[25] and to the surprise of the royal messenger, who had assumed she would be forced back to the river, the little party proceeded by land.

The adventure continued, but without Hortense, who could no longer risk staying on French soil and had returned to Chambéry, accepting the Duke Charles-Emmanuel of Savoy's hospitality and protection. Marie's route was punctuated by accidents where the overloaded hackney "tipped over twice although I did not hurt myself at all"; illness in her party, when "Morena had an attack of colic"; and second thoughts on the part of her trusted escort Marguein, who "seized by an affliction which was much more dangerous for me than for him . . . reflected very seriously on the negative repercussions that could result from my undertaking, for me as well as for him, and for his whole family, if we arrived in this way, against the will and the orders of the king."[26] Exhausted, Marie allowed herself to be persuaded to wait in Fontainebleau while Marguein went ahead to Paris to present letters to the king and his minister Louvois, who Marie hoped would show her more favor than Finance Minister Colbert had. They arrived in Fontainebleau on August 24, only to learn that the messenger who had been trying to intercept them since Lyon was not far behind.

There was nothing to be done but agree to meet with him in the small inn where their travels had come to a halt. Marie sat in her room alone, holding a guitar, which had somehow survived the rough roads intact. She listened to the proposals laid before her, then turned them down. She rejected all of the propositions and hypotheses regarding her own presumptuous confidence about her power to influence the king. And this time she invoked a precedent for her demands—other women who had been permitted to live apart from their husbands in retreat at a convent of their choice:

> I replied that I had not left home only to return so soon; that I had not made this decision based on frivolous pretexts but for good and solid reasons which I could not and would not relate except to the king, and that I hoped from the mind and the sense of justice of His Majesty that, provided I could speak to him just once, which was all I asked, he would easily be disabused of all the bad impressions that people had given him of me; that I was very far from flattering myself that I held the kind of power he had just mentioned; that I had neither enough merit nor enough ability to claim even the slightest role in the handling of his affairs, that I asked nothing more than to withdraw to Paris, and I restricted my ambitions to the space of a cloister, where I implored His Majesty to let me live among my relatives, as Madame la grande duchess de Toscane and the princesse de Chalais lived today and as a thousand other ladies lived who were widowed or separated from their husbands.[27]

Then, as the gentleman stared at her in astonishment, she lifted the guitar and began to play.

The following day she received a personal visit from Charles de Créquy. She must have watched with trepidation as he approached her little auberge, and felt humiliated as she saw the shock on his face as he entered her modest quarters. He greeted her with pity, "remembering the grandeur in which he had seen me in Rome, he confessed that he was surprised and touched by the change, and he lamented for me over the sad state of my fortune." But she was proud: "I mocked his lamentations straightaway and beseeched him to come right to the point, upon which he began to speak quite plainly."[28] The message he conveyed, Marie could have no doubt, came straight from the king. He told her that he did not want her to see him or even to enter Paris. He advised her to return to Grenoble and await an escort to return to Rome. And he specified that he had given his word to both Lorenzo and the papal envoy that this would be his decision. Marie could respond only by asking Créquy to beg the king's leave to enter the Benedictine convent in Lys, not far from Paris, and where her sister had previously resided. The following day, this permission was granted.

And so, to all appearances, Marie's tumultuous flight had ended with this royal refusal, which was nonetheless accompanied by a generous sum of money that Louis had delivered to his former love along with the promise of financial support for as long as she remained under his protection. Without further delay, Marie and Morena set out for Lys, as soon as the king's escort arrived to accompany them. As she accepted the purses handed to her, Marie could not prevent herself from commenting on the irony of the gesture, as was reported in a letter by Madame de Scudéry a few days later:

> Madame de Colonne is at the abbey of Lys. The king sent her a thousand pistoles and his gallant wishes via Monsieur de Créquy. In addition he also promised her a pension of twenty thousand francs. This is a gesture by the most gallant gentleman in the world. He wrote to her that he could not see her. She replied wittily to Monsieur de Créquy that she had heard of giving money to women in order to see them, but never not to see them.[29]

Although profoundly saddened by the turn of events (ten years later she would tell her friend Madame d'Aulnoy that she thought she would die of sadness at that Fontainebleau inn), Marie knew she would be cordially received by the abbess of Lys, and she was not disappointed. Her sisters Olympe and Marianne came to see her and remained there for days at a time. Although they had been critical of her flight from Rome in the beginning, now they brought her clothes and supplies, and paid her visits accompanied by as many friends as the poor abbess felt she could permit. Colbert had given the abbess strict instructions to limit the number of visits Marie received and to report to him daily on every detail of Marie's behavior and contact with the outside world. Anxiously, she tried her best to respect what she understood to be the king's wishes, but she was not an unkind person and had no desire to be a jailer. Her dutiful reports exhibit her reluctance to play this role:

As it is my duty to inform you of what happens here with regard to Madame the Constable, I take the liberty to tell you, Monseigneur, that since her arrival on Saturday night she has seen only three people: first, a gentleman of Madame the Countess of Soissons, named Bescheville, who came to bring her letters the next day. She only spoke with him for an instant and wrote her responses that were not more than ten or twelve lines each. She spent about a quarter of an hour with him. While he was here a valet of Madame Mazarin named Nolende arrived, bringing her some letters, he was coming from Madame de Bouillon's house and spent some time in the parlor with Madame the Countess's gentleman, which worried me, but . . . I thought, monseigneur, that since the king's orders were that she should be permitted to see her sisters, I should not refuse those people sent by them.[30]

Marie was grateful for the kindness of the Benedictine nuns. She busied herself with writing letters, to her sisters and friends in Paris as well as to Rome, to the Countess Stella and also to Lorenzo. Her husband was not happy to learn of her new residence in France. Although the French ambassador attempted to reassure him that Marie's presence in a French convent would help contain the damage to his reputation caused by her flight, he was particularly worried about her visitors. He did not have his own spies in place there, which perhaps is what eventually motivated him to grant her request that he send her more serving women. With the assistance of the Countess Stella, who helped mediate their communication, Marie obtained more clothing—laces, stockings, dresses, and a coat—along with the powders and perfumes that she missed from Rome. Immediately following her arrival at Lys she wrote to the countess asking for support in softening Lorenzo's attitude:

> My dear Countess I am much obliged to you for the trouble you take for me; Monsieur the Constable has no cause to complain either of me or of my conduct. He has written such a cold letter, supported by my brother, that I don't have the courage to respond. Nevertheless I am in a convent, as Madame Mazarin has relayed to him and where I will stay longer than he thinks. I am leading such a retired life that no one will have cause to talk about me and all those mean suspicions about me will be dispelled. I have seen and will see no one but my sisters though I could see other ladies if I wished, for they are not so scrupulous here as in Rome. But I am quite happy to see no one.[31]

After a few weeks, Lorenzo relented and permitted the requested packages to be delivered to his wife, accompanied by her Roman serving maids, at least one of whom, Nanette De Rocour, would soon write him secret letters reporting on Marie's movements and intentions. In September Marie wrote him a conciliatory letter expressing her gratitude:

The women have arrived with the things, which was very heartening; for I could see that on this occasion you willingly satisfied my wishes. I will not fail to look after them, especially Maria Maddalena, who has an opportunity to become a saint if she wants to, this convent being a model of virtue. Here I do not think you will be able to complain about my behavior, which is such that my very enemies will be compelled to praise it. I hope that you will be pleased and that more and more often you will have occasion to show me the esteem you have till now denied me. I assure you that I will forever hold you in esteem. Take care of the boys, kiss them for me and give them my love. . . . Please take care of the poor Countess and of the other women who stayed with you. In the meantime, I will always pray for you and the whole household.[32]

Such docility was not, however, characteristic of Marie. It would prove difficult for her to sustain it. Before long she learned that only her sisters had been permitted to visit her, and their visits became less frequent. She was aware that the abbess was being made to observe her every move. When in late September she received word from Colbert that she was also expected to pay for her expenses in the convent, she reacted angrily in a hasty letter accusing him of treating her worse than a prisoner. Immediately after sending the letter she regretted it, and sought the advice of the kind abbess, who wrote her own letter to Colbert attempting to repair the damage. But it was too late. Colbert had already shown Marie's letter to the king and Louis was not pleased by its tone. He had just sent his own letter to Lorenzo, in which he made it clear that he was not willing to take further action to force Marie back to Rome. Now he was presented with evidence of her ingratitude, and he decided to put an end to what many of his advisers had perceived all along as his overly indulgent posture. Five days later Marie was met at the gate of the convent by the ubiquitous Monsieur de la

Gibertière, the very same gentleman who had been sent to intercept her on her voyage from Lyon. This time he appeared "with a coach and an order to the abbess to let me out."[33] Her destination was Avenay, an ancient convent south of Reims, where yet another abbess waited to greet her new charge.

## ❴ 6 ❵

## SAVOY *and* BEYOND

*This Court is not at all happy with the departure of these two*
*ladies; the men because of the lack of respect that their wives*
*give them since they started frequenting these ladies, and the*
*women because they left without first solidifying the liberty*
*and advantages that they had procured for them.*

—Dispatch from Rome to the *Gazette d'Amsterdam,* July 12, 1672

WHEN MARIE HAD LEFT HORTENSE outside of Lyon, to continue alone into the heart of France toward Paris, Hortense had taken the shortest route to the border. After her close encounter with Duke Mazarin's chief military guard Polastron, she knew that for her, remaining in France was too dangerous. The offer of protection that had come from Duke Charles-Emmanuel of Savoy seemed to be her most attractive option. Savoy was an independent state, with its border territories extending to Turin in the east, Nice in the south, and the Swiss confederation in the north. It was a militaristic culture, with an imposing history dating from the fourteenth century, and per capita had the largest army of any European state. That the duke was capable of resisting political pressure from both the French king and Italian nobility was beyond a doubt. In addition to his reassuringly powerful status, he was also reputed to be a charming man, as dedicated to cultural entertainments as he was to defending Savoy's fierce independence in Europe. He seemed delighted at the prospect of drawing the Duchess Mazarin to the center of Savoyard society, knowing that her presence was bound to enliven the relatively small court at Chambéry, where he would be free to make frequent visits from his primary residence in Turin. And he knew her from the days when she had accompanied the French court on the ceremonial trip to the court of Savoy that was designed as an occasion for the two courts to consider a royal marriage of Louis XIV with Marguerite of Savoy, the duke's sister. During that visit, the fourteen-year-old Hortense had made a deep impression on the duke. He had not forgotten her, and had even at one point indicated to Cardinal Mazarin that he was interested in marrying her. But either his demands as part of the marriage deal were too great, or Mazarin had other plans for his niece already; in any event, the duke's overture had been turned down.

Charles-Emmanuel's delight in hosting the runaway Duchess Mazarin quickly developed into an obsessive fascination once he became more closely acquainted with her. Not satisfied with remaining in touch with his new guest via occasional visits and letters, he designated several emissaries to keep a close eye on her and to send him frequent reports of her activities. This served in part to guide him in how best to keep her happy (he gave her many gifts during the three years that she lived in Savoy), in part to assist him in the diplomatic maneuvering that he was obliged to undertake with France and Italy as a result of her presence in his state, and in part simply to satisfy his own insatiable curiosity about this intriguing woman.

A traveler approaching Chambéry in the seventeenth century would have been struck by the sight of the castle, perched at the edge of the city against a backdrop of the front range of the Alps to the east. To the west, flat marshland made the chateau walls themselves the outer limits of the town. It was a medieval, fortified castle, surrounded by a moat. The ducal residence was hidden behind turreted round towers and walls built of thick gray granite. The streets through the old city were narrow, barely wide enough to accommodate a small carriage, and a drawbridge was the only entrance to the castle. Inside there was a stone courtyard dominated by the startling facade of a chapel designed in a flamboyant gothic style, in 1672 a gleaming white after the cleaning and restoration that had been the special project of the duke's pious mother. The gardens that lay outside the walls provided the only other bright relief from all of the gray, with their paths following the rounded contours of the hill and lending a softness to the imposing stone structure.

At the end of August 1672, the Duchess Mazarin was greeted at the portal at the end of the drawbridge by Monsieur Orlier, the castle's governor, nervous but eager to provide the hospitality that the duke had ordered. Orlier's letters to Turin in those first days recorded his sense of surprise that the lady did not seem overly demanding:

> Madam Mazarin arrived on Sunday at around nine o'clock in the evening; she was welcomed to an apartment in the chateau and during these first days I have forgotten nothing in my services to her. . . . She shows much gratitude for the kindness that Your Royal Highness has shown her by granting her a retreat in his states. She greatly loves solitude, and it seems to me that she takes no pleasure in seeing people.[1]

In the first days and weeks Hortense was uncharacteristically retired, spending long hours in prayer and solitude in the splendid castle chapel. She exhibited little interest in receiving visitors. Charles-Emmanuel's informants were both mystified and amused, reporting that "if Madame the Duchess Mazarin goes on like this she will have to be sainted. Since Sunday she has twice confessed and taken communion."² Later Hortense would recount to her friends in London that this period in her life was one of reflection, study, and reading. At the end of her stay at the Chambéry court she would write her memoirs, and in the beginning she also wrote tirelessly, mostly letters to Paris and Rome to try to consolidate whatever small favor that Louis XIV and Lorenzo Colonna still felt for her. It was a delicate business. With Lorenzo, she wanted to support her claim that she had not instigated his wife's flight, and with the French king she was desperate to maintain his sympathy so that he would not rescind the financial support he had promised her. Still, she was incapable of being obsequious. In her letters to Lorenzo she denied responsibility and did not apologize for Marie's leave-taking, nor did she suggest that her sister's actions were without justification. She was careful, trying to explain Marie's thinking while avoiding overt accusations:

CHAMBÉRY, 14 OCTOBER 1672

. . . Please believe that I would never forgive myself if by caprice or by carelessness I had cleared the path for my sister to distance herself from you. Terror, or what I think was panic, based on counsel indiscreetly given and repeated many times, were the only counselors of this disappearance. My only part was keeping the secret. I believed that it would be a violation of good faith and intimacy to reveal it, and although in my own mind I give no credence to the subject that caused our departure, I did not want to oppose it, out of scruple and delicacy of friendship, preferring to risk my repose, my pleasure, and my wealth (the King wants to withdraw my pension for having followed her) rather than see her leave alone. I did not follow her to Lys, not finding security there. I retired to Chambéry, having for all company only the trees of a garden of the castle. They seem more agreeable than a forced religion. I wait patiently for Monsieur

Mazarin to be reasonable enough to draw me away, by granting me some very just conditions of which I would make very good use.[3]

In letters to Paris, Hortense turned to repairing any further damage she had done to her reputation at court. Working against her, of course, were the gazettes and private letters that were now freely circulating and inventing anecdotes about the runaway sisters. Even her other sisters, Olympe and Marianne, were restrained in their expressions of support. They busied themselves with visiting Marie in Lys and with writing condolence letters to their two abandoned brothers-in-law, holding out the hope of reconciliation. Soon after Hortense had left Rome, Louis had ceded to the demands of her husband that all monies sent to his wife be administered through him—a disaster for Hortense. She wrote in September to Louis from Chambéry, pleading with him to reverse his decision: "I beseech you, Sire, do not reduce me to the extremity of not knowing which way to turn. It is a matter of indifference to you that M. Mazarin have 24,000 additional livres of income, but to give that to me would prevent me from being the most unhappy woman in the world."[4]

Astonishingly, Louis agreed, and a grateful Hortense continued for a time to adhere to a new life of prudence and solitude. When in the spring of 1673 Marie came to Chambéry to see her, Hortense disappeared for two days in the country. Marie, hurt, understood that her sister was no longer willing to risk sharing the same path with her: "her affection had given way to circumspection and politic caution, and she hid from me for fear of being drawn into supporting my intentions."[5] But as the weather warmed and spring air penetrated the cold stone walls of the duke's castle, Hortense began to tire of her retired life and started to welcome the local nobility who had been soliciting her company. She began to accept the invitations to their salons and even more frequently, their hunting lodges, where she could freely indulge her favorite pastime. Orlier, governor of the Chambéry castle, would accompany the skilled huntress and horsewoman as requested by the Duke of Savoy, and as requested, he would send reports of their outings. He wrote of her skill in shooting and wrote about a tireless sequence of hunts for all manner of game in the hills around Chambéry: duck, geese, quail, rabbit, deer. Hortense delighted in her admirers, who called her a Diana of the hunt and followed her and her female companion Madame de Lescheraines as they rode on horseback through country villages at the end of a day's successful excursion. The duke sent her a pair of muskets as a gift, along with some admiring poetry.

Charles-Emmanuel's interest in theater and spectacle meant that he had gathered an excellent troupe of actors in Chambéry. Hortense soon became the guest of honor at their performances of the latest plays from Paris. She became more bold in her responses to the threats that the Duke Mazarin never tired of aiming at her. When she discovered that her husband had bribed one of her ladies-in-waiting to spy on her and to pressure her to yield to his demands, she threw the lady out. When in the autumn of 1673 her husband decided to make the trip to Savoy himself and demanded to see her, she locked herself in her rooms and declared that she "would rather die."[6] Mazarin could do nothing but return home, embarrassed, and attempt to cover up his humiliation by proclaiming that he had made the trip simply to obtain a necessary legal document from his wife that she had promised to give him in person.

It would be in Chambéry that Hortense would learn the card game called basset, newly arrived from Venice. It fascinated her, and she and Madame de Lescheraines would play long into the night. Basset was a gambler's game, based more on chance than on skill, and one could learn, win, and lose quickly. Hortense took to wearing a mask when she played, to disguise the changing expressions that she could not keep off of her face. The duke indulged her and helped her recoup her losses with his gifts. Soon she had new jewels, new clothes, and new servants, including a dark-skinned boy named Mustapha who would remain in her household for the rest of her life. He had come to Savoy probably from North Africa, as a captive from one of the frequent pirate raids off the Mediterranean coast. He would appear at her side in portraits that continued to be produced long after the Duchess Mazarin had left the Continent.

In early 1675 a new face appeared at the court of Chambéry, a writer by the name of César Vichard de Saint-Réal, just returned to his home city after ten years in Paris. Saint-Réal was a handsome man in his midthirties, and well educated—first by the Jesuits in Lyon and later in the salons and academies of Paris where he had sought to make his career as a novelist and historian. He had returned to Chambéry in a state of discouragement. It was not that his ambitions had been dashed in Paris, but in the years he had spent there it had seemed to him that his works had not been able to receive the sustained recognition they deserved. He was a good writer and was especially proud of his historical novel *Don Carlos,* which had sold well in the bookshops lining the arcades of the Palais Royal, next to the Louvre palace. He had done everything right, placing himself close to the court intelligentsia first in a position as assistant to Louis XIV's archivist and historian Varillas, then as a diligent visitor to the salons frequented by the most admired writers of the day. He enjoyed the company of the writers Chapelain and Ménage, and the well-placed Nicolas Colbert, nephew of the royal finance minister. In the late 1660s he had crossed paths with Duchess Mazarin in the salons of her sisters Olympe and Marianne. And he had achieved a certain status as a writer, even gaining a small pension from the king. But a quarrel with his patron Varillas, followed by the implementation of a new, more austere policy limiting the financial support that could be offered to foreign artists in Paris, led him to decide to return, at least for a time, to his native city.

There he approached his first encounter with the Duchess Mazarin with a combination of curiosity, self-confidence, and humility, for although he expected that she would welcome the company of a newly arrived Parisian, he also remembered that his position in Paris had never quite allowed him into the intimate circles of ladies of her stature.

She received him warmly but to his astonishment did not press him for news, and instead seemed primarily interested in learning all about him personally. He had heard about her adventures and troubles but when he expressed sympathy and interest, she replied modestly that these were not worthy of their conversation, not nearly as interesting as his own work and his own tribulations. It was not long before he was utterly smitten. Later he would describe the moment of their first meeting in a "letter on the character of Madam the Duchess Mazarin," which he published to accompany the printed edition of her memoirs:

> I was surprised at first that she didn't show herself to be overjoyed
> to see me in the way that is so common among people who have
> been distanced from the court, when they see someone who has just
> come from there. She received me with as much tranquility as the
> most indifferent lady from the country might have done. Instead of
> pestering me with questions on people and affairs in which she had
> an interest, she talked to me only of my voyage and other similar
> matters that were only to do with me.[7]

As his visits became more frequent, Saint-Réal observed the way that she accepted and even welcomed the inevitability of public exposure. At first this alarmed him, but he soon came to admire this quality as a sign of her courage, honesty, and unashamed pleasure taken in the company of others. Clearly she was a woman unlike any he had met before. "Although by nature she is quite private almost every hour of the day is public for her: the most secret spots in the house are as open as the common areas for those who visit her . . . her servants have become used to letting people come and go freely."[8]

Hortense had made another conquest. Saint-Réal's descriptions of her were openly adoring. When he described her eyes it was with the voice of a man who has fallen completely in love, and yet one who fears that his adoration will never be reciprocated: "The color of her eyes has no name. Neither blue, nor grey, nor quite black, but a blend of all of these. . . . When she stares at you, which happens rarely, you feel that a light has penetrated to the depths of your soul and you abandon all hope of hiding anything from her. . . . It is as though she were born to be loved, but not to love."[9] Over the months that followed their first meeting, Saint-Réal would spend many hours and days in her company. When she did discuss her own life, he urged her to write about it and offered his assistance, as one who had recent experience with the volatile world of both publishing and managing a public self-image.

Sometime in these months the Duchess Mazarin completed writing her memoirs and entrusted their printing and circulation to her new devoted friend. The book's publication would be the first time a French woman not of royal blood had written her life story with her name, as author, printed on the title page. The Duchess Mazarin knew of other women of her class who had written their life stories, but none, with the exception of one or two queens of France, had signed their names to their published autobiographies. If female writers circulated their works, it was to private circles of friends and even then, under cover of anonymity. And to commit one's private life to print was by definition a major transgression for a woman, a fact Hortense acknowledged in the opening paragraph of her autobiography: "I know that a woman's glory lies in her not giving rise to gossip," she wrote, "but one cannot always choose the kind of life one would like to lead."[10] It was as though she recognized that the cover of anonymity was not possible for her. But publishing her life's adventures was a way to make her own voice heard among the many others who were already spinning her story in public. She had already gone public with her life when she made her fateful decision to strike out on her own. Now she had to fight to retain the liberty she had taken such risks to preserve. The support of a powerful patron along with the assistance of a sympathetic and well-connected author in getting her story into circulation were opportunities that she embraced.

As she finished her memoirs, Hortense declared that in Chambéry "I have finally found the peace I had been seeking fruitlessly for so long, and where I have remained ever since, with much more tranquility than a woman as unfortunate as I should have."[11] This sounded like the voice of a mature writer at the end of her life's odyssey. But the Duchess Mazarin was just twenty-nine years old. And the calm she had found in Savoy would be only a brief pause in her tumultuous life.

Perhaps because of that peacefulness, to the citizens of Chambéry, Hortense may have seemed altogether too sure of the Duke of Savoy's patronage and protection. Members of Hortense's little itinerant household, having drawn closer to one another through the challenges they had faced in their travels, felt superior to the Savoyard pages at the court of Chambéry, and they let it show. Feuding developed between different camps. Members of the court who favored the Savoyard duchess, who found herself eclipsed in her husband's attentions by the exotic Hortense, were quick to pick quarrels with Hortense and her circle. Because Charles-Emmanuel was frequently absent from Chambéry, doing business in Turin, Hortense found herself increasingly exposed to hostility. By the time spring arrived in the cold mountain city, most of the provincial nobility in Chambéry who had been so eager for her company in the beginning appeared tired of her aristocratic airs.

Charles-Emmanuel, in Turin, received reports of confrontations between Hortense and his subjects over matters of protocol. Tensions escalated between members of Hortense's private household and the servants of the local elite. During carnival, brawls broke out. When Charles-Emmanuel demanded that apologies be formally made to the Duchess Mazarin, these budding resentments blossomed into hatred. Hortense soon recognized that Chambéry might not much longer be her comfortable haven.

In early June 1675 she wrote a letter to Finance Minister Colbert asking for an advance on her pension, and she began to plan for a departure, though she knew not where she would go. As it happened, the decision to leave soon was made for her. On June 12, Charles-Emmanuel suddenly died, at the age of forty; poison was suspected. In the interim until his young son Victor-Amadeus could reach the age of majority, the Duchess Jeanne-Baptiste of Savoy became regent. She had been forced to suffer Hortense's presence while her husband was alive, but after his death she wasted no time in sending word to Hortense that she was no longer welcome as a guest of the family. Hortense turned her sights toward England, where her cousin Mary Beatrice of Modena had married the king's brother. But she refused to leave immediately, showing herself to be unperturbed by the regent's demands and outwardly continuing her daily life as usual. Then in late October she departed suddenly and without fanfare, alerting almost no one and taking with her only a few members of her household. The ever-dutiful Orlier accompanied her on the beginning of her voyage but he was not informed of her final destination; indeed, perhaps not even Hortense knew at this point where she would end up, for the itinerary she would follow before arriving in London two months later was circuitous. "She left on the 22nd of this month to spend the night in Annecy and I accompanied her half way," Orlier wrote in a letter.

> The next day she is going to Geneva where she will stay for awhile, awaiting news, and from there she will go toward Bavaria. She took with her only half of her household and left the others at the castle,

with the intention of sending for them in three weeks or a month. She is quite happy going away, she said goodbye to no one and left just before dawn through the castle garden.[12]

Had Saint-Réal been one other person to whom she confided her departure? Nothing is certain, but he did leave Chambéry soon after, heading for Paris. There he acted as her negotiator at the court and even with Duke Mazarin, attempting to help the couple arrive at some kind of satisfactory truce. Saint-Réal also devoted himself to seeing to the printing and translation of her memoirs. When, in January 1676, the Duchess Mazarin arrived on the coast of England after nearly three months of dangerous flight across the war-torn states of northern Europe, César Vichard de Saint-Réal was not far behind. The English translation of her memoirs appeared in London only weeks later.

If Charles-Emmanuel had not spent as much time with Hortense in Chambéry as he would have liked, this was due at least in part to the efforts he was making in Turin on behalf of her sister. Marie had not remained long in the abbey of Avenay after having been exiled there from Lys. She had understood that further attempts to move closer to Paris would be rebuffed. Avenay had other disadvantages: it was not as comfortable an environment as Lys, it was more difficult to receive visitors there, and she complained of the "bad air" that made her feel constantly ill. Though she made an attempt to occupy herself with worthy projects, such as reading and studying with her chaplain Boniel, her letters expressed a combination of sadness and irrepressible stubbornness. She confided her thoughts in letters to her dear friend the Countess Ortensia Stella. The king, she wrote, "has made me leave Lys to go to Avenay which is further from Paris by another 25 leagues, and where I am not well, as the air is awful and the place so deserted that one can have nothing that one wants. All this to get me to agree to return to

Rome—it is not the way. I have more aversion for Rome than for all the convents in France, as you know better than anyone."[13] Marie was acutely aware of the danger that anyone in whom she confided might be acting in the interests of her husband. From the moment she and Hortense had left Rome, Lorenzo had focused on mustering a network of agents, spies, mediators, and supporters to help him pressure her to return or at least keep him informed of her intentions and movements. Ortensia was a person she trusted; another was Philippe. Before long her brother arrived in Avenay, to all appearances to rescue her, and he did not have difficulty persuading her to return with him to Nevers. Still, no sooner had they arrived that he informed her that he needed to go to Venice on business and that she had to find a convent in which to stay in his absence. Marie was surprised but compliant, asking only that she be allowed to stay in Lyon, where she could find a religious residence to her liking. This was in all likelihood the outcome Philippe had hoped for from the beginning, for he had been in secret correspondence with Lorenzo and had promised to get Marie close enough to the Italian border that she might be "persuaded" to return to Rome.

Marie was angry and hurt to discover that this was the stratagem. But she was learning to use her own tactics. She pretended to concede, wrote a letter to Lorenzo declaring that she would agree to return, and made a show of setting out for Italy in January 1673. In Chambéry she suddenly stopped. She requested that Hortense arrange to send a letter to Charles-Emmanuel asking for his protection. On this occasion, Hortense did not run away. She arranged for the delivery of the message and Marie was gratified to receive the duke's welcome in response. She continued her voyage southeast, not toward Rome, but toward Turin. Philippe, dismayed that he had failed in this attempt to please Lorenzo, who he had thought would inevitably be the victor in this dispute, was further surprised to learn that Louis XIV would not object to Marie's refuge in Savoy.

The king had sent a respectful message to Charles-Emmanuel, addressing him as his "brother" and declaring only that he assumed Marie would be working in Turin toward an accommodation with her husband: "I take joy in knowing that she has chosen a road leading her to a place where she can address her accommodation in person. You will give me great pleasure in exhorting her to attend to it as quickly as possible, as I am persuaded that this is the true road to happiness that I wish for her. I look forward to this sign of your friendship."[14]

Lorenzo's response to the news that Marie would be received in Turin was less friendly. He insisted angrily, if somewhat helplessly, that his wife at least be housed in a convent, a demand that both Marie and Charles-Emmanuel quickly agreed to, and so she settled for three months in apartments prepared for her in the Convent of the Visitation in Turin. This was not exactly the arrangement that Lorenzo had hoped for. Marie was free to come and go as she pleased, at first in the city and then eventually to Chambéry once again to see Hortense. But on this occasion Hortense was afraid to meet her.

Hortense had perhaps concluded that Marie's political position, like her own, was weakening. In any event, the reunion of the sisters was enough to panic both the French king and the Prince Colonna. Louis sent orders barring Marie from continuing toward France, and Lorenzo, frustrated and enraged, plotted to have her incarcerated somewhere that she could not so easily escape. Charles-Emmanuel at first was unruffled, and he whisked Marie away to his country hunting estate of La Veneria, but after another month he succumbed to what by now was heavy political pressure from both France and Italy. Reluctantly he escorted a resentful Marie back to her convent lodgings. He decided to make some effort to effect a reconciliation. The only way to do that, he was convinced, would be to get Lorenzo to come to talk to his wife. Lorenzo preferred to send more agents instead, demanding that they discern his wife's secret intentions and report to him.

This was a task that no one seemed able to accomplish. Who could say what Marie intended to do? Marie herself may not have known her own plans from day to day, except that she was determined to remain independent of her husband. She also was learning how to manipulate or mystify the spies her husband sent after her. It was useful to be spontaneous and unpredictable, even contradictory, when her freedom depended on hiding her intentions. After her failed effort to visit Hortense, even some of those closest to her were no longer in her confidence. Nanette De Rocour, one of the maidservants Lorenzo had sent to Marie, and who had remained with her through her travels, continued to send reports on her mistress's behavior to Lorenzo, as she was being paid to do. But she could not shed much light on it. Or maybe Marie and Nanette were collaborating and concocting false information to keep Lorenzo in the dark. Nanette wrote to him:

> I am much obliged to Don Maurizio for the care he has taken of me, and I know that Your Excellency had the kindness to order him to do so. Madame came to dine with me yesterday and she sat on the edge of my bed with me. I don't know what good humor seems to have come over her. . . . As soon as she appeared in my room she told me to get well soon, because she wants to go into Savoy. I asked her what she wanted to do there and she said that she would enter a convent, that the Visitation was impossible and that she could not stay the summer there, with only one room for her and for me. In Savoy there is a much larger convent than all those we have already seen and she wants to go there. . . . I will do what I can to find out why she wanted to go to Chambéry.[15]

Lorenzo's other spies were even more helpless to explain his wife's mind. "I must confess to you sir," one wrote, "there is nothing more difficult than penetrating the sentiments and objectives of Madame the Constabless. . . . Monsieur Don Maurizio and I still think that Your Excellency should not delay in making a surprise visit to her as that might have a very good effect."[16] But despite a chorus of urgings to this effect, Lorenzo stopped short of making a personal appearance. He knew his wife, and he could not tolerate even the thought of enduring the sort of humiliation to which Duke Mazarin had been reduced in his foiled efforts to recover Hortense. He was much too proud to risk being turned away at the door of whatever refuge Marie had managed to find. And so Marie and Lorenzo continued their cat-and-mouse game, she sometimes openly defying him, spending the money he sent her as soon as it arrived, knowing that his pride would not permit him to leave her in poverty, and he pushing that confidence to the limit, alternately satisfying and denying her requests. Charles-Emmanuel, meanwhile, insisted that he had known nothing of Marie's intentions from the moment of her arrival in Turin, of which he had learned, he said, "only when she was very close and at the gates."

During this time, Marie revealed some of her private thoughts to Ortensia Stella, ever her most trusted correspondent. In February she wrote from Turin, reflecting on Hortense's apparent attempts in Chambéry to lead a life of restraint and so keep her husband at bay. As for herself, "my poor Countess you know that when one has done a thing such as I have done at my age, it is better to die than fail to sustain it. Madame Mazarin was only twenty when she left Paris, but I had passed six candelabras and thus should know what I was doing."[17]

From the Convent of the Visitation, Marie resumed her letter-writing campaign to persuade Louis XIV to revoke his orders excluding her from France. The newest in the parade of treacherous Colonna agents to visit her in Turin, Carlo Emanuele d'Este, Marquis of Borgomanero, assured her that even her husband was attempting to persuade the French king to allow her to enter France, for he felt that there was more hope of controlling her in France than in Savoy. No permission was forthcoming, however, and Marie, ever restless in her pursuit of a destination where she could truly enjoy her liberty, allowed herself to be persuaded by Borgomanero that her best alternative would be to go to Spanish Flanders. The Marquis of Borgomanero was a member of the Este family of Lombardy, a family that, like the Colonnas, served the interests of Spain in Italy. Lorenzo, Borgomanero told Marie, would approve of moving to a state more closely allied with his own political interests, and yet she would be able to remain at liberty there. Marie wanted to believe this but she took some precautions. Sending Nanette and a small group of other servants ahead to a town on the banks of Lake Maggiore, she chose a different route for herself. It was an unlikely choice, and a much more difficult route north, through the Great Saint Bernard Pass, but her diversionary tactic proved wise. Unknown to her, Lorenzo had pressured authorities near Milan to intercept his wife's traveling party and they, not recognizing Nanette as Marie's lady-in-waiting, mistakenly detained her for a week until the confusion was dispelled. This mix-up gave Marie's party time to advance deep into the Alpine pass, "not having so pleasant a time on the mountain of Saint Bernard," as she wrote.[18]

It was late November 1673, just eighteen months after Marie and Hortense had first left Rome, and now Marie was back on the road, this time in winter, at a very dangerous time for any traveler to undertake such a voyage. France was at war against the Quadruple Alliance of the Dutch Republic, Spain, the Holy Roman Empire, and Brandenburg; the war had begun in late spring of 1672, precisely when the sisters had left Italy. In addition to "snow and along dreadful paths lined with precipices," as Marie described the Great Saint Bernard Pass, the ever-present threat of bandits or agents sent to arrest her, and the uncertainty of finding anyplace that could offer her safe haven, there was in northern Europe the likelihood of encountering soldiers. Borgomanero, who was accompanying Marie, was even more nervous than she. The group took circuitous routes as they progressed toward Brussels, even though Marie argued for more direct paths. This meant that Marie found herself passing through "Frankfurt and then to Cologne, going far off the most direct path in order to please the marquis de Borgomanero and the abbé Oliva, who did not wish to run into the siege of Bonn and who wanted to avoid encountering the Spanish and French troops who had set out with provisions at the same time as we had."[19]

Marie was impatient with these prudent measures, and chafed against "the contrary nature, the unbearable slowness, and the unnecessary precautions of the Marquis."[20] In Cologne, she welcomed their encounter with a French regiment that was assigned to undertake peace negotiations and included two French statesmen, Honoré Courtin and Paul de Barillon, with whom she took counsel on her own predicament. Courtin and Barillon did not trust Borgomanero. Marie later reflected that she should have listened to their advice against going to Flanders, and their suspicions of Borgomanero, who continued to urge her on. Their concerns proved justified almost immediately upon her arrival outside of Brussels, after a long ride through conflict-ridden territory, escorted by French troops. In Flanders the party was greeted by an emissary of the Count of Monterey, then governor of Flanders, who informed them that preparations were being made to house Marie in a convent.

This was not what she had been led to expect. At the very least she had hoped to choose her own place of retreat, religious or otherwise, in exchange for agreed-upon restricted liberties that Lorenzo had indicated he would permit. Borgomanero feigned surprise and made protests, but Marie soon saw that she had been trapped. She was escorted to the neighboring port of Antwerp and taken to the citadel built into the eastern wall of the fortified city. It took her two days to realize that she was nothing but a prisoner, with guards in the corridor outside her door and all messages intercepted. Borgomanero seemed to be taking a cruel pleasure in her discomfort.

Only letters from Lorenzo were permitted to reach her. And hers reached him, angry, accusatory letters against Borgomanero:

> The Marquis invents all manner of things to keep me here, I have never known a more treacherous or malignant soul, and you would say even worse if you had witnessed all that has happened. . . . for the love of God, and for the kindness that you have shown me in the past, don't let me be subjected any longer to this affront of being arrested, write to the governor that you agree to my going to a convent in Brussels, I promise you I will not leave without your consent.[21]

In letters to the Duke of Savoy she was more explicit in her accusations.[22]

> I am reduced to this state because of the excessive passion that the Marquis de Borgomanero had for me, I will not disguise that from you. All my people are witness to this, and because I did not reciprocate and I mocked him, this is his rage and hatred. If I had treated him better I would be more fortunate. . . . Even Monsieur Fouquet was not given more guards nor was he more constrained than I am.[23]

When after two cold months in the Antwerp citadel the Count of Monterey finally agreed to prepare lodging for her in a Brussels convent, Marie was no longer inclined to trust anyone. She wanted only to be released, and agreed to the move, asking first that Nanette and Morena be permitted an advance look at the residence that was being prepared for her. They came back to the citadel reporting that the place was not really a convent, it was a worse prison, and that Borgomanero had even arranged for extra bars to be put on the windows of the two rooms prepared for them. Desperate, en route to her new abode Marie asked to be allowed to go to the adjoining chapel to pray: "I went into the church of the convent on the pretext of saying my prayers there, and I immediately declared to the captain of the guards who was escorting me that I would not leave the spot where I was."[24] The count and other mortified city officials came to plead with her to leave the chapel. Finally she was persuaded that they would take her by force if she did not comply. Her only consolation was that she could now receive letters more freely than in the citadel, and hope that the ones she wrote in reply would reach their destination. She resumed her correspondence with Hortense:

BRUSSELS, 17 MARCH 1674

My dear sister, your two letters gave me great comfort and the courage to suffer all that might befall me. . . . You will know that I have been brought to Brussels to be kept in a more secure prison. I had taken refuge in the church, declaring that I would not leave except to be taken to a convent. The Count of Monterey came and told me that I would be taken by force and that he had permission to do so. . . . I was obliged to obey him for fear that violence would be done to me. I am now behind four walls. All of my people have been taken from me except for my women whom I clung to by force. I am not allowed to speak to anyone, man or woman. . . . All my letters are opened but I say nothing that I would not want everyone to know. Would that it had pleased God that I believed you and never left the land of the good cornettes.[25]

The situation was unsustainable, even for the hard-hearted Monterey, supported by a vengeful Borgomanero. Once the count received word from Lorenzo that Marie could leave and continue on her route of exile to Spain, he was relieved. As soon as her escort, a relative of Lorenzo's, arrived in Antwerp to meet her, Monterey was only too happy, as the papal envoy reported, to be "released from this awkward situation in which he had put himself."[26] As for Marie, she prepared herself for another voyage and another convent.

# HORTENSE'S LONDON

*[She has arrived] like Armida in Godefrey's camp. Everyone speaks of her, the men with admiration and the women with jealousy and concern.*

—Henri de Ruvigny, French ambassador to England, in a letter to the French court

*6 September 1676. Supped at that Lord Chamberlain's, where also supped the Duchess Mazarine, famous beauty and errant lady (all the world knows her story).*

—Diary of John Evelyn

*I*N 1675, CHARLES II OF ENGLAND was forty-five, and a man fully enjoying the pleasures of royal middle age. His youth had been a series of lost battles, personal traumas, and political humiliations. After his father, Charles I, was beheaded in the English Civil War of 1649, young Charles had mustered an army in Scotland and marched on England, but was defeated by Oliver Cromwell at the battle of Worcester in 1651. Forced into exile, Charles made an adventurous escape but lived in poverty in France and the Spanish Netherlands until 1660, when he was restored to the throne and subsequently crowned in a magnificent ceremony in Westminster Abbey. Since that time, he had progressively maneuvered British interests closer to the French and managed to sustain a complicated web of political alliances, including a formal alliance with Holland and Sweden and a secret treaty with Louis XIV. He had become skilled in dealing with an ever more powerful Parliament, usually by circumvention rather than direct confrontation.

In 1662 Charles had married the Portuguese Catherine of Braganza, a devout woman soon obliged to tolerate her husband's adulterous affairs, as the poet John Dryden wrote, "The best of Queens, the most obedient wife. . . . His life the theme of her eternal prayer." The couple were childless, but by 1675 Charles had already fathered several children with mistresses whom he publicly acknowledged: Louise de Keroualle, Duchess of Portsmouth, favored by the French interests; Barbara Villiers, Duchess of Cleveland; and Nell Gwyn, the celebrated actress. Although he was Protestant, Charles was close to the Catholic factions in England, and his ties to France were strong. He had lived at the French court, and his sister Henrietta had married Philippe d'Orléans, brother of Louis XIV. The greatest personal loss of his life had been Henrietta's death in 1671. Charles had loved Henrietta more than any other, and it took him years to be able to conceal his grief at the mention of her name.

When Charles heard that the runaway Duchess Mazarin was traveling to England, he was intrigued, as was everyone else who heard about her escapades. Once the duchess was back on the road, she was back in the limelight. She had decided, before her predawn departure from Chambéry, that her destination would be London, for several reasons. In London she had a relative in the royal family, Mary Beatrice of Modena, whose mother, Laura Martinozzi, had long ago accompanied her young cousin Hortense on the galley ship taking them with their mothers from Italy to France. Cardinal Mazarin had arranged a fine Italian marriage for his niece Laura, who became Duchess of Modena. Laura's daughter Mary Beatrice, who in 1675 was just seventeen, had two years before been sent to

England to become the second wife of the widowed Duke of York, brother to King Charles II. Mary Beatrice was lonely at the London court. Her marriage to an heir to the throne was regarded with suspicion by the anti-French faction, increasingly concerned by the expanding power of Louis XIV and his Catholic allies in Europe. From Chambéry, Hortense had corresponded with Mary Beatrice, and also with Lord Montagu, the English ambassador to the court of France. For different reasons, both urged her to go to London, where she would be welcomed by a growing French expatriate community and enjoy the safety of being at a distance from her husband's legal pursuits. Lord Montagu was interested in undermining the influence wielded at the court of Charles II by his mistress Louise de Keroualle, and he thought the Duchess Mazarin would provide a diversion at the very least, and more likely an overt competitor for the king's attentions and confidence. As for Mary Beatrice, she welcomed the chance to have her lively older cousin by her side while she waited to give birth to her first child. It was to arrange her move to England that Hortense lingered in Chambéry after the Duke of Savoy's death, and she was bound for London as she set out on that chilly October morning.

The route she would choose to get there, however, was anything but direct. She did not want to risk traveling through France, so she planned to leave from Holland. But she took her time, nearly three months, to get to London, first going through Geneva and then crossing Germany and the Dutch states, along the way making contact with acquaintances who reported home on these stages of her itinerary. The slow pace of her travels seemed to taunt her husband the duke, while the French public relished in the spectacle. Rumors flew that "the Mazarine" was approaching Paris, only to be contradicted in the next gazette posting or letter delivery. Madame de Sévigné wrote breathlessly to her daughter on November 20, "Here is a little note from the Count of Saint-Maurice, which will

inform you of the news of the Mazarine. I am assured that at this
moment she is six leagues from Paris. What folly! What folly!"[1]
Though Hortense skirted the borders of France, she did not attempt
to disguise her travels in the least. When her party approached
Geneva after a difficult voyage on snowy mountain roads, she paused
long enough to acquire an elegant escort and fresh horses, then made
an entrance designed to cause a stir. Her old friend Marie-Sidonie
de Courcelles, herself again on the run to escape her own husband,
arrived in Geneva two weeks after Hortense passed through the
city, and the event was still being talked about. "It is a great misfortune to find oneself pursued to all corners of the world," Courcelles wrote in a letter to Paris, "but what is extraordinary is that
this woman triumphs over all her disgraces with an excess of folly
that has never been seen. After experiencing this misfortune she
thinks only of pleasure. Arriving here, she was on horseback, wearing
a wig and feathers, with twenty men in her escort, talking only of
violins and hunting parties, in short, anything that gives pleasure."[2]

Hortense had written in the opening line of her memoirs that "a
woman's reputation depends on not being talked about," but then
she proceeded to write and publish her own life story, and from
that point on she would continue to live as though the act of going
public was a destiny that she embraced. Although she might feel
that she had lost control of her reputation, she was learning how
to manipulate her public image. The image of herself that she now
projected was not that of a fragile prey to those who would hunt
her down but rather a strong huntswoman herself, in her favorite
guises as the goddess Diana, or as an Amazon. Most frequently on
her travels she simply dressed as a man but without much concern
for the efficacy of the disguise. This was the persona she maintained
throughout her continued voyage through war-ravaged Germany,
as her adoring friend Charles de Saint-Evremond would later ex-
claim, "She had to cross wild, armed states, calming some and com-

manding the respect of others. She spoke none of the languages of these peoples, but they understood her."[3]

She finally arrived at the Dutch port of Brill in December 1675 and prepared to embark for the coast of Britain. Travel on the English Channel was fraught with dangers typical of open water at the time: violent storms; French, Dutch, Spanish, and English ships vying for control of the trade routes; and pirates, hijackers, or ordinary thieves. Once on land, seafaring voyagers were in no less danger until they were well inland. Entire villages had been abandoned along the Atlantic coast because of the threat of marauders arriving by sea. Inevitably, adventure awaited Hortense, this time a violent winter storm lasting five days, forcing her vessel to land at Solebay, a considerable distance from their intended port of entry into England. She was exhausted. Her servant Mustapha and the others in her little party were in even worse condition.

When the Duchess Mazarin finally arrived in London on New Year's Eve in 1665, she was on horseback, wet and muddy, and at first mistaken by onlookers for a postal courier because of the men's clothing and long cloak she was wearing. Her arrival made an immediate impression, within days being reported in London gazettes and circulated in pamphlets. One pamphlet recorded excited discussion in a coffeehouse between Englishmen (or "coffists," as they were called) and Frenchmen about her dramatic arrival by postal horse:

1ST COFFIST. Have you not heard of the courier arrived three days since with a retinue that marked him for a man of great quality?

2ND COFFIST. I saw him and his attendants alight from their post horses, terribly weather-beaten, having rid in the late storms. . . .

1ST FRENCHMAN. I will tell you that the person you saw was indeed an extraordinary courier and one of great quality.

2ND FRENCHMAN. In truth it was not a courier, but a very illustrious *coureuse*.

1ST FRENCHMAN. The courier you saw alight, booted and spurred, covered with a great coat and still more covered with mud, was the fair Duchess of Mazarin herself.[4]

This "new Queen of the Amazons," as the coffists went on to label her, who had survived a difficult journey "on a post horse and in the depth of winter," was a courier without a packet of letters. It was as though Hortense was staging her own arrival, drawing on the familiar sight of a postal horse to stress her impressive capacity to move about freely. The package she was delivering to the shores of England was her own person, a *coureuse,* or loose woman, as the Frenchmen had jokingly called her.

Who would become her next protector? This was the question to which her new public turned. Henri de Ruvigny, the French ambassador, wrote a letter on January 2, 1666, describing the sensational news and speculating on its political implications:

She embarked from Holland in a paquebot that the storm pushed to Solebay, a hundred miles from here. She arrived day before yesterday in London wearing a men's riding habit and accompanied by two women and five men, not counting a little Moor who eats with her. M. de Montagu, who met her in Chambéry three years ago and who since then has been in correspondence with her, went to meet her ten miles from here. He has his plans, and not being a friend of the Duchess of Portsmouth, he is causing great anxiety. There is much speculation. What is certain is that Montagu is advising her. . . . We hear from a valet of the Count of Gramont, who saw her arriving in her riding clothes, that she has never been more beautiful.[5]

From the time he heard that the Duchess Mazarin was headed for England, Ruvigny had been worried. With Lord Montagu advising her, it was certain that she would be encouraged to do what she could to weaken the favor that Louise de Keroualle enjoyed at the English court as Charles II's mistress. Ruvigny had a comfortable relationship with Louise, she was happy to pass on information to France through him, and she was relatively pliant, usually ready to take her cues from Paris. The dramatic arrival of the Duchess Mazarin on British shores threw the French ambassador into a panic. He decided that the best course of action would be to find a way to send her home, and soon. The only means to accomplish this, he reasoned, would be to grant the conditions that she had always demanded for her return: the restitution of her wealth and property and, most important, as part of her protection from her husband's vengeance, a residence where she could live independently and come and go as she pleased. The ambassador sounded out King Charles, who was quite aware of the speculation swirling around him about Hortense's irresistibility, and reported that the king was reassuring. But Ruvigny was not easily reassured. He noted every expression on the faces of the king and his courtiers since Hortense had "arrived at the court of England like Armida in Godfrey's camp."[6] He observed that the duchess spent most of her time by the bedside of her cousin Mary Beatrice for her lying-in. King Charles was also visiting his sister-in-law, and with increasing frequency.

By the end of January, Charles had added his own personal appeal to the king of France that Hortense be provided an income worthy of her station and that was hers by right. Ruvigny could only nervously echo the request, but Louis XIV promptly turned it down and charged his ambassador with informing Hortense of his decision. In the next letter from Ruvigny, the French king learned that Charles had supplied the money that he had denied, a gift, Ruvigny added timidly, "that will have a very adverse effect on Madame the Duchess of Portsmouth."[7]

And indeed it did. The consequences fell also on Ruvigny, who was recalled to France and replaced by Honoré de Courtin, a mature and politically astute courtier who had enjoyed the favor of Louis XIV since the king's youth. And although Courtin claimed to agree that the best course of action would be to return the Duchess Mazarin to France, soon he was spending long hours in her company and writing letters to her husband reassuring him that his wife was conducting herself with all propriety. "Madame your wife gives so little thought to her beauty, her coiffure, and the clothes that might flatter it, . . . that it is easy to see that she has no interest in making any use of it in any way that could give you the slightest cause for concern."[8]

Courtin's reports to the king and his minister Arnauld de Pomponne were more blunt. King Charles, he wrote, had assured him and Ruvigny "that he would not be won over. But she is beautiful. . . . All those closest to him talk only of her merits. It will be very difficult for him to resist temptation much longer. . . . The best thing would be for her to cross the sea again. It matters little to Your Majesty that she not sleep with M. Mazarin, and that she be given fifty thousand francs, but it matters a great deal to you that in the meantime England not join your enemies."[9]

And so Hortense had occasion once again to reflect on how her life resembled the plot of a novel. Washed up on the shores of England by a storm, this mysterious and foreign noblewoman was heralded as an immediate threat to the reigning royal mistress. At one time, when King Charles II had been living in exile in France many years earlier, he had indicated that he might want to marry this young niece of Cardinal Mazarin. At that time, Mazarin had declined the offer from a suitor who was a deposed king with an uncertain future. But the episode had an important place in Hortense's public image, as well as in her own self-image. As she reminded her readers in her memoirs, "Everyone knows about the proposals that were made several times, to marry me to the King of England."[10]

By the time the Duchess Mazarin arrived in London, Charles had long been labeled "the pleasure king" by some of his subjects. His political adversaries in Parliament associated the king's lax ways with immoral influences, primarily French and Catholic, from the Continent. The king's sensual looks were often caricatured in pamphlets and broadsheets, where his more lofty pursuits of pleasure and learning were rarely acknowledged. He had been the most important patron of architect Christopher Wren during the ambitious projects for rebuilding London after the Great Fire of 1666. Charles had founded a national school of mathematics and nautical science. He was an enthusiastic supporter of new scientific experimentalism in botany and agriculture, and in 1660, he founded the Royal Society of London, a learned society for science. Under Charles II, London became a flourishing cultural capital for theater and the arts.

By 1675, the king had learned to navigate the treacherous factionalism pitting Protestants against Catholics. He was sympathetic to the Catholic faction but may have formally converted only on his deathbed. He was not a ruler easily angered by petty offenses or lapses in protocol, and he encouraged an informal atmosphere at court. In matters of politics, religion, and personal affection, he was known to be tolerant. His connections with the French court remained strong, not the least because England had become a haven of tolerance for courtiers who had not been so fortunate at the court of Versailles. Hortense could count herself as one of these, but at the same time the French king's advisers viewed her as a possible ally, a potentially useful pawn who could act as an inside informant and exert influence on Charles should she become close to him.

On this subject there were mixed feelings. Some of the French envoys were enthusiastic about the idea. Others were more cautious, recognizing that the Duchess of Portsmouth was already a useful, more pliable presence close to Charles who could be relied upon to serve the interests of Louis XIV, whereas Hortense Mancini had shown herself to be anything but dutiful. But everyone clearly enjoyed watching what would happen. Inevitably, those who were close enough to observe and report on her were also inclined to fall under her spell. Ruvigny had panicked at the spectacle of her triumph and had to be recalled to France. Hortense's friend from Savoy, the writer Saint-Réal would not stay long in London after Hortense's arrival, when he found himself reduced to the status of just one in a long line of admirers.

To no one's surprise, Hortense became the king's mistress not long after her first meeting with him. Though she kept her residence at Saint James's Park, close to Mary Beatrice, she was frequently at Whitehall, the king's residence. She had arrived in January 1675, and by August she had been given an apartment at Whitehall, the same one that had been previously occupied by the king's mistress Barbara Villiers. Louise de Keroualle remained at court but was reported to look perpetually unhappy. Before long Louise was advised by her friends that if she wished to retain any favor at all with the king, she would have to receive the Duchess Mazarin and seek her company. It was a bitter pill, but the Duchess of Portsmouth took it, humiliating herself by making a show of enjoying outings and visits with her French compatriot. There could be no better public evidence of Hortense's newly acquired power at the court of England.

As usual, Hortense appeared unfazed by the envy and resentment that her new status was generating all around her, but she also seemed to be quite enjoying herself. Her pleasure, even in this privileged instance, took on a reckless aura, as she showed no inclination to devote herself exclusively to the king's company, though she was said to be almost constantly with him. By late spring, as the damp London winter finally began to dissipate, the king and Hortense were taking frequent promenades together along the Thames.

In the same months that her relationship with Charles was developing, she befriended the young Countess of Sussex, Charles's illegitimate daughter by Barbara Villiers. Hortense and the young girl became inseparable. Anne was just fourteen and had been married off a year earlier to Thomas Leonard, a Gentleman of the King's Bedchamber. The new Lord Sussex was fond of cricket and of country life; he was not drawn to the sophisticated pleasures of the capital city. Lady Sussex had opposing tastes, and she became infatuated with Hortense. The two of them were frequently together at Saint James's Park. Hortense delighted in this passionate friendship and neither of them seemed to mind that they were said to be lovers. Hortense taught Anne how to hunt, and the two of them took fencing lessons, practicing together in the park on one occasion even by starlight, when they were spotted in nightgowns, with swords drawn.

It was a mark of Charles's famous tolerance and libertine leanings that he did not put a stop to this, though it was also true that no one at the time would have thought it overly scandalous that two women could have had a sexual attraction to each other. Physical beauty, when it was powerful enough, was thought to quite naturally attract both sexes. Saint-Evremond would write admiringly that "Hortense has claimed lovers of both sexes." But what Charles did not tolerate, in the end, was Anne's decision to refuse to return to her husband when he eventually tried to summon her back to their country estate. The young countess was forcibly removed by her husband's guards from the Duchess Mazarin's household and sent to France to be incarcerated in a convent.

Once in London, Hortense had first been lodged in the Saint James palace in the center of the city, residence of the Duke and

Duchess of York, where she was warmly welcomed. Soon afterward, Mary Beatrice's husband, James, would purchase a spacious house in Saint James's Park, next door to the palace, and he invited his wife's fugitive cousin to live there with her household. Hortense moved in with Mustapha, Nanon, a number of other servants, and her growing collection of pets, including hunting dogs and exotic parrots. Soon she was receiving visitors. One of the first to arrive was Saint-Réal, who provided a collection of books for her library and stood ready to serve as her loyal squire, though he was quickly deflated. Another was Honoré Courtin, the newly appointed French ambassador, who took to spending hours at a time in the duchess's salon and library. Visitors were particularly attracted to the openness of Hortense's household, the same quality that Saint-Réal had described in the flattering letter he had published with her memoirs. Visitors could come whenever they wished and settle into a room with others or find a corner of the library in which to read in solitude. There seemed to be few restrictions on who could come and go, and there was no set day of the week when she would receive visitors and no early hour when visitors were required to leave. This was a unique and intriguing practice. Courtin reported to the French court that "we always stay there until midnight, the house is very pleasant, and living there is very comfortable. . . . I occupy a large chair by the fire-side with one of the books that I take from the library that the abbé de Saint-Réal has established. . . . Madame Mazarin's temperament is as attractive as her appearance."[11]

For many of the visitors to Hortense's salon in those years, she came to symbolize a kind of enviable female freedom, albeit a freedom that was perpetually threatened by an uncertain future. Anne of Sussex was one young woman who had been inspired to follow the dangerous path her friend had taken. Saint-Evremond wrote a portrait describing Hortense's daring flight from her husband as an adventure that should inspire other women. The writer Marie-

Catherine d'Aulnoy described the Mazarin residence as the center
of all that was most interesting and vibrant in London society, declaring it "the meeting-place of all that was illustrious and witty in
London: I went there often. Everyone recounted news there, there
was gambling, good food, and the days passed like moments."[12]
Fiction writers and playwrights modeled their heroine's escapades
on those of Hortense. Marie-Catherine Desjardins, who had been
Hortense's friend in Paris, wrote the pseudomemoirs of an adventurous runaway woman who had the same initials as the Duchess
Mazarin.[13] They were immediately translated into English. Years
later, Susanna Centlivre would stage her play *The Basset Table* about
a salon like the Duchess Mazarin's. There, a character named Lady
Reveler presided over a diverse social group where gambling mixed
with music, poetry reading, and discussions of the new science. As
the years wore on, Hortense's endless struggles with her husband
also became the focal point for discussions by feminist writers such
as Mary Astell and Aphra Behn about women's rights in the legal
institution of marriage.

During her first years in London, Hortense continued to negotiate for the income that had been promised her by Louis XIV, but
her efforts were continually frustrated, no doubt in part because it
was known that Charles had granted her a pension. She lived
comfortably, even long after her liaison with the king had ended.
She took pleasure in the fascination that she continued to exert
over London society during those years of the Restoration. Saint-
Evremond collaborated with musicians, composers, and Hortense
herself on at least eight short operas performed in her residence
between 1678 and 1692. The Duchess Mazarin often sang in
these productions. She embraced her reputation as hostess to an
unusually diverse society of artists, foreigners, political figures,
and royalty, as well as travelers and tourists of all social stations.
Her reputation as a powerful and paradoxical woman only grew

and became more linked with legend as time went on. The writers and painters among her friends helped to foster this reputation, as Saint-Evremond wrote that "Madame Mazarin had the air, habit, and equipage of a Queen of the Amazons; she appeared equally equipped to charm and to fight."[14] Hortense was painted in exotic fashion, as Cleopatra and as Diana, goddess of the hunt. As a French woman of Italian origin at the English court, she already was easily cast as mysterious, foreign, and more than slightly dangerous. Added to these traits were her personal penchants for hunting, swordplay, gambling, and exotic pets, and the constant stream of mixed company in her relaxed household. The most stunning painting of her produced during her early years in London was a huge oil canvas (ninety by seventy inches) by Benedetto Gennari, *Duchess Mazarin Dressed as Diana,* which she probably commissioned and hung in her lodgings. In the center of the painting she sits in a languid pose, bare-breasted and with her long dark curls hanging loosely over her shoulders, holding a spear. Unlike the goddess Diana she is surrounded not by nymphs but by hunting dogs and four dark-skinned boys dressed as pages. A parrot is perched on a fountain behind her. The pages wear silver collars identical to those worn by the dogs. One of the pages, the only one who is not smiling, is a young man, older than the others, and he stands behind the duchess, collecting water from the fountain as he gazes at her.

This figure is thought to be Mustapha, one of only two people in her circle who were consistently described as loyal to her. As a servant, whose status was in effect that of a slave, he was not in a position to freely choose his loyalties. Her other loyal follower was Saint-Evremond. Saint-Evremond embraced the publicity her presence generated in London. He wrote essays dedicated to her and letters advocating for her in her widely published legal disputes with her husband. In verse and in prose he used terms stressing characteristics that seemed always to be linked with her: foreigner ("beautiful Roman"), strong woman ("Amazon"), traveler ("adventurer and vagabond"), independent soul.

Hortense's friendship with Saint-Evremond was an unusual one. Saint-Evremond had been living in London since 1662, when he had fled France fearing arrest for having published an attack on French foreign policy under Cardinal Mazarin. In France he had been known as a reckless but accomplished writer, philosopher, poet, diplomat, and wit, whose downfall came, as one friend put it, "because he did not know how to hold his tongue."[15] He was also a libertine whose closest friendships had been with other figures famous for causing scandals: Ninon de l'Enclos, noted for her culture and learning as much as for her philosophy and practice of free love, and the Count of Grammont, expelled from France for publicly criticizing the early years of Louis XIV's reign and attempting to seduce the king's mistress. When Saint-Evremond first met Hortense, she was twenty-nine and he sixty-two. His letters to Ninon de l'Enclos and other friends in Paris showed that, like everyone else, he was infatuated with the duchess, but unlike her other new admirers he had no illusion that he might be able to consummate the relationship. Even his affectionate friends described him by then as an old man no longer capable of attracting lovers, though his personal physician, Pierre Silvestre, described him as "well made," a man who had "retained even to a very advanced age, a natural and easy carriage." He had a fondness for direct speech and undisguised opinions, a distaste for the elaborate protocol of the court, and a sharp eye for anything that might make a good subject of ridicule. "His eyes were blue, keen, and full of fire," wrote Silvestre, "his face bright and intelligent, his smile somewhat satirical. In youth he had had fine black hair, but though it had become quite white, and even very sparse, he never would wear a wig, and contented himself with wearing a skull cap."[16]

Saint-Evremond wrote incessantly but rarely published, viewing the profession of "author" with some disdain. His works were written for his friends, and if they circulated any further it would be because his friends saw to it both during his lifetime and after his death. Hortense was happy to find in him much that she missed of Paris: "His conversation was gay and easy, his repartees lively and incisive, his manners good and polite; in a word, one can say of him that in all things he showed himself to be a man of quality."[17] The two were kindred souls. He saw in her much of his own propensity for risk and love of pleasure, and in her life's adventures a vindication of the bold criticism of absolute authority that was a hallmark of his own philosophy and writings. They became close friends; he advised her on negotiating the unfamiliar labyrinth of London society and then stood by like an indulgent uncle when she ignored his counsel. His character was a perfect contrast to that of Cardinal Mazarin, and it seemed fitting that his own exile had been precipitated by his attacks on the prime minister. To Hortense he made no secret of his hatred of this particular member of her family. He no doubt had chuckled when he read in her memoirs that her response to the cardinal's death was "Thank God he's croaked." Among the many literary tokens that Saint-Evremond would offer to Hortense as gifts would be a collection of bitter verses aimed at her uncle's memory.

The writer and the Duchess Mazarin conducted a lively correspondence throughout her life in London, even as they saw each other often on a daily basis. When in 1689 Saint-Evremond finally received official permission to return to live in France, he declined, saying that he had found all he needed in London: "In the country in which I now am, I see Madame Mazarin every day; I live among people who are sociable and friendly, who have great cleverness and much wit."[18] Of Hortense's letters to him, none remain, but many of Saint-Evremond's written to her have survived, and they give us an intimate look at her life there. He also wrote to many others about her, adding considerably to the quantity of reports on her life and descriptions of her person that were already circulating throughout Europe.

From the beginning, he expressed his delight in this newcomer to London society, who inaugurated something close to a Parisian salon, but freer, frequented by an even more diverse and cosmopolitan array of visitors. He was pleased by her immediate success with Charles II and encouraged the liaison for its obvious benefits to Hortense's personal security in England. He was amused by the efforts of the French envoys to draw her into a more political role, and was not surprised when she proved to be too much of a free spirit to excel at either espionage or diplomacy. He was concerned about her strong fondness for gambling and drink, but he never tired of having to draw her away from the gaming table to more serious conversations. Gaming and intellectual pursuits went comfortably hand in hand in Hortense's salon, and indeed in many of the salons of her day. It would not be until decades later that gambling became the subject of extended and disapproving moral treatises. To be sure, religious groups condemned the popularity of gaming, but to the epicurean Saint-Evremond the danger of gaming for the Duchess Mazarin was simply that she could not afford to lose, and losing was inevitable. And he personally could not understand how one could be drawn to gambling over the supreme pleasure of finding oneself at the center of endless clever conversation.

The friendship between these two was alternately playful and serious. Saint-Evremond knew that Hortense was fond of chivalric romances like *Amadis of Gaul,* and he read with her from *Don Quixote,* suggesting to her that he was like the besotted knight and she his elusive Dulcinea. Hortense entered into the game, for years signing her letters to him "Dulcinea to Don Quixote," and he signing his "to Dulcinea, from the sad-faced knight." His friends took to calling him "Madame Mazarin's knight," or "the champion of Madame Mazarin." When, some years after her arrival, she confided in him that she was thinking of joining her sister in her Madrid convent, he wrote her a desperate, adoring, and outraged letter:

How is it possible for you to leave persons who are charmed with you, and who adore you? Friends that love you more than they love themselves, to go and hunt after unknown people you will not like, and who perhaps will insult you? Do you consider, Madam, that you are going to throw yourself into a convent, which the Constable's Lady, your sister, abhorred? If she returns thither, 'tis because she must either choose that, or death; whereas, in order to go to it, you will leave a court where you are esteemed, where the affection of a gracious and good-natured king affords you a kind treatment, where all sensible and judicious persons have both respect and friendship for you. Think well on it, Madam: the most happy day you will pass in a nunnery, will not be worth the most melancholy you pass here at home.[19]

Early in their relationship Saint-Evremond was already advising his friend concerning how best she should manage her pleasures at court—not that his advice was always heeded. In late 1676 he penned an essay titled "On Friendship," which he addressed to Hortense, and in which he counseled her to better manage her liaison with Charles II, which appeared to be threatened by her flirtation with a newcomer to London, the Count of Monaco. "If my wishes were realized," he wrote, "you would be ambitious, and would govern those who govern others. Become Mistress of the World, or remain mistress of yourself."[20] He knew that King Charles was indulgent with his new mistress and tolerant of her fondness for receiving all who were inclined to attend her late-night social gatherings. The king's own visits to the duchess in her little house in Saint James's Park were frequently even later, after the other guests had left. He would return to his own rooms at Whitehall at dawn. Neither Charles nor Hortense was inclined to jealousy. Nor was the king surprised that his mistress found herself surrounded by men who loved her.

But Saint-Evremond, an astute observer of men and of royal egos, urged Hortense to be more strategic. When the lovesick Count of Monaco announced his decision to leave England out of despair for the love of Duchess Mazarin, her friend knew that the king would take notice. Hortense responded precisely as her enemies had hoped she would. She took pity on the count, began to encourage his melancholy overtures, and persuaded him to stay.

This move was impulsive and of course ill advised. She was finally in a position of safety, protected from a forced return to her husband, and she was letting herself be drawn by her love of pleasure into a relationship that could only damage her newfound security. Perhaps she thought that the infatuated king, who publicly embraced his libertine reputation, would tolerate an infidelity with another man as easily as he had accepted her intimacy with Anne of Sussex. Hortense seemed to believe, too, that her connection to Charles II had been somehow predestined and was invulnerable, determined at the start from the moment he had first seen her as a young girl at the French court.

The strength of their new bond did in fact endure longer than many would have predicted. The king was satisfied at first that Hortense's affection for the Count of Monaco was not serious, even when the count reversed his plans to leave England, and as Courtin urgently reported to the French court that Monsieur de Monaco seemed unwilling to leave Madame Mazarin. Saint-Evremond intensified his warnings to Hortense. But Charles continued to keep the Duchess Mazarin close to him, even seating her behind him at the opening of Parliament in 1677. It was only when Hortense's liaison with the Count of Monaco became so open that the king felt himself mocked that he withdrew his affection.

In the summer of 1677 Hortense's old friend Marie-Sidonie de Courcelles, herself newly arrived in London, wrote letters home detailing what to her seemed to be Hortense's foolish relinquishing of the position of royal mistress in favor of an affair with a visiting nobleman of little consequence. She described Monsieur de Monaco as physically ill with love, and Hortense in "solitude," having incurred the anger of Charles II. "The king," she wrote, "was yesterday making loud jokes about it, saying that the service of Madame Mazarin was too difficult. . . . It was killing her husband as well as all of her noble lovers; Monaco is having dizzy spells just like Mazarin did."[21]

Marie-Sidonie and others predicted after this episode that Hortense would have no choice but to return to France. "She is even more unhappy than I and sees no one," wrote Marie-Sidonie. But her prediction was not borne out. For a time Hortense made a show of devout repentance while appealing once more for her husband to send her funds. But Charles had not cut her off entirely. He continued to provide Hortense with enough financial support to remain in the house in Saint James's Park that was dubbed the "little palace."

Soon life was almost back to normal, except for the French ambassador, Courtin, who was discouraged and exasperated by his inability to predict with any accuracy what the duchess would do next. He had been informed of his recall to France and the arrival of his replacement Paul Barrillon at about the same time that Marie-Sidonie had arrived in London. Courtin wrote a rueful letter to the French minister Pomponne: "Madame de Courcelles arrived here two days ago; England is the refuge of all women who have quarreled with their husbands; it will be a fine affair for Monsieur de Barrillon."[22]

Social life in the "little palace" was only the livelier without Courtin's daily presence in the library. But it was a period of increasing hostility toward Catholics in England, and by extension toward French and Italian residents there. The pope was routinely burned in effigy. Protestant Parliament was hostile to the king's policies promoting religious tolerance, and there was great anxiety about the succession to the throne. Charles had no legitimate children and the heir apparent, his brother James, was Catholic and married to a Catholic of French and Italian origin. Between 1678 and 1681 hysteria mounted surrounding a supposed Catholic conspiracy to assassinate Charles II, with accusations of this "popish plot" brought by Titus Oates, a Protestant clergyman. At first Charles dismissed the accusations as ridiculous but was pressured by Parliament into hearing them. Before it all came to an end in 1681, with Oates arrested and convicted of perjury, fifteen people were falsely tried and executed.

Many highly placed foreign Catholics found themselves threatened by accusations of complicity in this fictitious conspiracy, among them the Duchess Mazarin. In November 1678, Barrillon wrote Louis XIV, "I think that Your Majesty will learn with some surprise that Madame Mazarin was named today by Oates as an accomplice in the schemes formed against the state and religion. The King of England mocked this accusation and spoke to me of it as something that was utterly ridiculous. But he says the same of the Lords who are in the Tower and have been tried by the courts."[23]

Among those tried and executed was Edward Coleman, secretary to Hortense's cousin Mary Beatrice of Modena. Charles attempted to dismiss most of the accusations, but he was unable to protect Catholic noblemen from exclusion from the House of Lords. It was not easy to count on his protection, so Hortense considered her other options. She was in contact throughout this period with her sister Marie, by now in Madrid, living in a convent where she was considered a secular pensioner who could leave at will, and where she felt comfortably connected to the court of Spain. For a few months it seemed that Hortense's best course of action might be to join her sister in Madrid. Her friend Saint-Evremond sent her a letter railing against convents, even liberal ones, and pleading with her to abandon such a notion. Even the pleasure of reuniting with her sister, he wrote her, would be short-lived; they would reminisce for a few days and then she might easily find that further conversation would be forbidden her, for after all, he warned, "one of the rules in a convent is that pleasurable contacts must not be sustained. . . . After you have spoken for three or four days about France and Italy, after you have talked about the King's passion and the weakness of your uncle Mazarin, of what you thought you would be and what you have become, . . . of your flight from Rome and the unhappy successes of your travels, you will find yourselves locked in a convent."[24]

Saint-Evremond's eloquence may have worked its magic: Hortense did not leave England. A few months later Oates was thrown in prison, and those friends who were counseling the duchess to leave to avoid persecution were relieved.

Over the next several years Hortense resumed her pleasurable life, punctuated by what had become her almost routine appeals for the restitution of her dowry. Money continued to be her biggest challenge. The "Mazarine" salon was one of the earliest examples of what would later become a vogue of gambling spots in London and Paris, often hosted by women. Her salon became famous as a gambling site, or "gambling academy," as it was often termed. Hortense became known for her big wins, and even more notorious for her losses. She began to accumulate debts while showing no inclination to curb her passion for the game of basset, all the rage in London's racier social circles by the end of the seventeenth century. Looking back on the heady years of Restoration society from a more

sober vantage point in 1714, Theophilius Lucas compiled an en-
cyclopedia of famous gamblers titled *Lives of the Gamesters*. Hortense
Mazarin was the only woman he included.

Her social circle also continued to be noted for literary and political discussions as well as musical performances in which Hortense
participated as performer and singer. In the 1680s Hortense's home
continued to receive a steady flow of visitors from the Continent.
Some were simply curious to see this "famous beauty and errant
lady"; others were writers, artists, and scientists drawn to the salon
over which she and Saint-Evremond presided. Her salon became a
focal point for popular discussions of science and art, and for pre-
publication readings of French writers newly translated into English,
and English into French. Saint-Evremond, ever attentive to his
friend's attraction to danger, wrote verse praising her happy tran-
sitions from the gambling table to more elevated interactions. When
Bernard de Fontenelle's dialogues on astronomy, *Conversations on
the Plurality of Worlds,* first appeared, Hortense was obsessed with
it and could talk of nothing else for days. "No one would dare speak
of Basset even for a moment," wrote Saint-Evremond. "All is moon,
sun, circle, orb, and firmament."[25] His French audiences read of
her salon with pleasure and came to regard it as an outpost of
French culture and sociability: "It is true that people often argue,"
he wrote, "but it is more reasoned than heated. It is less to contra-
dict people, and more to shed light on the subject, more to enliven
conversation and less to embitter the mind. . . . Madame Mazarin
spreads over all a kind of easy air, free and natural; one would say
that things just proceed of their own accord, so difficult it is to see
their secret hidden order."[26]

These were good years for Hortense. But in the winter of
1684–1685 two dramatic events occurred to darken her happiness.
The first was another casualty of her personal charisma. Among
the visitors from France was a young relative, Philippe de Soissons,

the seventeen-year-old son of her sister Olympe. The boy had quickly become infatuated with his aunt, so much so that he developed a strong antipathy for one of her admirers she particularly favored, a visiting Swedish baron. Young Philippe challenged the man to a duel and, to everyone's astonishment and horror, fatally wounded him. Hortense was furious and inconsolable, draping her rooms in black and refusing to leave her lodgings. Young Soissons was forced to flee on the spot to avoid arrest. The event damaged Hortense's ever-fragile but mending connections with the French court, as well as with her own family. "Who would have thought that the eyes of a grandmother could still wreak such havoc," wrote Madame de Sévigné.[27] (At thirty-nine, Hortense already had children who were married.)

In London she was more easily forgiven, at least among her friends, including the king. Just a few months later she was already back at Whitehall sharing a gaming table with Charles and two of his mistresses. On a night in early February 1685, John Evelyn was received at the royal residence and recorded in his diary the shock and disapproval that the spectacle inspired in him: "I can never forget the inexpressible luxury and profaneness, gaming, and all dissoluteness, and as it were total forgetfulness of God (it being Sunday evening) which this day I was witness of, the King sitting and toying with his concubines Portsmouth, Cleveland, and Mazarin, a French boy singing love songs in that glorious gallery, whilst about twenty of the great courtiers and other dissolute persons were at basset round a large table."[28]

Six days later, King Charles died after an apoplectic fit, probably caused by kidney failure. He was fifty-four. On his deathbed, he converted to Catholicism.

# MADRID

*Madrid, 23 May 1677*
*Most Excellent Lady,*
*I hereby inform your Excellency, by order of the king,*
*that . . . the king sees no impediment to Your Excellency*
*choosing . . . in order to live there, a decent habitation in a*
*healthy place with clean air, pending the approval of the*
*Constable. His Majesty will do all in his power to lend favor*
*to Madame in this enterprise, for her greatest satisfaction.*

—Don Bartolomeo de Legassa, secretary to Carlos II of Spain

*Here we do not treat our wives as you do in Italy. Your wish*
*to put her in a prison is not enough to see it done.*

—Archbishop of Caesarea, papal nuncio in Madrid, to Lorenzo Colonna, March 1677

A YEAR BEFORE HORTENSE FIRST LEFT Chambéry for England, Marie had managed to extricate herself from her "prison" in the Brussels convent and was headed for Madrid. The Spanish capital was a compromise destination, and the only one acceptable to Lorenzo Colonna because of the strong network of family and political allies that he enjoyed there. Marie was willing to go to Spain because she hoped she would be able to find protection and welcome at a court where ties to France were also strong. And she thought that if she lived in Madrid, her husband might come to see some value in their separation, because there she could work for the family's interests and cultivate contacts that would benefit their sons. Lorenzo himself was expected to make regular voyages to the Spanish capital, and Marie hoped he would bring their three boys with him, or send them to her in Madrid for prolonged visits.

Lorenzo had agreed to his wife's travel to Spain with the stipulation that she be escorted by his half-brother Don Ferdinando, who was under strict instructions to report on her every move. From the moment of his arrival in Brussels, Don Ferdinando had already managed to provide Marie and her household with more comfortable living conditions. So, as Marie and her entourage set sail from the harbor of Ostend in Spanish Flanders on a warm June day in 1674, there was general goodwill and optimism that they were headed toward a brighter future. They were passengers on an English merchant vessel headed to the Atlantic coast of Spain. The winds and weather favored them, and after only nine days of smooth sailing they landed in San Sebastián. Marie was able to set out immediately by carriage for Madrid. She received a welcoming message from Spain's queen regent, Mariana of Austria, and not long after that a message from the Don Juan de Cabrera, Admiral of Castile, the second-highest dignitary in the kingdom, who announced his intention to receive her personally and to provide her with her own residence. It appeared that Marie finally would realize her most fervent wish, "to live at peace in a house of my own." She was escorted first to the Casa de Huerta, the splendid country residence of the admiral just east of the capital city and surrounded by expansive gardens, where she happily settled in.

The landscape of Spain that Marie crossed as she rode in carriages relayed from San Sebastián to Burgos, Alcobendas, and finally to Madrid was stranger than she had anticipated. In the 1670s, although Spain was still arguably the most powerful realm in Europe, it was a poor country, with roads that were much rougher than those of northern Europe. Mule-drawn carriages bumped along at a slow and deliberate pace. When Marie entered the carriage that was sent for her, she had to push aside several layers of heavy curtains. Women who traveled were not supposed to be seen, nor were they expected to try to see the sights outside their carriage window. In the hot June sun, the voyage was stifling.

But the admiral's gardens soon helped her forget the uneasiness of her voyage. She noted that her luxurious surroundings at the Casa de Huerta were, as she put it, "decorated with a very great number of the richest and most beautiful paintings there are in all of Europe."[1] This was reminiscent of her Roman days. She was not in a hurry to leave, though she quickly was becoming aware of some of the more dramatic differences in what was considered acceptable behavior for Spanish women compared with that of French or Italian ladies. Though she had chafed at the restrictions on her freedom in Rome, in Spain they were far more severe. In the admiral's gardens she could wander as she pleased, but outside the enclosed walls of their residences, noblewomen were not permitted to walk about alone. The most familiar structures in the city were convents and monasteries—Madrid had more than fifty in 1674, at a time when the population was under 150,000. Marie's friend the writer Marie-Catherine d'Aulnoy would record her impressions of Spain in a travelogue reflecting on her own voyage to Spain a few years later:

> Highly placed ladies go on promenades in public only in the first year of their marriage, and then only with their husbands. The lady in the back of the coach, the husband in front, curtains all around, and the lady heavily covered . . . sometimes at night there are great ladies who go out *incognito*. They even go to the Prado on foot once night has fallen. They cover their heads with white woolen mantillas embroidered with black silk.[2]

Marie regarded this new world with trepidation. She had been in Paris when Louis XIV's Spanish queen had been introduced to the French court, and she had heard the stories of the rigidity of the queen's manners and the stiffness of her clothes. Royalty in Spain cultivated a frozen, godlike demeanor that stood in odd contrast to the impoverished, almost rustic atmosphere that prevailed just outside the palace walls in the capital city. Madame d'Aulnoy remarked in her travelogue that Madrid seemed to be inhabited only by the very rich or the very poor: "There are only seven or eight streets filled with merchants. You will find no boutiques in this city, except for those that sell sweets, liqueurs, jams, ice water and pastries."[3] Spanish courtiers always seemed hungry and ill-mannered at table; they "ate like wolves" and were permitted to take away food from the lavish banquets held at court. The ladies, constrained by their heavy clothing, "after stuffing themselves with candied fruits, filled five or six kerchiefs that they had brought expressly for that purpose."[4]

It was a foreign culture, but Marie was determined to find a secure place in it. She focused her attention on being received at court and wrote letters to the queen regent requesting an audience. She studied the Spanish fashions and had new veils and dresses made for herself, complete with the uncomfortable whale-bone girdles and hoops that served as undergarments and gave the dresses their awkward geometric shapes. Spanish women's dresses of the day were constructed on a kind of frame made up of several hoops that supported multiple layers of fabric. She insisted that her servants also observe the Spanish fashions, which they found trying. Nanette wrote a letter to Lorenzo complaining that she had been punished for not wearing her uncomfortable new dress all day:

> I believe it is my duty to tell Your Excellency why I was thrown out by Madame, for a thing so small you will hardly believe it, it was for having put on my dressing gown at ten o'clock in the evening after

having worn my Spanish dress all day. No one could see me. . . . She
said I could go to France if I wanted to dress in the French style,
and I assure you, your Excellency, that no one dresses more in the
Spanish style than I![5]

Marie was determined, and perhaps more irritable than usual
with some in her household, as she reflected on her next move. She
pressed the admiral to help her find a suitable independent lodging,
a house, she proposed, on the grounds of a convent, of course. She
remained at Casa de Huerta but was eager to move on with her
plans. The admiral was a relaxed and gracious host, even a bit too
leisurely for the impatient Marie. She noted a "certain slowness"
in his character and worried that it might be easier for him to keep
her there rather than to press the queen to grant her request.

As she waited for her opportunity to be received at court, Marie
decided one evening to take a little outing accompanied only by
Morena, to explore the surrounding area. Even the easygoing admiral, when he found out about it, considered this an overly bold
move. The papal envoy to Madrid, who along with Lorenzo's relatives was keeping a close watch on Marie's movements, was quick
to report the misbehavior to Cardinal Altieri: "Yesterday, unbe-
knownst to Don Ferdinand or the admiral, Madame Colonna, who
is residing in his home, went off alone in a carriage with her Turkish
maid on a promenade by the river. Everyone was astonished. . . .
This action if it becomes known will scandalize the court, where
one never sees a lady in public."[6] After this incident, though, the
admiral was not quite so slow in helping Marie to receive her audience with the queen. When in August 1674 her request finally
was granted, Marie caused a stir by appearing in a heavily orna-
mented dress in the Spanish style, complete with a huge rectan-
gular hoop (the French called it a "princess guard") supporting
yards of heavy fabric. She could not have looked more Spanish.
On the last day of August she received her authorization to take

up residence in a small house adjoining the convent of Santo Domingo el Real in Madrid.

The Constabless Colonna was well aware that in her new living arrangement she was still being closely observed by agents of her husband—in fact, one-half of her modest house was prepared as a residence for Don Ferdinando—but she was still optimistic that this move would mark the beginning of her new independence. She had not been writing to Lorenzo in her first months in Madrid and had concentrated instead on developing her own network of contacts. Her memoirs later would record her own effort to be hopeful despite the very clear signs that this new residence was not a place from which she could freely come and go: "I was given the house that adjoins the convent; half of it was made into my apartment, to which a hatch and metal bars were added, and the other half was left for the abbé Don Ferdinand Colonna and for the rest of my servants."[7] But, she added, "I made new acquaintances in the convent and felt fairly happy there." In a letter to the Countess Stella, who had remained at the Colonna palazzo as a dependent, she also tried to underline her satisfaction:

I have received the lace you sent me which is very much to my liking. . . . Take good care of my children, and never doubt that you are all in my thoughts. I am nonetheless doing very well in this country. The air is the most perfect that I have ever breathed, and I am also very comfortably lodged, not bothered by the nuns, I go to see them when I please and they cannot come see me unless I request permission for them. There are often ladies who come to see me, otherwise I see no one in the parlor except for nuns or priests, for the Spanish don't favor grilles like the Italians do. But I care little about that. Adieu, fair Countess, always count on my friendship as it is entirely yours,

—M.M.C.[8]

For these first few months, things seemed to be going well. When Lorenzo had authorized her move to Spain, Marie had hoped that he would allow her to play some role in looking after the family's interests there. She had already been able to obtain from the Spanish queen honors for her sons, including, for the ten-year old Marcantonio, the title of commander of two companies of cavalry. Lorenzo had not discouraged her efforts, seeming to recognize that Marie could be useful. She also had asked that the papal envoy procure special permission for her to leave the convent lodgings once a week. No one seemed to have any objection to this and the formal request had been sent to Cardinal Altieri in Rome. But Lorenzo was toying with her. Although he allowed himself to be persuaded that she could serve as a kind of family representative in Madrid, he was determined to allow her that function only on very restricted terms. Unknown to Marie, he had decided to oppose granting his estranged wife even the small freedom of weekly promenades. He had written to the Spanish court and made his wishes clear to both his family in Madrid and to papal advisers in Rome. Altieri was forced to tell the papal envoy that there was nothing he could do to moderate Lorenzo's stance: "Monsieur the Constable refuses the requests of Madame his wife, and I will write to her without saying precisely that, but in such a way that she will understand."⁹

By March, it was clear to Marie that her hoped-for liberty would not be realized. Her other fervent request, to be permitted to finally see at least one of her sons again, was also denied. In her memoirs written two years later, the memory was recent and still painful:

I learned subsequently that the Constable was far from giving me satisfaction for my earnest entreaties that he send me my second son so that I could travel with him to Flanders, where the two companies of cavalry that Her Majesty had granted him immediately upon my request obliged him to go. Vowing, doubtless, to make me return to Rome by thwarting me in everything, he had written to Her

Majesty and to the Admiral, who had endeavored in their letters to make him condescend to what I asked, that he did not wish me to go out of the convent, that he begged Her Majesty not to permit me to do so, that I was safe and secure in Madrid, and that he did not want to risk seeing me at liberty anywhere else.[10]

In 1675 she resumed her letters to Lorenzo, this time taking a different tone. Now she made no attempt to disguise her anger and hostility:

Now I realize from your letter that you are always trying to fool me with empty promises about my return to Italy, when instead you should be content to do what is necessary and not always be giving me different orders when you invite me. I am not the one who keeps changing; I always say the same thing. If I complained about the Admiral, it was for a good reason, when despite my repeated requests to see him, it was never possible for two whole months, even though I always respected him and followed his instructions in everything. As for my travels, do what God inspires you to do now; you who have the ball in your hand, play it, while fortune conspires against me. . . . Maybe one day that will change.[11]

Three years had now passed since Marie had left. In Rome, Lorenzo was finally resuming the lifestyle at the palazzo Colonna that he had cultivated during Marie's presence. For the 1675 carnival he hosted his first theatrical production since his wife's departure. The Roman newsletters announced that "the house of signor Constable is freely open for staging plays." Reports of the festivities reached Marie's household, and Nanette wrote to the Countess Stella that in Madrid, Mardi Gras was not quite so much fun, "as you told us that you had a grand carnival I will tell you that we had a good and nice holy week, and while I like Madrid well enough, for your love, my dear Madam and that of everyone, I would have better liked to see your carnival."[12] Meanwhile, Lorenzo continued his close contact with informants in Madrid, continuing to provide Marie with some funds but conceding nothing regarding her disputed *libertà*.

In June 1675, news arrived of the unexpected death of Charles-Emmanuel, the Duke of Savoy, another blow to Marie. She had maintained a close correspondence with him and he had continued to sympathize with her while remaining baffled and fascinated by this woman he termed the "bizarre Colonna." He had sent her gifts in Madrid and taken delight in the reports of her pleasure at receiving them. He had continued to politely urge her to return to Rome, while at the same time trying to persuade Lorenzo to grant her principal condition for returning, that she be permitted to live apart from him. Charles-Emmanuel's sudden death meant that Marie, like her sister Hortense, had lost a powerful ally.

Further complicating matters, Marie's determined optimism had caused her to overestimate her own ability to find either friends who would welcome her in their homes or an abbess who would permit her to live in a convent from which she could come and go as she pleased. Spanish convents were not as congenial to taking in secular women as were those in France. But she stubbornly persisted in lobbying on her own behalf and found some allies in unlikely places, even among Colonna relatives who were as concerned about calming the family reputation as they were about satisfying Lorenzo's demands to have Marie shut up in a strict cloister or imprisoned. Gradually she began to obtain some favors from her husband's relatives, ever eager to minimize damage to their public image. She also curried favor with courtiers close to the royal family, many of them with ties to France, which was gaining increasing influence in the Spain of the 1670s. From behind the locked doors of her little house at the convent of Santo Domingo el Real, Marie occupied herself with her writing. Mostly it was letters to Lorenzo, in which she continued to try to persuade him to send her their sons and to allow her to transfer to another house, one outside the convent walls. The queen, she assured him, had no objection to her plans: "You will see in her letter how she wants to comfort me and therefore awaits your approval [of] a house at some distance from the convent but with more space outside, where I could get more exercise and enjoy the cool of the evening; whereas here the nuns close the doors at 9:00 so that I cannot even go into the garden. What is more, the house where I am staying is extremely hot in the summer."[13]

Lorenzo did not immediately refuse her outright. He and the Countess Stella continued to send her the many small items she requested—cedar fans, perfume, laces, portraits of her sons, copies of portraits of herself that she could give as gifts—and Marie sent back gifts for everyone, especially the children: "The special mail will bring you a box with a black vase that the first lady-in-waiting gave me, and since it is highly considered I am offering it to you, together with some small tablets for burning and some little bowls and saucers for chocolate, one for each of the boys."[14]

By August it was clear that Lorenzo would not allow his sons to make the trip to Spain. Marie responded angrily, and yet continued to plead:

I was not expecting an answer different from the one you gave me, for by now I am accustomed to your subtle games with me; nor will I plead with you to let me live in Madrid in a house. . . . Since the nuncio has not yet left I want to hope that you will have time to arrange whatever is necessary with regard to my little boy and that he will be able to leave with him. . . . I want to hope that one way or another you will send him.[15]

It was in this period, too, that Marie may have learned of the true nature of the relationship that had developed between Ortensia Stella and Lorenzo Colonna. Many years later, in his will, Lorenzo would acknowledge the two illegitimate children he had fathered with the Countess Stella. The first had been born in 1674, just before Marie's arrival in Madrid. Never in the long correspondence that Marie and the countess would maintain throughout their lives is there any sense of bitterness between the two women. Over the years Ortensia continued to serve Marie faithfully as a conduit to the Colonna household, interceding with Lorenzo and continuing to obtain his permission to send Marie a variety of requested items, from clothes to serving maids and pet dogs. On occasion, but not often, she also saw to it that Marie received promissory letters for delivery of some money, just enough to prevent the Colonna name from being tainted by the estranged wife's poverty. All these expenditures were meticulously recorded in Lorenzo's accounting notebooks. It would be the Countess Stella's signature that would continue to appear on the household records whenever items were withdrawn to be mailed to "Madama," and it was to her friend that Marie would continue to confide her worries about her children, about Lorenzo's rejection of her requests, about gossip that might reach him. Ortensia had her own risks to face and her own calculations to make. Many years later, as we shall see, Marie would acknowledge that she understood them.

Sometime in 1675 Marie received a copy of the memoirs her sister had published in France. The printer, "Pierre de Marteau" of Cologne, was a familiar pseudonym used by many printers in France who wanted to publish a book that was likely to sell but that might get them in trouble with royal censors. The Duchess Mazarin's book was an exciting novelty, not only for the inside information it provided about the family of Cardinal Mazarin and her own notoriously bad marriage, but also because it was a private memoir published by a woman who acknowledged her own authorship, something that had never been seen before in France. Manuscript and print copies were quickly circulated in several languages all over Europe and Britain. From Spain Marie read her sister's account of parts of her own life, including her romance with Louis XIV, her marriage, her years in Rome, and the adventures on the road the sisters had shared. Marie had become accustomed to being the subject of gossip, to being spied upon, and to having her movements documented by gazetteers and private agents, but it was a new experience to see herself as a subject in a book, described sympathetically by someone close to her who had risked her own reputation to write it. In the first lines of her memoirs, Hortense wrote that she was fully aware that to defend her own reputation was inherently impossible for a woman: "I know that a woman's glory lies in not giving rise to gossip," but to remain unknown was not her destiny. "One cannot always choose the kind of life one wishes to lead, and there is fate even in the very things that seem to depend most on conduct."[16] The book was a sensation, provoking curiosity for more information about the runaway sisters. Within months another memoir appeared, also printed by "Pierre de Marteau," titled *Memoirs of M.L.P.M.M., Grand Constabless of the Kingdom of Naples.* Its sales were no less successful than those of the first one, and this book, too, arrived in Madrid at the door of the lady by whom it was supposed to have been written.

Marie read it with astonishment. Clearly the author was someone who had known her life in Rome quite well, someone who could provide details of her daily occupations, her friends, her movements. The memoirs were prefaced by a letter signed only with the initials "N.N.," claiming, in the conventional style of popular fiction, that the author had simply come into possession of the memoir: "I am sending you by express mail the Memoirs of Madame the Constabless Colonna, so that they don't fall into anyone else's hands by the same accident that has put these and those of the Duchess Mazarin in your hands. These two sisters, having some connection in the disaster that has befallen their husbands, have also been fated to have similar accidents befall them."[17] Marie continued to read: "As I saw in Rome a good number of the things that she recounts, I recognize the sincerity of her story."[18] As she delved further into these "memoirs" of her own life, her agitation grew. Who among those close to her had the audacity to assume her voice and to write of her life as though she herself were telling it? Worse, the telling of it was just convincing and plausible enough for readers to believe she herself had written it, but the image the memoir conveyed was not the one she would have chosen; it was not how she saw herself or how she wanted to be seen. Many of the facts of her life were either invented or distorted. The memoir itself started with her impersonator describing the "idleness" in which she was living in a Spanish convent and the timid reluctance with which she agreed to write the story of her life to comply with the request of a "noble" protector: "I could have no higher ambition than to acquire a protector such as you, whose merit knows no bounds."[19]

The memoir went on to describe, in melodramatic terms laced with references to mythological figures, her thwarted romance with the young king: "And so it was that my unhappy destiny led me, who could have been a Venus, to be not even one of the Graces. My eyes fill with tears and my heart, choked with distress, stifles any happiness when I even think of it."[20] The fake memoirs described Marie as having become "too dangerous for the public good" once the king was betrothed, suggesting that she would have become a royal mistress after the marriage. Readers were told that she had to be married off to an "Argus" who would keep a close watch over her. Marie's impersonator had described her as taking pleasure in arousing her husband's jealousy, and Lorenzo was characterized as being driven nearly mad with jealousy, accusing everyone from Marie's valets and servants to her brother of courting liaisons with his wife.

The book also liberally exposed the gossip and scandal that had circulated around Marie and Hortense in Rome, describing dramatic feuds between Hortense and her sister over the Courbeville affair and between Lorenzo and Marie over her relationship with the Chevalier de Lorraine. Marie is described as uncertain and helpless after her flight, wanting to follow her sister to England. Marie read on, about the many jealousies that Lorenzo had suffered on her account, about his suspicions of her liaisons with her musician Coresi and the Chevalier de Lorraine, and about her own quarrels with her husband over his amorous adventures with Roman ladies. This gossipy narrative was punctuated by pathetic expressions of regret and resignation, culminating with her impersonator's expressed desire to return "to France to be near the King," and with her sad contemplation of the "thick walls" of the Madrid convent that now contained her, and her hope that she could "dig" her way out like famous prisoners had done.

This was too much for Marie. She wasted no time in taking up the battle against whatever damage the imposture had done, publishing her own version of her life's adventures, which she titled *The Truth in Its Own Light; or, The Genuine Memoirs of M. Mancini, Constabless Colonna*. And so she joined Hortense in her move to go public with her life and attempt to reclaim her reputation. In the first paragraph she took on her detractors and decried the lucrative book market that encouraged writers to produce such calumny:

As there are no actions upon which the light of public scrutiny shines more harshly than upon those of people in high places, there are also none that are more exposed to censure, nor more easily the target of malicious gossip, and especially in France, where the lampoons meant to libel and to blacken the reputations of those of our sex sell very well, and pass for works of court gallantry. But although I was not unaware that there is nothing in the world so sacred that these sorts of works will not attack it, I believed I was beyond the reach of their blows, both by virtue of time and through the propriety of my actions, until I received word from France that there was in circulation a book about my life under my name. This news, along with certain circumstances of which I had been informed, made me curious to see it, and the sight of it has since changed the pique and indignation that I had felt about it into the greatest contempt in the world for its author; for I needn't say here, for those who know me, that there is not a single adventure in it which is not made up, and as far from my character as it is from the truth.[21]

Lorenzo Colonna had seen the first memoir, and a manuscript copy had been translated into Italian for him. We do not know how he reacted to it, but it is clear that Marie felt that her life story in her own words could only be better received by him, for she sent him her own manuscript even before it was printed and was eager to receive his impression of it. She explained to him that it was important to correct the image that the first version had created, declaring in a letter that "I have been obliged (to counter the ridiculous and impertinent story that is circulating under my name) to give to the printer a true relation of my life."[22] She included, often briefly but suggestively, even episodes in her life that he might have preferred to see passed over in silence, including her romance with Louis XIV. On this moment in her life she stated forthrightly, "As far as the king is concerned I could not have explained myself in less detail, because we are dealing with such a public event that it would be worse to keep silent about it."[23] Describing the romance, she recounted episodes illustrating the king's "kindness," his chivalry, and "the indulgence with which he treated me in everything."[24]

Marie had been particularly angered by the fake memoir's closing scene, which described her situation in Madrid. There she was depicted as a virtual prisoner, pining away behind impenetrable stone walls and pathetically fantasizing about how she might dig herself out. By contrast, she ended her own memoir with a pointed objection to this sort of representation of both her character and her situation. She insisted on the ease with which she had escaped any such efforts to contain her, starting with her unauthorized sorties from the convent:

> I learned that the constable was far from giving me satisfaction for my earnest entreaties that he send me my second son, . . . He had written to Her Majesty and to the Almirante, who had endeavored in their letters to make him condescend to what I asked, that he did not wish me to go out of the convent, that he begged Her Majesty not to permit me to do so, that I was safe and secure in Madrid, and that he did not want to risk seeing me at liberty anywhere else. I have already said somewhere in this history that it is in my nature to be infuriated when I am thwarted, so one can well imagine the resentment and the pique that this news caused me. . . . On top of that, certain malicious individuals, in order to do me a bad turn and thereby gain his good graces, wrote to him that I wanted to run away and that I would do it inevitably if I were not closely watched. These rumors, together with the other reasons which I have declared above, made me decide to go out of the convent, to show that the efforts to hold me would keep me locked up there only so long as I was willing. So one day when Don Ferdinand had gone out with all my servants, I had my maids open in an instant—and it was my maids, mind you—those strong, those thick, and those high walls which the author of my history contends were the only obstacle to my flight.[25]

If Lorenzo was not particularly pleased with his wife's portrayal of his own role in these events, he apparently did not tell her so directly. Marie wrote in one letter to him, "I am pleased that the book has been to your liking,"[26] and he made no objection to Marie's publishing successes. Even in Rome, she had been known as a writer, having authored two astrological almanacs. From her convent residence in Madrid she managed, quite remarkably, to have her memoirs printed in Saragossa and translated into Spanish for a second edition. The book quickly appeared in English in London, where a public familiar with the life of the Duchess Mazarin was curious about her sister. But although Lorenzo did not try to interfere with the book's circulation (an attempt that in any event would certainly have failed), he worked feverishly to place stricter limits on his wife's own freedom of movement. Marie learned of these obsessive efforts during the summer months of 1677. She in turn had written her own petitions to the Spanish court and used her book as testimony before a special tribunal of government ministers that had been formed to consider how to respond to the conflicting requests being put forth by the haughty constable and his fugitive wife. Other members of the French community in Madrid wrote home about her presence among them and her stubborn struggle to build her own network of alliances to counter her husband's influence with the Spanish court. The papal nuncio Savo Mellini, who had arrived in Madrid shortly after Marie, was sympathetic to her. This archbishop of Caesarea was a young man, in his early thirties, and impatient with some of the more severe approaches to marital discord that prevailed in Rome. Responding to Lorenzo's demand that Marie be locked in a fortress if she could not be contained in the convent, he wrote:

> I already indicated to your Excellency how difficult it would be to execute the thought you continue to have that Madama be locked up in some tower or castle. Your Excellency cannot fully understand the respect in which women are held here. . . . The Marquis of Astorga and Don Pietro of Aragon . . . have told me that the State

Council has totally rejected your Excellency's proposal as being a practice unheard of in Spain.[27]

Lorenzo persisted. The envoy was obliged to repeat himself in subsequent letters throughout the summer. "That you find it strange that a husband can't pay to have his wife put in a fortress, I find totally in keeping with the practices in Italy," wrote the archbishop. "Here, however, one approaches wives using different methods."[28] Marie, meanwhile, made Lorenzo aware that she knew he was conspiring against her:

> You told me nothing in your last letter, but nothing has been hidden from me about the secret attempts you have made against my freedom, writing to the king to have his majesty shut me up in a fortress and writing to the ministers to carry out this request . . . by restraining me thus, using such extreme means, you intend to suppress a will that would surrender, were I treated differently. I am alerting you now that a memorandum has been written concerning me in the council of state and I am waiting to hear from you regarding their consultation.[29]

On May 23, 1677, the Spanish council of state delivered its judgment, which satisfied neither party. On the one hand, Marie was authorized to "choose for herself a decent residence in a healthy environment with good air," but on the other hand, this authorization "awaited the approval of the constable."[30] The council seemed to want to indicate its opinion in the matter, but without directly challenging Lorenzo's authority. However, Marie wanted a more definitive decision. She immediately left her Santo Domingo residence, without authorization, as if to prove her own freedom. Fleeing to a small house she had been given by a noblewoman she had befriended at the court, she was pursued immediately by Don

Ferdinando. The papal nuncio followed close behind and managed to negotiate her return to the city with the promise that she could live in Don Ferdinando's house that was just within the convent walls but did not have bars on the windows. Even the Spanish prime minister, Don Juan of Austria, was drawn into the dispute.

Marie had reason to believe the new prime minister would be in a position to act more decisively in her favor than the queen had been. The year 1677 had been a disruptive one for the Spanish government. Having reached majority, the sixteen-year-old Carlos II was eligible to govern, but incompetent. The queen mother found herself marginalized by the ever-declining popularity of her prime minister and her son's increasing reluctance to follow her orders. In January the popular Don Juan José of Austria, illegitimate half-brother to Carlos II, arrived in Madrid at the head of an army and exiled the prime minister to the Philippines and the queen mother to the Spanish province of Toledo. Carlos promptly made him prime minister. Up to that time, Don Juan's career had been largely a military one. He had shown himself to be a skilled negotiator, in both victory and defeat. Neither political nor domestic intrigue was daunting to him, and he understood how the two could coincide. His own illegitimate status, and his hatred of his father's wife, would continue to propel him in his political decision-making until his death. When called upon to address the dispute between Lorenzo Colonna and Marie Mancini, he made a political decision that he thought could lead to a resolution of the domestic divide. The Constable Colonna, ever susceptible to flattery and honors, was appointed to the position of Viceroy of Aragon, the same position that Don Juan had just relinquished to take on his new role as Spanish prime minister. In that capacity, Lorenzo would be required to take up residence in Saragossa for part of the year, with inevitable trips to Madrid. Marie had always said she would consider reuniting with her husband if certain

conditions were met. Lorenzo's agents had always told him that
an essential gesture would be to meet with her in person. Now it
seemed that these conditions might be realized. Lorenzo prepared
for a voyage to Spain, and Marie for the longed-for reunion with
her sons.

## { 9 }

# DIVORCE

*Madama continues to talk of divorce and other crazy notions.*

—Don Ferdinando Colonna, letter to Lorenzo Colonna, February 4, 1677

*Relatives took action, religious advisers became involved, the king's authority intervened, nothing was able to persuade Monsieur Mazarin. Must the wife be eternally subjected to the caprices, ravings, and false revelations of the husband?*

—Charles de Saint-Evremond, *Factum for Madame the Duchess Mazarin Against Monsieur Mazarin Her Husband*

IN THE YEARS FOLLOWING the death of King Charles II in 1685, tensions between England and France increased, despite the early efforts of Charles's brother, the Catholic James II, to strengthen ties between the two nations. But James was obliged to defend his succession to the throne from the beginning. He had served in the French army during the period of exile that he and his brother had spent in France, where he was also drawn to Catholicism. Anti-Catholic factions in Parliament attempted on more than one occasion to exclude him from the line of succession. Once he assumed the throne, Parliament viewed him as a threat to English liberties. For the Duchess Mazarin, living in London, James's accession to the throne had to some extent enhanced her status and security there; after all, the new Queen Mary Beatrice of Modena was her cousin's daughter, and Hortense had played the role of affectionate aunt to the younger woman since her arrival in England fourteen years earlier. The Duchess Mazarin had been close to Mary Beatrice during her early years at the English court. Hortense's apartment at Whitehall placed her near her cousin throughout Mary Beatrice's confinements during pregnancy. Despite multiple pregnancies, James and Mary Beatrice had not been fortunate in children. Mary Beatrice had suffered several miscarriages and had given birth to five children, four of whom died in infancy, by the time she was twenty-four. The Duchess Mazarin had attempted to help Mary Beatrice cope with her grief when the queen returned from a voyage to Scotland in 1681 to learn that her one surviving child, Isabella, who had celebrated her second birthday just six months earlier, had suddenly died of smallpox. Three years after Mary Beatrice assumed the throne, she still had not produced an heir.

Standing to inherit the English throne if no heir was produced were James's two Protestant daughters by his first marriage. Then Mary Beatrice became pregnant once again in 1687, and the news provoked anti-Catholic rioting. When a healthy son was born on June 10, 1688, wild accusations began to circulate almost immediately. This was a queen, after all, who had proven herself unable to produce a viable male heir—this birth was not possible; the baby must be a changeling! Despite the testimony of more than thirty witnesses who had been present at the birth (challenges to its authenticity had been anticipated), many citizens were convinced that the newborn James Frances Edward was an impostor.

It is likely that the Duchess Mazarin was among those present at the much anticipated birth of Mary Beatrice's son. She heard the news of the parliamentary resolution accusing James and his wife of secretly conspiring to introduce an infant who was not theirs into the birthing room, and she must have reacted with astonishment and indignation. But by then the public sentiment against King James was irreversible.

In November 1688, William of Orange, husband to James's daughter Mary by his first marriage, invaded England with an army supported by the Protestant factions, and the government of James II collapsed. The royal couple fled to France with their infant son, where Louis XIV offered his protection and his country residence of the Chateau de Saint-Germain-en-Laye. William and Mary were Protestant, and members of the French Catholic community remaining in England found themselves much less likely to be treated with favor by the new king and queen. When William of Orange was proclaimed king on February 13, 1689, one of his first moves was to grant permission to Charles de Saint-Evremond and his community of French friends to remain in London without fear of reprisal. This was a gesture of generosity to a group of expatriates who themselves had, more often than not, acted as thorns in the side of the French king. Hortense was among them. But some members of the House of Commons were less generous. In July they petitioned William to have Hortense removed from the kingdom. William responded only by asking the duchess to vacate the apartment that had been set aside for her visits to Whitehall when Mary Beatrice had occupied the palace. For the time being, she remained in her residence in Saint James's Park and continued to host a vibrant salon.

Starting in 1685, when the throng of French émigrés arriving in London became predominantly Huguenot, the society that had continued to gather in the Duchess Mazarin's salon had changed. In that year, Louis XIV revoked the Edict of Nantes, the royal declaration of religious freedom that his grandfather Henry IV had designed to put an end to the French Wars of Religion. In renouncing the edict, the king outlawed Protestantism in France. Waves of wealthy exiles fled to Holland and England. The Duchess Mazarin's reputation for making her home a crossroads of diverse social groups became even more pronounced, as her salon drew visitors from an ever-broadening array of social, linguistic, and religious backgrounds. But her own future in England seemed to be uncertain at best. And her husband, observing her weakened position there and the increasing political tensions between France and England, decided to make another attempt to force her repatriation to France.

And so as the deposed James II began to amass troops in France for an assault on England and an attempt to regain his throne, the Duke Mazarin was gathering his own forces for a retaliatory attack on his wayward wife. His arms of choice were drawn from the dense network of legal assistants, judges, lawyers, and courtiers who over the years had come to know Armand-Charles de la Meilleraye as a reliable source of income. The Duke Mazarin enjoyed keeping an array of legal suits constantly in process. In his religious frenzies he had been compared to Molière's Tartuffe, and in his eagerness to litigate he evoked Molière's Misanthrope, who didn't even mind losing court cases because his losses showed the world that he was being wronged. In this instance, Armand-Charles's enemy was a wife who, though not enamored of litigation, was nonetheless as tenacious as her husband. She had continued, even through the years in England when all her friends were congratulating her on having escaped the clutches of a madman, to press her own arguments for legal independence and recovery of her dowry.

It had been more than twenty years since Hortense had run away from the Mazarin palace, and now Armand-Charles watched as her kinswoman Mary Beatrice was welcomed to the court of Versailles. He joined in the chorus of praise for the exiled Catholic queen, writing her a letter declaring his intent to bring Hortense back from the "road to perdition" that she was following in England. "I see no alternative but that of placing her under my lawful power," he wrote. "Pride caused the rupture between us, license has sustained it, and intrigue has strengthened it."[1] It was a long, rambling letter, rehashing all of the accusations that Hortense had made against him, accusations he knew she had shared with Mary Beatrice. He refuted them one by one, but if he hoped that Mary Beatrice would lend him her support, he went on to undermine his own position with crazed declarations of his determination to "persecute" his wife: "I swear it here: menaces, prayers, rewards, punishments, the loss of fortune or even of life itself will never deter me from being the persecutor of Madame Mazarin. But you must also believe me when I say that if she is willing to return to me I shall be the most gentle, the most humble, the most tender husband that anyone could ever imagine."[2]

Such declarations did not bode well for a reconciliation. But the duke remained convinced that the time was right for a definitive legal confrontation that would force his wife to return to him. France and England were at war, and the French Catholic community in London was increasingly vulnerable. The religious basis of the conflict gave more zeal to the duke's determination to extricate his wife from England. He hoped for the support of the French king in his efforts, but he was aware that the general feeling at court was that Hortense should return to France without being required to return to him. Most people regarded the duke as eccentric and fanatical, if not mad. After a chance encounter with him when she was traveling near his country estate in Brittany, Madame de Sévigné had written to her daughter: "I cannot describe to you how extravagant the man is, he is mad, he dresses like a pauper. . . . We tried to persuade him that he should get his wife out of England . . . but he keeps repeating that she has to return to him. To him! Good God. Saint-Evremond is right when he says that she should be excused from the usual rules, one has only to look at Monsieur Mazarin to see why."[3] If the opinion of the refined public was against him, the legal system, the duke felt, might not be so sympathetic to his wife. Throughout the 1680s he increasingly had been resorting to the courts to resolve the many quarrels and conflicts that plagued his tormented life. Even his own grown children, exasperated by the disarray of their father's financial affairs and his propensity for giving away vast sums to religious extremists and monastic orders, had entered into litigation against him.

The duke's next move was to engage the services of Claude Erard, a Parisian lawyer famous for his successful suits against aristocratic women by using sensational attacks on their reputations. Although divorce would not be legalized in France until the Revolution one hundred years later, a married couple could receive a legally authorized separation (sometimes called a "divorce") that determined the division of common property. But the guidelines for such agreements were extremely variable depending on the magistrate or legal court conducting the review and the persuasiveness of arguments lawyers prepared. Lawyers presented their arguments to the presiding magistrate in writing, and because some of their briefs were also printed for public distribution in pamphlet form, lawyers became known for their rhetorical skills. Erard excelled at this. For the Mazarin case he also published his arguments as a pamphlet or "factum" that was widely circulated and immediately translated for broader distribution in England. His presentation decried every decision the Duchess Mazarin had made over the two decades since she had left her husband. He held her up as a bad example to all women, a libertine and a gambler, a woman who kept the company of vagrants, foreigners, and traitors to their country and religion. The salon that was so admired by visitors to London became a den of iniquity in Erard's description: "Madame de Mazarin made of her home a public bureau of gambling, pleasures, and gallantries, a new Babylon where people of all nations, all sects, speaking all sorts of languages, marched in confusion under the banner of fortune and sensual delight."[4]

A principal counterargument presented by Hortense's lawyer, Sachot, was that his client was legally entitled to recover her dowry because she was under the protection of a kinswoman. Legal tradition (Roman law) dictated that women who left their husbands without permission risked losing their dowry, unless they took up residence with another member of the family. Erard ridiculed Sachot's claim, insisting that the intention of the law was that a wayward wife reform her behavior under the supervision of a relative:

My principal response to this objection draws on the sort of life that Madame Mazarin has led close to the Queen of England. First, did the Queen summon her to London? Has she retained her there? On the contrary, if Madame de Mazarin had followed her counsel, she would never have left her husband's house, or rather she would have returned there very promptly. It was chance that drew her to London, after having visited a multitude of other states, or rather she went there only out of the desire to put the sea between herself and Monsieur de Mazarin, and to not occupy the same continent as he. For it was her good fortune that led her to find the Queen of England, who was willing to tolerate her and to offer her charity, in the hopes that her presence and the consideration that Madame de Mazarin bore her, would moderate her behavior. But how has the opposing party used this favor? In what way has she lived close to this great Queen? Was she attentive to her person? Did she follow her in her charitable and pious actions? Did she imitate her example? Nothing has ever been more opposite. The Queen was entirely occupied with matters of salvation and eternity and with the exercise of our religion. Madame de Mazarin was entirely occupied with the follies of the age and seemed to have no other desire than to damn herself and others.[5]

The eloquent Erard pursued his points relentlessly and at length, clearly basking in the favorable position in which his client now found himself. With Mary Beatrice of Modena now in France, and England engaged in a religious war against France, it was not difficult to insinuate that Hortense's continuous absence was tantamount to treason, even heresy: "Is the Prince of Orange her relative? All those gamblers, those libertines, those Presbyterians, those Episcopalians, those Quakers; in a word, those people of all religions except the true one, who fill her house, are they her relatives? Let her explain these relations of which we are ignorant. But there are none, it is only the love of independence that keeps her in that country."[6]

It did not take long for the Grand Council to find in favor of the duke. Hortense's lawyer was forced to present arguments extending beyond those based on legal precedent or custom, which meant that Hortense lost the legal battle but won the sympathies of many. The discussion turned to popular opinion: What were the limits of a woman's obligation to a deranged husband? When should a feuding couple be encouraged to divorce? Did a woman not have an absolute right to control her own dowry? Readers of the pamphlets on both sides of the English Channel, already familiar with Hortense's story, were drawn into this case, which now became an occasion for public debate about a woman's right to independence from an unhappy marriage. Sachot evoked the duke's intolerance, his disturbed behavior, his destruction of the property of Cardinal Mazarin. Saint-Evremond seized the occasion to produce his own *Factum for the Duchess Mazarin Against Monsieur the Duke Mazarin Her Husband,* in which he decried the "injuries and calumnies" aimed at Hortense "and the English nation" by her husband's lawyer. He retold the story of Hortense's life beginning with her uncle's misguided choice of a husband. He itemized the dissipation of the cardinal's wealth in the hands of a crazed man "who always had the devil present in his dark imagination." And he argued for the "natural" right to divorce a spouse who is clearly insane:

The first misfortune of man is to be deprived of his reason, which is necessary for human society. The second is to be obliged to live with those who are without reason. These two calamities occurred in the unfortunate marriage of Monsieur and Madame Mazarin. . . . When the husband is an extravagant, unjust and inhuman, he becomes a tyrant and breaks the tie he has contracted with his wife. The separation is done by right; judges do not do it, they simply publicly confirm it by solemn declaration.[7]

Factum and counterfactum centered on the Mazarin case would prolong the public debate over legal separation and divorce for decades to come. This case for legal separation became the first of its kind to be aired in the international media, and it generated published treatises and arguments about the legal rights of women in marriage. In her famous response to John Locke's theory of natural law, the feminist philosopher Mary Astell composed the essay "On Marriage" and opened it with the story of the Duchess Mazarin. In Paris, the playwright Jean Regnard produced a play called *The Divorce,* in which he incorporated arguments from the trial.

The judgment in favor of Duke Mazarin was rendered on December 29, 1689. Hortense was ordered to return to France and take up residence temporarily in the convent of Sainte-Marie de Chaillot, then return to her husband. She was in a difficult position, with considerable debt. "I would rather die," she wrote to her sister Marianne, "than return to M. Mazarin, and I would have almost as much aversion to spending the rest of my days in a convent."[8] She was offered the option of joining Mary Beatrice of Modena in her residence in exile at Saint-Germain, but the prospect of living so close to Paris and a legally fortified Armand-Charles made Hortense nervous. Saint-Evremond argued vigorously against it. And though she was burdened by debt and uncertain of her future in London, she did have a strong coterie of friends there. Saint-Evremond and others were willing to loan her considerable sums of money.

In letters written to friends and family in France, Hortense eloquently pleaded her own case (some thought her letters bore Saint-Evremond's mark). "I stayed longer than I should have and as long as I could with a husband who was so opposed to me; in the end I left for good reason a man who I had been attached to out of obedience. My just disengagement cost me the wealth that the world heard so much about, but liberty is never too dear for those who deliver themselves from tyranny."[9] She pointed out that even were she to return to France, she could not do so legally without first settling her debts in England. She wrote Marianne, her brother, Philippe, and Philippe's wife asking that they attempt to persuade the duke to help settle her debts, but Mazarin's response was clear: he was interested in only one outcome of the legal case. He wrote to Marianne:

> I declare to you that I am pursuing and will continue to pursue justice until I receive a judgment that provides a remedy that all the useless negotiations have not been able to provide, which is to force her to do her duty. That is the only motive that leads me to take this action, and if she had an ounce of courage she would come to France and dispute the matter with me here, instead of cutting such a miserable figure in England.[10]

None of the efforts of the many parties involved in this legal battle led to a significant change in the couple's ongoing estrangement. The duke had won his case, but he could not forcibly bring his wife to Paris. The duchess failed to retrieve some of her lost wealth, but her friends continued to provide her with financial support, and she refused to return to France. After James II invaded England from France in a failed attempt to recover his throne, the war between the two countries expanded, postal connections were broken, and communication was difficult. Hortense held on to her life as best she could, moving to a smaller home in Kensington in 1692 and an even smaller one in Chelsea in 1694. All the while she continued to host her famous social gatherings, attract a steady stream of visitors, and give her favorite pleasure, the gambling game of basset, her increasingly obsessive attention.

Hortense had managed to remain in contact with Marie over the years since they had parted ways in Chambéry. In London, Hortense and Mary Beatrice had both been surprised to learn how much the English public already knew about the Mancini family, beginning with the sensation that had been caused by the story of Marie's tragic romance with Louis XIV. Hortense's memoirs, then the two versions of Marie's life story, were translated and published in England almost as soon as they were written. And as both sisters boldly tested the range of options available to them once they had made the decision not to return to their husbands, each was also aware of the moves that the other was making, and they consulted with each other. When Marie felt trapped in her Madrid convent, she proposed, on more than one occasion, that she be permitted to join Hortense in London, and when Hortense became depressed about her prospects in England she wrote to Marie that she was considering joining her in Madrid. Both of them eagerly received reports of the other from travelers to the courts of England and Spain, who brought news based on personal contact as well as what was available in the gazettes, always eager to print news of the fascinating sisters.

Unlike her sister, Marie had managed to orchestrate a reunion with her husband and children, which took place in July 1678, when the constable arrived in Madrid to officially accept his new appointment as Viceroy of Aragon. The two had not seen each other in more than six years, nor had Marie seen her sons, who by now were twelve, fourteen, and fifteen years old. Lorenzo's traveling party also included Ortensia Stella, Marie's close friend and Lorenzo's mistress. If Hortense read the *Gazette of Madrid*, she certainly would have been surprised by its account of the couple's warm reunion. "The very day of his arrival," the gazette reported, "Signor the Constable stopped at the convent of Santo Domingo el Real where Madama is living. They exchanged the most lively expressions of joy and tenderness, which lends more hope for their imminent reconciliation."[11] It was publicly understood that the two had reached an agreement whereby Marie would accompany her husband to Saragossa and there arrangements would be made for them to live in the same city, but separately. Another convent was acceptable to Marie, provided that she would not be cloistered. As expected, Lorenzo wrote to the pope formally requesting approval for the arrangement. But what was not known was that he had also written a letter to Cardinal Cibo in Rome asking him to ensure the refusal of his own request. By this duplicitous move he hoped to save face and be perceived as conciliatory, while also guaranteeing that he could force Marie back to Rome.

It was a long time before Marie realized what a cynical trap had been laid for her. Lorenzo stayed in Madrid for eight months, sending Ortensia and his sons ahead to Saragossa. It seemed to observers that the couple were working toward some kind of mutual agreement, if not reconciliation. Marie entered into the discussions Lorenzo was having with the Duke of Medina Celi as the families arranged the marriage of Filippo Colonna to Laurencia Medina Celi. The Colonna couple paid court to the new prime minister, Don Juan of Austria, and King Carlos. Lorenzo tried to position himself as safely as possible between the young king and Don Juan's ministry, which looked favorably on him but was itself vulnerable to reprisals from the exiled queen regent. Don Juan's term in power was in fact short-lived. On September 17, 1679, he died suddenly, possibly of poisoning. By then Lorenzo had left for Saragossa, leaving Marie in Santo Domingo el Real with instructions that she remain cloistered there.

Throughout the winter, spring, and summer months of 1679, Marie would correspond with the Colonna household in Saragossa, keeping in close touch with the Countess Stella there. Marie attempted, at a distance, to take on some supervision of the education of her sons, designating the countess as her representative. "Do not hesitate to make use of the permission I gave you," she wrote her friend, "and if you don't want to act in your own name use mine, for I very much desire my children make a favorable impression through their fine qualities."[12] Marie insisted that her children receive good instruction in Spanish; she pressed Ortensia for information about who was tutoring them. She wanted her sons to write her in Spanish and noticed when their letters seemed to have been dictated by a tutor who was not competent in the language. "Tell me honestly," she wrote to Ortensia, "who dictated that letter that he wrote to me? I have never seen anything so contrary to the Spanish style."[13] There is an intimacy and affection in all of these letters, expressed not only for her sons but for Ortensia as well. Marie thought that plans were being made to have both women live in Saragossa, with Marie being granted a residence separate from her husband there. To Ortensia, she said only that she would like to be able to see her, though it is not clear whether the two of them had seen each other in Madrid. "I have for you all the friendship that you could wish," she wrote, "but it will not be without regret that I leave Madrid where I would be more happy to see you than there, as I don't know how I will feel there and here I am in good health, which is not how I have felt in other places."[14] The two women exchanged gifts, the countess sending an assortment of goods to Marie and also to her serving maid Nanette. "I cannot tell you how I admire you," wrote Marie on March 18. "Nothing is more beautiful and in good taste than the box that you sent me and all that was in it. The boxes of soap, the powders, the two agnus dei, the box of whale oil creams, all arrived safely and I send you a thousand thanks. . . . Nanette thanks you also for the punctuality with which you sent her the package."[15] Ortensia had brought gifts with her on the voyage from Rome, and she also sent her items obtained in Saragossa that were difficult for the cloistered Marie to obtain in Madrid. On January 21, when Lorenzo was still in Madrid, Marie wrote to the countess inquiring about her son Marcantonio, who had been ill.

> I have learnt about Marcantonio's illness and his recovery at the same time, if it had not been so I would have been much afraid. Embrace all three of them for me and tell them that it would be the greatest consolation in the world to have them here, for I love them and wish for them to continue to give me cause for affection. They must learn Spanish well, and do all their lessons. . . . I am waiting for the powders and also some guitar cord. . . . See if there is someone who would like to sell some to me and I will buy it. In the meantime please believe that I bear you the same friendship that you have always known from me.[16]

Marie's hesitation about any arrangement that would take her from Madrid was due in part to her sense that her political contacts stood a chance of improving there. The year 1679 was a crucial one in Spain's gradual reconciliation with France, with which relations had historically been more belligerent than peaceful. It was a period of great political uncertainty but also one in which Spain's position in Europe was recovering strength. Early in the year the Spanish had signed a treaty with France. Louis XIV sealed the alliance with the betrothal of his niece Marie-Louise d'Orléans to the eighteen-year-old Carlos II, and the French faction in Madrid looked forward to a period of prosperity and influence. The marriage was conducted by proxy at Fontainebleau in August 1679, and on January 13, 1680, Marie-Louise made her ceremonial entrance into Madrid. Along with other French courtiers, Marie Colonna was on the balcony of the home of her brother-in-law the Marquis de Los Balbases, watching the lavish parade. The royal entrance was stunning in its colorful display of wealth and military strength. Marie-Louise, mounted on horseback and weighed down with layers of heavy, rich fabric and jewels, passed under a series of arches that had been built for the occasion. It took all day for the different militias, titled noblemen, and liveried squires to pass through the city. Marie watched in fascination, delight, and, like so many others who knew both the lovely sixteen-year-old Marie-Louise and the sickly, half-crazed Carlos, with pity.

In Saragossa, Lorenzo learned of his wife's presence at the festivities that accompanied the arrival of the French princess. He had known that Marie would not be able to bear remaining cloistered as the city celebrated the royal marriage. In fact, he had told her she could leave the convent to join the spectators on that occasion, but he changed his mind. He had obtained a letter from the pope denying Marie permission to live on her own, and he decided that he would use this written document to see that she was placed behind walls that were more secure. He knew that he could count on the assistance of the Marquis de Los Balbases, who was no friend of Marie, though he was adept at pretending to be when it was useful to him. Balbases had known Marie since she had married his wife's brother. Marie's distrust of him was tempered by their long acquaintance and her fondness for her sister-in-law. But now, as ever, the marquis was ready to do Lorenzo's bidding, and Marie somehow got wind of her husband's plan. Not knowing where to turn, she at first simply grabbed Morena, got into a carriage, and rode several times around the city, trying to decide what to do. Marie had been assured by a messenger from the newly arrived Princess Marie-Louise that she would have her support at the court of Spain. So she decided to ask for asylum from the French ambassador. Marie arrived at his home in a state of great agitation. The ambassador's wife, Madame de Villars, described the episode in a letter to a friend:

> She circled around the city in her carriage and alighted at our doorstep. So here she is with us, saying that she doesn't want to leave and that we would not want to put her in the street. She would be happy to speak with the papal nuncio. We gave her dinner and I did my best for her because in fact she is a pity to behold in the state she is in.[17]

Madame de Villars had not seen Marie since her own arrival in Spain, and at first she did not recognize the constabless. But when Marie lifted her veil she realized who it was:

> She approached a window with Monsieur de Villars and beckoned me toward her. . . . I remembered vaguely having seen someone who looked like her. Monsieur de Villars cried out, "It is Madame la connétable Colonna!, and I immediately began to pay her my compliments, but that was not her style. She came right to the point. She was crying and asked that we take pity on her. Let me say two words about her appearance, she has a lovely figure. A scarf in the Spanish style that covered just enough of her shoulders, and what shows is very attractive: her hair is in two long black tresses, tied up at the top with a beautiful ribbon the color of fire; the rest of her hair in great disorder, barely combed; beautiful pearls on her neck; an agitated air that would not be seemly on another but on her is quite natural and spoils nothing.[18]

Villars wrote to Louis XIV asking what he should do, and received a curt reply indicating that the king was not unsympathetic but did not want the lady to take shelter with the French ambassador. When the Constable Colonna was notified, he made a show of exhibiting a similar ambivalence. At first he had Marie sent to a small convent outside of the city, then he went to Madrid and escorted her back to the convent of Santo Domingo, surprising her friends by coming "every day to visit her and talk with her in the parlor, and behaving as gallantly toward her as a lover would do for a mistress."[19]

Marie did not know what to make of this. But by now she was familiar with her husband's capacity to keep her in a state of high anxiety, which he proceeded to do for several more months. She could count on the influence and protection of her French supporters and friends only to a limited extent. Even the young Queen Marie-Louise, who seemed to have a fondness for her, had not yet established a solid base of authority for herself at court. In her first year in Madrid, she was preoccupied with the difficulties of adapting to a grotesque marital life as well as some of the more extreme manifestations of intolerance and conservatism at the Spanish court. On June 30, 1680, she had been forced to accompany her husband as he presided over a huge mass confession and conviction of heretics in the Plaza Mayor. The procession included 120 accused prisoners and resulted in the burning of twenty-one condemned for heresy— the largest auto-da-fé ever conducted by the Inquisition.

Lorenzo Colonna's conciliatory behavior toward his wife lasted only until he had managed to finalize the terms of his son's marriage to the daughter of Duke Medina Celi, a negotiation that included securing a substantial financial contribution from Marie's own dowry. As soon as the marriage contract was concluded, Lorenzo returned to Saragossa, leaving Marie to reside in the house he had occupied in Madrid. For a few weeks Marie enjoyed the freedom of visits with the many French travelers newly arrived at the Spanish court, and the particular affection of the queen, who as the court was leaving for the Escorial palace outside of the city assured her that she would continue to be safe in Madrid. But a few days later, on a chilly October night, Marie awoke to the sound of her doors being broken down by the king's guards, who presented her with orders to go to the Alcazar fortress, in Segovia, to be locked up. Marie fought, grabbing a knife from the table next to her bed and managing to inflict a wound on one of the guards, but in the end she was dragged by the hair to a carriage where Don Ferdinando Colonna waited to escort her, along with Morena and another serving woman, to prison. Marie's friend the writer Madame d'Aulnoy would later remember the outrage that she felt upon hearing the news:

> She was driven all night in this way to the Segovia fortress, with two of her women, with no consideration for her rank or her reputation, even though she had done nothing to be treated so, she was at the time living in her husband's house, her only crime had been to refuse to return to Rome with the constable. . . . There were few people who did not sympathize with her suffering, saying that the promise that had been made to the queen was betrayed, that the king's name was used just to satisfy the animosity of Los Balbases. . . . This affair was a great shock to everyone and I knew all of the details because I was a good friend of that lady, who was good, in no way spiteful, and what people said about her was true, that she had never done harm to anyone but herself.[20]

The Alcazar, an austere medieval fortress perched high on a steep crag outside of Segovia, was the most secure prison imaginable. But with the help of her servant Morena, who was with her there, Marie managed to smuggle out letters. She wrote to anyone she thought might be able to assist her: Roman cardinals, Spanish royalty, French family, and friends. In London and Paris, Marie's family received the news. Hortense knew that her own influence with

Lorenzo was nil, but she was the first in the family to write to him
in protest:

> All the family has been extremely surprised to learn that Madame
> the Constabless has been put in prison at the very time that we were
> rejoicing in the prospect of an accommodation that seemed to be
> absolutely sincere. This thing, sir, seems so unimaginable to me that
> I can hardly believe it and I need to be informed of it by you per-
> sonally in order to give it credence. It seems to me that my sister
> has suffered too many misfortunes and does not deserve this last
> one. I pray, sir, that it will not be as great as suspicious people are
> saying that I should fear.[21]

Lorenzo found himself flooded with similar letters pleading with
him to come to his senses. The nuncio in Madrid, Savo Mellini,
wrote to Rome that he was concerned for Marie's health. It was an
unusually cold winter, and as the nights became colder she remained
locked behind the hard stone of the Alcazar. Months passed, offering no new hope of softening Lorenzo. Louis de Mercoeur, the
husband of Marie's deceased sister Laure-Victoire, wrote him at
the end of December, "I beg of you, do not refuse the moderation
that everyone is asking of you and that she deserves."[22] Marie's
sister Olympe was more explicit: "Things have reached a point
where there is no longer any hope for a reconciliation, which is why
I ask you to take a noble and durable position. . . . In the name of
God do not reduce her to despair. If my poor sister were to die
while she is imprisoned you would never console yourself for all
that everyone would say."[23] Meanwhile, in Madrid, Marie's
strongest ally, Queen Marie-Louise, could only watch in frustration
as her own attempts to assist her were ignored.

This went on for more than three months. Festivities celebrating
the coming marriage of Filippo and the daughter of Medina Celi

were being held in the family residences while the mother of the groom remained locked in a cell, cold and hungry. Then suddenly Lorenzo sent a letter to the queen declaring that he would be satisfied if Marie were to return to Madrid and once again enter a convent, this time not as a pensioner but as a novice, where she must take her vows and commit to remaining for the rest of her life. He declared that he would follow suit and enter the Order of Malta as a monk, if the pope so desired. The prospect was preposterous. No one could think of two people less inclined toward religious life, and most thought that Marie would refuse, but she was so weak and her living conditions so deplorable that she agreed, then was made to wait until mid-February while Lorenzo argued over the details.

By March 1681, Marie had entered the novitiate of the convent of San Jeronimo in Madrid. Madame d'Aulnoy was present at the solemn ceremony and visited her friend often in subsequent months. In her *Memoirs of the Court of Spain*, she describes Marie's return to Madrid and her life in the convent:

> She was brought back to Madrid on February 15 1681, where she immediately was shut up amongst the nuns of the Conception of the Order of St. Jerome. She was so afflicted at her misfortunes that she would see nobody but her children. She told them she looked upon herself to be the most unfortunate creature in the world and that she was going to do a thing which might cost her the repose of her life, that she beheld the consequences of it with terror, but that nevertheless she was resolved to undergo it, because she had given her promise. In effect, she went down into the choir where everything was prepared for the ceremony, and she took upon her the habit of a novice, but with a formal design to die rather than make profession. She wore a petticoat of gold and silver brocade under her woolen robe and when she was not in company with any of the nuns she would throw her veil aside and put a coif upon her

head after the Spanish mode, dressed with ribbons of all colors. Sometimes it so happened that the bell rung to chapel, where she was obliged to make her appearance by the rule of her order, and the mistress of the novices coming to inform her of it, she clapped on her frock and veil over her ribbons and her loose hair. This made a very odd and comical figure and nobody could have forborne laughing at it had not her miseries on the other hand drawn the compassion of all persons that knew her, for indeed her condition was very necessitous, she wanted money, had but mean eating, and yet worse lodging.[24]

Lorenzo remained in Madrid just long enough for the marriage of his son on April 20, 1681, a sumptuous affair conducted in the absence of Filippo's mother. The Madrid gazettes reported that "the young seigneur was much afflicted, for he loved her tenderly. The day after the wedding the new couple went to the convent and were greeted with demonstrations of tenderness and joy by this most excellent of mothers."[25] Lorenzo then returned with his family and entourage to Rome. It remained to be determined what steps he would take to fulfill his part of the bargain, to take vows in the Order of Malta. Early in the following year the gazettes announced that Lorenzo had received a papal dispensation permitting him to join the order without taking vows of chastity and poverty and without embarking on the requisite pilgrimage to Jerusalem. He had managed finally to orchestrate a separation that suited him.

For the next few years Marie remained in Madrid, living in the convent but perpetually postponing the moment she would be expected to move forward from novice to nun. It did not take her very long, after Lorenzo's departure, to draw more effectively on the strength of her contacts at court and her friendship with Queen Marie-Louise. She was able to see people, even take excursions by carriage outside the convent walls. A succession of

French ambassadors came to visit her in her chilly room at San Jeronimo: "when the Constabless took me to her room I thought I would freeze to death," wrote Madame d'Aulnoy, "it was really nothing but an attic."[26] The papal nuncio Mellini was sympathetic, instructing the nuns to be lenient with Marie, and responding to letters from Rome inquiring about when she was going to take her vows, saying that it would be a sin for her to do so until she was ready. She was allowed to receive presents, blankets, shawls, and embroidered clothing that she wore under a habit that she kept only loosely covering her shoulders. She recovered her lost gaiety and began to enjoy amusing her visitors and friends. She acquired a little spaniel, adorned with bracelets, collar, and even earrings all made of gold. Even King Carlos, who seemed powerless to arrange her release, was envious and immediately declared that he wanted a dog just like hers.

Lorenzo was occupied in Rome with other concerns, so he did not give his usual attention to the reports he was receiving from Madrid. He had not returned to Rome with his wife, but the palazzo Colonna did have a new mistress in the person of Filippo's bride, Laurencia, and the couple began to make their residence a centerpiece of Roman society comparable to what it had been under Marie and Lorenzo. The theater that had been constructed while Marie lived there was restored and once again became the site of concerts, operas, and plays. But Lorenzo struggled to resume his former supreme status among Roman nobility; he was no longer consistently invited to lead the cavalcade in the annual *chinea*. He no longer seemed to be held in high favor by Pope Innocent XI, who was perhaps impatient with Lorenzo's history of demands regarding his broken conjugal life. He spent increasingly longer periods on his country estates. When in 1687 he wrote to Cardinal Cibo, secretary to the pope, to press once again for Marie's return to Rome, Cibo addressed a perfunctory letter to the nuncio in

Madrid but Mellini's response indicated how weakened Lorenzo's position had become. "Nothing can diminish the aversion that she feels toward her husband's home," he wrote. "Furthermore, if anyone should solicit His Majesty to put Madame in that fortress again, I think it would be a request that would never be granted, because the queen is entirely on her side and would never permit that such violence would be used on her again."[27] The result was quite the opposite of what Lorenzo had wished for: Marie was moved to more comfortable lodgings with the Order of Calatrava in Madrid, where she enjoyed the freedom to enter and exit as she wished.

Late in 1688, Lorenzo found himself grief-stricken by the sudden death of a close friend, and he could not manage to recover from his sadness and shock. He called for priests to attend to him as he contemplated his own mortality. He began to follow daily exercises of piety, going out into the streets to give money to the poor and instructing his confessor to provide funds and shelter to prostitutes if they would promise to reform their errant ways. He felt his own health declining, even when told that his symptoms were not serious, and he became increasingly preoccupied with what his confessor described as "the violence and disorder of his past life."[28] By March his illness was taken seriously by everyone. His sons and sisters gathered in the palazzo, where Lorenzo addressed each of them, giving his blessing to his children and urging them to reform their faults and not imitate their father. One of the priests asked him to say something about his wife, and as the confessor recounted in a report prepared later,

> He replied at once in the presence of everyone that he had always loved her in the depths of his heart and that he greatly regretted not having given her more satisfaction in everything, that he urgently wanted his feelings to be conveyed to her; then he added that he had written a letter in which he declared his feelings for her. Calling

his son from the next room he recommended to him, in everyone's presence, the respect and love that he owed "his most excellent mother," and he left her to his care and that of his brothers.[29]

It was perhaps this letter from Lorenzo, given to their son to transmit to her, that inspired in Marie the grief that she expressed when she learned of her husband's death in April 1689. The international gazettes were filled with reports of the event coupled with accounts of Marie's reaction to the death and reminders of her travels and her husband's mistreatment of her. The French *Mercure historique et politique* reported that

> Madame the Constabless Colonna seemed greatly afflicted by the death of her husband and it is said that she would see no one but the Marquise of Balbases. If the tears of Madame Colonna are quite sincere, one could say that this lady is very generous to regret a husband who kept her locked up in a convent while she seemed in no way destined for the cloister, and this husband further had seemed so unbearable to her that she took great risks to get away from him.[30]

In her private letters to Filippo and to Ortensia Stella, Marie expressed genuine sadness and certainly more grief than Lorenzo's sister, who could only comment that her brother "had lived like an assassin and a hedonist."[31]

Lorenzo's death must have seemed to the Duke Mazarin one more indication that the time was ripe for him to make one final desperate attempt to force his own wife to return to him. He had followed closely all of the tactics Lorenzo employed, and noted their failures. When he wrote to Mary Beatrice of Modena to declare his own intention to bring a legal case against Hortense, he seemed to be passing judgment on the strategies to which Lorenzo had resorted. He was not interested in committing his wife to a convent, where he feared she would be allowed visitors and salon-style conversations. He wanted her returned to his personal supervision. By the end of the year Armand-Charles had been vindicated by the courts. But like Lorenzo, he would find that only death would bring a definitive resolution to the battle he had been waging.

# ( 10 )

## "DUST *and* ASHES"

*And yet I did not lose heart for having seen my attempts at freeing myself turn out so badly, and conscious that freedom is the richest treasure in the world and that a noble and generous spirit must stop at nothing to acquire it or to recover it after having lost it, I applied my efforts once again to obtaining it.*

—Marie Mancini, *The Truth in Its Own Light*

HE DECISION OF THE Grand Council court in Paris had been in favor of the Duke Mazarin, but the duchess refused to obey the order to return to France. She remained in London, close to the court of William and Mary, though not in favor there, and she no longer had access to the apartment at Whitehall. To her friends, she expressed no regret over being excluded from the new elite society surrounding the king and queen, which everyone said was anything but animated. William suffered from asthma, which seemed to be aggravated by the damp palace air. Almost immediately after arriving in London in 1689, the royal couple commissioned Christopher Wren to expand the buildings of Kensington palace to make it a more suitable residence for them, and the court was transferred there at the end of that same year. When fire broke out and destroyed much of Whitehall palace in 1698,

William was quite content to know that he never would have to return to that chilly and damp residence along the banks of the
Thames. The Duchess Mazarin moved her own residence to 15
Kensington Square sometime in 1690. It was a smaller house than
her "little palace" in Saint James's Park but was located in a rapidly
growing and fashionable district just down the street from the new
royal palace. She maintained this residence for a time as her lodging
close to the court but sometime in 1693 acquired another, more
modest home on Paradise Row in Chelsea, where she spent an increasing amount of time in the years that followed. It was an effort
to economize, bemoaned by Saint-Evremond and others who found
the neighborhood isolated and entirely too far from the hustle and
bustle of the city. Hortense dismissed their worries and held to
her habitual lifestyle, continuing to host regular social gatherings
in her new home and making her own way about the city without
concern for the dangers of returning home alone late at night. She
held chamber concerts, some of them short operas with such titles
as *The Chelsea Concert* and *The Basset Scene*, that played out on stage
the conversations, music, and gambling for which her gatherings
continued to be well known.

During this time, France and England were at war, and would
remain so until 1697. Within London, many friendships of long
standing were broken and new alliances formed. Hortense was accustomed to loyalty in her friendships. If she had survived different
regimes and cultural environments in the years since fleeing from
Paris, it was not because she knew how to cynically manipulate
different political interests. Her feelings were never hard to read,
and she had pursued her pleasures openly, confronted her enemies,
and held fast to her friends. Saint-Evremond had little luck persuading her to pay court to the new figures in power and to forget
those who had fallen from it. You must do as I do, said the old
exile: "I always have an unwavering attachment to the present gov-

ernment of the country in which I reside." Hortense laughed at him, but their friendship withstood these rough years. They saw each other almost daily, and wrote letters when they were apart. He sent her his favorite books and they continued to discuss the ones they both enjoyed—*Don Quixote,* and historical tales of the loves of Henry IV—and he persisted in his affectionate mockery of her stubborn fondness for pastoral romance. She became annoyed with him for producing verse praising only the English victories in the war, and he replied that the French victories did not inspire him.

When the French won the battle of Namur, Saint-Evremond stubbornly refused to share in Hortense's satisfaction. Hortense's daughter Marie-Olympe had a husband fighting with the French. In August 1692 he was killed in the battle of Steenkerque. Hortense was corresponding with her London friends from Bath, where she was taking the waters to try to heal a leg injury from a fall. Saint-Evremond wrote to her that her salon habitués all had come together to bemoan the sad military news, and then finished by drinking cheerfully to her health: "We drank to your health thrice: we started with approval, from approval we went to praise, and from praise to admiration. As tenderness and pity are normally mixed with praise, while drinking we regretted the misfortune of your condition, and I had difficulty stopping all the murmuring against Providence for having made the daughter a widow, instead of the mother."[1] And so it went—the circle of friends sought above all to keep their pleasures alive during the difficult war years.

Political positions were hardening on both sides. In his advanced age, Louis XIV was increasingly intolerant of religious practices that were not Catholic. After he revoked the Edict of Nantes in 1685, thousands of Protestants had fled the country, causing France to lose precious resources and a significant portion of its educated population. In England, William of Orange, after the death of his wife, Mary, in 1694, embraced a harder line in favor of the Protestants, as he strove to strengthen his hold over Parliament. When the Nine Years' War ended with the Treaty of Rijswijk in 1697, the English had won important concessions from Louis XIV, including his recognition of William as king, but it was a fragile peace, not destined to last for long.

Although the Duchess Mazarin watched her own financial and political support weaken, she nonetheless had the pleasure of realizing that her public image as both wronged wife and female libertine continued to fascinate. Although moralistic condemnation of the lifestyle she had embraced continued and even increased, the cause of unhappily married women, which she had come to symbolize, was aired more openly in the 1690s than ever before. Several prominent women brought divorce cases before the House of Lords, and forced or unhappy marriages were discussed and acted out on the stage in plays by female playwrights. Even writers who took a more conservative view of marriage, such as the philosopher Mary Astell, who lived down the street from Hortense in Chelsea, acknowledged that the Mazarin case illustrated circumstances that no wife should have to endure.

Marie had managed to remain informed of Hortense's life through the years, sometimes sporadically, but she knew her sister's fortunes were in decline. In a letter to Countess Ortensia Stella, she conveyed her sister's good wishes and reported on her difficult situation:

> Madame de Mazarin asks me especially for news of you and tells me that she still has a great fondness for you. Since she thinks I am in Rome, she asks me to pay my compliments to Cardinal Guici and assure him that she will never forget her obligation to him. Please have someone tell him that. It is she who has been in a very bad state for some time, she has no pension, and no help coming from any side. It is only gambling that sustains her.[2]

A series of letters by Saint-Evremond to the Duchess Mazarin and other friends provides the closest look at what her life had become by the spring of 1699, in the months leading up to her death. Her old friend was appalled to see her take so little care for her health, as she began to drink in amounts that even for him seemed excessive. He was terrified at the prospect of outliving his younger companion, who by then was fifty-three. She spoke to Saint-Evremond of taking a final "retreat" that might bring her "relief," and he replied to her anxiously, trying to maintain the light tone that had been the foundation of both of their approaches to life in what is thought to be his last letter to her:

> The horrible retreat that you speak of would be no more so for you than for me. When you are happy, I am satisfied; when you have cause to grieve over your condition, it is reason for me to grieve over mine. Your strength makes me believe that you will endure for a little longer the poor state of your affairs; and your good sense should keep your mind from latching on to the hope of imaginary and false relief. Hope, Madam, that your troubles will come to an end. Leave beer aside, drink your wine, and let Mustapha lift your spirits with his usual inspiration that he draws from drink. That works better against ill fortune than the consolation offered by Seneca to Marcia.[3]

Was she grieving over a death, as the reference to Seneca might suggest? Was she unable to live with the inevitable signs of her own declining beauty? Or was she simply overwhelmed by the diminished state of her financial affairs, as the letter also indicates? When she refused company, it was clear to her friends that Hortense was depressed. By the beginning of June 1699 she was spending most of her time in solitude, drinking alarming quantities of her favorite eau-de-vie. By mid-June she was refusing to eat. Her behavior was not merely self-destructive; it had become suicidal. Saint-Evremond would later write a poem about her death in which it is clear that he believed she had deliberately killed herself by drinking.

Throughout June a flurry of letters circulated warning that she was ill. Her sister Marianne set sail from France to join her, as did Hortense's son, Paul-Jules. The Paris gazettes reported the news: "Madame the Duchess of Bouillon has just taken leave of the king who has given her permission to go to England to see her sister"; "we hear from London that Madame Mazarin is dangerously ill. The Duke of Meilleraye, her son, has rushed to join her, saying to his friends that he was taking money to her, which she badly needed." Meanwhile, Saint-Evremond persisted in his efforts to cheer his ailing friend and dissuade her from her sinister intent. But all was in vain. When Marianne arrived on the Dover coast, she was informed that her sister had died just days earlier, on July 2. Hortense's son had not arrived in time to speak with her. In her last days, she had refused all medical care and all visits, including that of a priest, and died, as one letter said, "without any manner of concern for what was past or what was to come."[4] Anyone arriving from France to claim her body could expect to confront her creditors. Marianne did not even disembark; her boat returned straightaway to France.

Saint-Evremond was inconsolable. "No one here speaks of Madame Mazarin's death without also speaking of your grief," wrote one of his friends. His lifelong friend Ninon de l'Enclos wrote him long, consolatory letters full of praise for a woman she had come to know only through Saint-Evremond's descriptions:

What a loss for you, Sir! If one didn't risk losing oneself it would be impossible to ever find consolation. I am so sorry for you, you have just lost a beloved companion who sustained you in a foreign land. What can be done to make up for such a misfortune? Those who live long lives must see their friends die. After this your mind and your philosophy must work to sustain you. I felt this death as though I had the honor to know Madame Mazarin. She thought of me in my troubles; I was touched by her goodness and what she was to you attached her to me. There is nothing to be done and there is no remedy for what happens to our poor bodies. Conserve yours.[5]

Saint-Evremond was left without his dear companion, and also without the huge sums of money he had loaned her. After a few months he was able to reflect with his characteristic dry wit on the position in which he now found himself. His French friends were urging him to make the return voyage home to live out his remaining years, where the aging king would surely forgive him the reasons for his exile, long in the past, but he declined.

Madame Mazarin cared little for the injustice that Nature did her; for no one ever died with so much resignation and fortitude. I am afflicted every day by her loss. . . . The thought of what she owed me has no part in my sorrows. When I think that the niece of Cardinal Mazarin had need of me at a certain time in order to survive, I think Christian thoughts that will serve my salvation, even if they are useless in getting me repaid.[6]

The question of the duchess's debts had in fact provoked a macabre final chapter in the story of her life's adventures. Almost as soon as Marianne's boat had landed on the coast of France, the Duke Mazarin decided to officially claim his wife's body and have her returned to him, once and for all. But he was hindered by a tangle of legal impediments. Several of Hortense's creditors (though not Saint-Evremond) had engaged lawyers to prevent the disposal of her body without due payment of her debts. As one news gazette reported, the body of the duchess was "arrested": "Her body was first embalmed and it is thought that it will be sent to Paris to be interred in the church of the College of Four Nations, where there is a beautiful mausoleum for Cardinal Mazarin, her uncle and founder of this college. A few days after her death an individual to whom she owed money had her corpse arrested."[7] Armand-Charles found himself in an absurd situation: having steadfastly refused for decades to send money to Hortense while she was alive, he now was being forced to pay her expenses after she was dead. Faced with this dilemma, and to the surprise of many, the miserly duke decided to pay, though he negotiated a reduced sum, while Lord Montagu and other friends of the duchess contributed additional amounts. The duke finally welcomed Hortense home two months after her death, when the coffin carrying her remains was returned to him.

The ensuing spectacle was even more astonishing and eccentric, as all who knew the Duke Mazarin had come to expect. As if carrying out his revenge on Hortense's defiant ability to travel where and when she pleased, he traveled with her corpse throughout northern France, to all the places where she had so hated accompanying him during their marriage. Slowly and ceremoniously he transported the casket to each of his provincial estates before finally, four months later, allowing himself to be persuaded to deposit the coffin in the small church of Notre Dame de Liesse, near one of his country chateaux. The church was a pilgrimage site, housing a statue of the Virgin brought back from the Holy Land during the crusades. For years, until the duke's death in 1713, Hortense Mancini's coffin became one of the relics before which pilgrims prayed. In 1714 it was transported for burial next to her husband and uncle in the College of Four Nations in Paris.

When Marie learned of her sister's death, she was still living in Madrid, having returned there after briefly attempting, for a few months after Lorenzo's death, to live once again in Rome in the family palazzo with her son Filippo and his family. But the ghosts were too present there, and she was not inclined to play the largely invisible role of dowager princess. Still, she had been happy to find herself reunited with her sons. Carlo, the youngest, had come to Madrid immediately after his father's death to persuade her to return. His career was assured in the priesthood, with a likely advancement to cardinal. Marcantonio, too, had found success as a military officer. Marie's family was paying her a pension drawn on her dowry, which was adequate to give her the independence she had always craved. So she returned to Madrid, now free to make her own life there, and committed to serving her family's interests from afar, which she did with considerable energy. She maintained a regular correspondence with Filippo, offering advice on everything from household budgets to fashion to remedies for various health ailments. Filippo was patient, and satisfied to retain his connection with his mother, and indirectly with his Spanish in-laws, in this manner. When Filippo's wife, Laurencia, died, childless, in 1697, Marie supported his quick remarriage to young Olimpia Pamphili, daughter of one of the wealthiest families in Rome and niece of Pope Innocent VIII. The Colonna dynasty seemed assured.

Throughout these years Marie also maintained her close contact with Ortensia Stella. Filippo, perhaps not surprisingly, had been not particularly inclined to continue supporting his father's longtime mistress after Lorenzo died. It was Marie who urged him to treat her fairly, as indeed Lorenzo had requested in his will, where he also had officially recognized his paternity of two children by the Countess Stella. Ortensia had written her friend immediately after Lorenzo's death and Marie had responded, "I am more than persuaded of the sincerity of your affection and your feelings, having no doubt that you have as much interest as I in the loss that I have suffered, and that for the same reason it must be equally sensitive for you."[8] Surveying the consequences of Lorenzo's marital infidelities, Marie took a position that was not unlike that of many women of her time and social class. It was common to tolerate a husband's infidelity with a person of a lower station. Marie had left her friend vulnerable to pressure from Lorenzo when she had first decided to flee with only a few servants to accompany her. There seems to have never even been a question that the Countess Stella would join her. Instead, the two women had helped each other acquire what they each needed from Lorenzo's household. In the 1690s Marie continued to receive through the mail her favorite perfumes, powders, gloves, fans, jasmine oil, and other cosmetics from the countess. Ortensia urged her to return to Rome, and Marie replied affectionately that her friend should join her in Genoa, that she still could not tolerate Rome:

> I can't manage to tear you away from your fine house, household, and friends. But I would not like being in a city where the strife of business and the rigorous justice of priests is not to my taste. . . . Long live republics, and long live Spain and the good Countess, whom I love tenderly.
>
> C. Colonna[9]

Ortensia would ultimately call upon her old friend to help her in a vastly more delicate matter, asking that she persuade Filippo, the new Constable Colonna, to provide for the livelihood of her children who had been fathered by Lorenzo. And Marie did so, writing to her son and then, when the countess reported that he had not yet made any accommodation, lending further support and advising her on how to proceed:

> I am most annoyed to see that your troubles continue when I thought that it was all concluded as you had written to me in your last letter. The best thing is to have patience and be careful not to let these things be exposed to the public. That's what I advise you

in all friendship; I have also written Marcatelli asking that he dispose my son to do all that is reasonable. Please God that he will be able to give you some relief, as I will always do whenever the occasion presents itself. I have just written another time with this mailing to the Constable that he may see fit to give you what he can in all good conscience. Try to be accommodating as well, better to get something quietly than to get nothing after many scenes in court. Adieu, I hope that he will soon give you the happiness and repose that you need,

The C.C.[10]

Marie's efforts, though, were not sufficient to assure Ortensia's children of the income that had been promised them in Lorenzo's will. Ortensia and her son brought their case before judges in Rome in 1692 and won a settlement the following year. Although Marie managed in these years to remain involved and play a respected role, from a distance, in her family's affairs, the political climate in Spain had changed abruptly after her friend and ally Queen Marie-Louise died suddenly in 1689, at age twenty-six, of an attack of what seemed to be appendicitis. She had borne no children, so the disturbed and probably impotent King Carlos was married off quickly a second time, to the German Princess Mary Anna of Neuberg, who was selected for her likely fertility (her mother had borne twenty-three children). But no progeny came from this royal marriage either. By 1699 everyone was watching Carlos's demented behavior and speculating about what was likely to be a highly contested succession. The new Queen Mary Anna, with whom Marie had worked to ally herself, was not popular. She was prone to hysteria and suffered from the relentless pressure to conceive a child with an uncooperative husband; it was thought that she faked her miscarriages. She was perpetually leaving the court to seek relief in the homes of foreign nobility, who whispered that when she left she always seemed to carry off with her several objects of value.

Marie spent time with French visitors and residents of Madrid, including the mother of her friend Madame d'Aulnoy. Madame d'Aulnoy's mother, Madame de Gudannes, was not a good adviser to Marie; though she was certainly a very intelligent woman, she was noted for her duplicity and the ease with which she could play double agent when called upon to provide secret information. At different points in her career she had been employed by the French, the Spanish, and the Italians to acquire secret information of one kind or another. Her spying inevitably ended with her being thrown out of the country. As a political operator she had acquired a certain power over courtiers who feared blackmail, but she was hardly the best source of information or advice for someone like Marie. It was exciting, though, to participate in the conversations she hosted in her garden next to the family residence of the Admiral of Castille, where Marie had first been sheltered upon arriving in the city. Marie spent many mornings in this garden until Gudannes was suddenly and unceremoniously escorted out of Spain.

The death of the childless Carlos II in 1700 brought to a head tensions over the succession. Carlos himself had favored the French over the Austrian faction and on his deathbed designated Philippe d'Anjou, grandson of Louis XIV and Marie-Thérèse of Spain, as his heir. The young French prince would make his triumphal entry into Madrid on February 18, 1701. The new King Philip V drew around him and his thirteen-year-old bride, Marie Louise Gabriele de Savoie, a close coterie of French advisers and supporters. Marie wanted to be among these, and she angled for a position as governess to the young queen, but it was not to be. Louis XIV took a personal interest in selecting the French circle that he wanted to be able to control Spain. Marie's loyalties to France were hazy at best, and hers was not the exemplary life that would make an ideal centerpiece for the education of a princess.

And so in the decade that followed, Marie found herself once again traveling throughout Europe. In each spot where she settled, she found herself always a little too attracted to risk and intrigue, a little too trusting of all who offered her their friendship. In 1702 she rented a house in Avignon, where she met a shady character named Don Alfio Morando de Mazarin, who claimed to be a long-lost relative with strong ties to Versailles. Within three months she had signed over her rights to several important family legacies, much to the consternation of her sons. Later she fell almost as quickly in the thrall of another confidence man, this time a monk named Father Florent, whom she obliged by introducing him to various important and wealthy personages whom he proceeded to rob, shamelessly.

It was to bring suit against this renegade that she returned to Paris in 1704, for the first time in forty-four years, and the last time in her life. She found herself once again close to the French court and king. But neither Marie nor Louis made any attempt at a meeting. She did write to her son of how she felt to be once again in the city of her youth: "You will be surprised to know I am so close to Paris, in one of my brother's houses in the country, just a half league away. . . . Paris is well worth being seen by everyone. I find it much more beautiful than I had left it. The streets, the bridges, and the buildings are like nowhere else."[11] It would be only in the last two or three years of her life that Marie seemed to finally settle into a more peaceful rhythm for her existence, visiting her sons but living in her own homes in Genoa and Livorno, and returning frequently to her beloved Venice.

It was in Pisa, Italy, on the morning of May 10, 1715, that the Reverend Father Ascanio was interrupted at his duties in the church of Santo Sepulcro by a servant come to tell him that Princess Colonna was in the city and was summoning him to the home of her relative the Duke Salvati. Ascanio was surprised. He had known Marie Mancini Colonna since the years immediately following the death of her estranged husband, when she had first dared to return to Italy from her long exile in Spain. She had found in this intelligent Spanish monk a sympathetic listener and adviser whenever she was in Pisa, and had come to rely on him for advice on matters legal as well as spiritual. He had counseled her on the writing of her will. But her sons and family residence were in Rome, and Ascanio had not, on this occasion, received any advance notice of her visit. As he walked to the Salvati palazzo he must have been perplexed and perhaps concerned, reflecting sadly on the lady's age and on the recent events that had befallen her, and marveling at the energy that kept this inveterate traveler perpetually on the road. Just a few months before, she had suffered two bereavements, first that of her younger sister, Marianne, Duchess of Bouillon, and then an even heavier blow, the death of her eldest son, Filippo. Marianne's death had been sudden and entirely unexpected. Of the surviving Mancini siblings, she was known as the one with the most charming temperament, always lively, always seeming innocent and youthful. Upon receiving the letter informing her of this death, Marie must have thought back to many moments in her own adventurous life when her young sister had been one of her few loyal friends. Filippo's death had been less of a surprise, as it came at the end of a long illness, but he was her firstborn son. He had been the first to forgive her for leaving her children behind when she fled her husband's household, and in later years he had been her most faithful family correspondent. Father Ascanio had heard that Marie Colonna had made a hurried and exhausting voyage by carriage from Livorno to Rome, arriving just in time to hold her son in her arms as he died.

Now this seventy-five-year-old woman had traveled from the residence where she had been living in Livorno, and was back in Pisa, urgently asking to speak with him. The good priest was sympathetic, but he also had other obligations to attend to and his own health was failing. He knew how demanding she could be and prepared himself to urge her to be patient. He was not ready on that day for the intense and lengthy conversations that he knew she would require. When he arrived at the Salvati residence, he later wrote in his report of the events, he

> beseeched her Excellency not to visit him as was her habit, because it was the day that the courier was scheduled to come take the mail going to Spain, and the Reverend Father would be extremely busy. I repeated several times to Madame that I would ask her to think of me as *dead* on that day, and having said that I returned to my lodging thinking only of the writing I needed to do, and not dreaming that Madame was to make that impossible.[12]

At noon she suddenly appeared in his doorway, saying she had been praying at the Carmelite church and wanted him to explain a passage from the gospel to her. "I satisfied this pious request," he reported, "and then accompanied her back to the Salvati residence, again repeating that I wanted her to think of me on that day as being in the other world."[13]

But at the end of the day she appeared once more at the door of the Santo Sepulcro priory, and this time she simply stared intently at Father Ascanio and the papers and books surrounding him, before collapsing on the floor. Doctors were called, but they could do nothing to reverse the attack of "apoplexy," or stroke; they could only lift her onto the monk's cot, where she died a few hours later. It was left to Ascanio to alert her household in Pisa and write a letter reporting the sad news to her two surviving sons and their families, while Marie's personal chaplain, Father Delmas, was summoned to take the inventory of her belongings at the time of her death, beginning with the objects she had brought with her to Pisa and finishing with a list of the items in her household in Livorno.

Anyone who didn't know the owner of these materials would have understood, at first look, that they were the property of a noblewoman with considerable wealth. But examined more closely, the inventory of the deceased's personal belongings had some mysterious aspects. The contents of the lady's wardrobe were impressive—they included a vast amount of fine clothing and luxury items, and there was perhaps even more than the usual array of laces and rich fabrics: satins, velvet, Indian silks and cottons, and finely embroidered linens. Their owner had traveled and had exotic tastes. She possessed numerous Spanish mirrors, combs, and fans, which were carefully packed in a small metal chest lined with green velvet, and she had two soft velvet cushions for her little pet dogs. She had traveled from Livorno to Pisa in her personal carriage, designed in the modern style with glass windows, and upholstered in the traditional red velvet. Back in Livorno she left several other means of transportation, unusual for an elderly widow: along with horses and mules she owned a light two-wheeled carriage designed for speedy travel and a small movable seat called a flying chair, which could be rigged to whisk its rider from an upper floor down the open stairwell to make a dramatic appearance when receiving guests. She was educated: there were books, mostly translated volumes of classical Roman authors such as Juvenal and Virgil. In Livorno there were also many fabrics and tapestries but almost no works of art— no family portraits or paintings decorating the walls, a most unusual absence for a person of her standing, and especially for a noblewoman who had been famous as a great art patron. The galleries of paintings and statuary in the palazzo Colonna were the envy of the European nobility, and Marie and her husband alone had amassed more than 4,000 works of art. But as a woman who had made the radical choice to abandon her husband's household, Constabless Colonna had forfeited all claim to the treasured possessions she had acquired during her marriage, a legal restriction that her sons had continued to observe even after their father's death.

In fact, most of the items in the inventory Father Delmas prepared were designated as legally owned not by Marie Colonna but by her sons, to whom they were to be returned after her death. Among the objects held in her own name were only two of any exceptional value, but they were stunning. It was striking, too, that she had carried these items with her even on what was essentially a personal business trip to take counsel from Father Ascanio. Though the two items were small, Father Delmas, who knew the stories behind them, must have been struck by their beauty and by the incongruous decision that had been made to bring them on this particular voyage. The first was a pair of diamond-encrusted brooches, exquisitely designed, which had been offered to Marie as a wedding gift from her husband, Lorenzo. And the second was a magnificent strand of royal jewels, thirty-five large pearls that had been given to Marie in 1659, one year before her marriage, by Louis XIV.

"I do not know that I have any debts," Marie had written in her will, "but if I do they must be paid forthwith by my heirs." What pride and what struggle she had felt and undergone in the fifty-five years since these two prize jewels had come into her possession, and how determined she had been to keep them in her possession through her life of wealth and poverty, independence, despair, and exhilaration. In her memoirs she had described these objects as pieces of her identity, the only jewels she had taken with her on that warm day in 1672 when she fled her husband, never to return. "And so I set out on the twenty-ninth of May, carrying no more on my person than seven hundred pistoles, my pearls, and some diamond pendants." In her travels the jewels only made her more vulnerable to the constant risk of robbery or capture, but she had always seemed to view them as a charm, somehow protecting her from danger. Father Delmas, studying them, would have appreciated the strength and beauty of this strand of gems that had survived such an adventurous and volatile life's itinerary. The pearls were legendary, like their owner and like the king who had given them.

The pearls had stayed with Marie throughout her years in Rome as wife to the Grand Constable Colonna. She had worn them as she sat for portraits done by the celebrated artists who found patronage from the Colonna family: Pierre Mignard, Jacob-Ferdinand Voet, Carlo Maratta, Gaspard Dughet. She had taken them with her when she and her sister Hortense became fugitives, causing her servants much anxiety but somehow having a magical and quieting effect on the two ladies, who had amazed their small entourage by calmly going into the woods and falling asleep as they waited for the boatman who had promised to take them to France.

Even during her most difficult years in Madrid in the 1680s, when Marie was desperate to find allies against her husband's efforts to have her imprisoned, she had kept Louis's gift close to her and even worn her pearls in the most incongruous of circumstances. When Father Delmas recorded the pearls in his inventory of Marie's possessions at death, he knew her intentions for them. She had made it clear in her will. They were never to be sold, and must remain in her family for all time.[14]

A few months after Marie's final conversation with Father Ascanio, on September 1, 1715, Louis XIV died of a gangrenous infection, bringing to an end his fifty-five-year reign, at the time the longest in European history.

Even in death, Marie wanted to leave a trace of a life committed to mobility and independence. She left instructions that she be buried wherever she was when she died. Her youngest son, Carlo, carried out her wishes, arranging her burial in Pisa. Inside the church of the Santo Sepulcro on the floor just inside the main door, the attentive visitor may still find her tombstone with the simple marker in Latin that she had requested:

MARIA MANCINI COLUMNA, Pulvis et cinis.
*Maria Mancini Colonna*, dust and ashes.

Marie's wishes for a modest marker for her grave, and for a final resting place wherever her life's travels came to an end, seem to reflect a peace that she managed to achieve in her later years, and an acceptance of the unpredictable and vagrant life she had come to see as the only one that would give her the freedom she desired. The events surrounding Hortense's death and burial, on the other hand, seem to dramatize just how grotesquely difficult her risky life choices had been. Yet both sisters had decided, early in life, to pursue adventures that were unprecedented for women of their time, and that they knew would lead, inevitably, to more exposure to public condemnation than they could even dream of. They embraced the notoriety that came to them, publishing their own memoirs in response to the many accounts of their lives being circulated by a European society that found them fascinating. They were frequently at the center of public controversies, admired by libertines, feminists, and free-thinkers but viewed by others as frivolous at best and threats to civil society at worst.

There were many "firsts" in the lives of these two sisters. They were arguably the first media celebrities, in the earliest years of journalism, when news of prominent people and current events was just beginning to be given circulation in print. Hortense was the first Frenchwoman not of royal blood to print her life story under her own name, and Marie followed suit one year later. Marie was already a writer who had seen her work into print, having been arguably the first woman in Europe to author a book on astrology. The 1689 legal dispute between the Duke and Duchess Mazarin became the first divorce case to be aired in the media. Hortense was the first woman to be included in turn-of-the-century treatises about famous gamblers. The sisters were among the first women to travel for pleasure, adventure, and escape. Both sisters served as examples to the first generation of free-thinkers and feminists in France and England who were broadening an older philosophical discussion on the equality of women to include a critique of marriage and arguments for the rights of women to live, own property, and move about independently. The claims that they made for their own autonomy became part of these public debates.

In the years following the end of Louis XIV's reign, there was an explosion of writing about his court and the lives of those who had helped him to create it. From the beginning, historians had trouble figuring out what to make of the two notorious nieces of Cardinal Mazarin. But even their most severe judges acknowledged the impact the two women had made on the imaginations, and often the lives, of their contemporaries. Some echoed the warnings of Pope Innocent XI, who had declared ominously that the Mancini sisters exemplified a new "class of women."[15] Others would give a more positive spin to that assessment, labeling the sisters "les illustres aventurières"—an epithet that paired their scandalous adventures with their education and accomplishments in the world of high culture. That women could have "adventures" of their own choosing, leave their families in favor of a life on the road, and then survive, even find pleasure in the risks that accompanied such choices, was viewed as the stuff of fiction. Hortense and Marie would continue to surprise, scandalize, and delight all who came into contact with their amazing stories. From the beginning of their adventures the sisters had recognized that their lives, in Hortense's words, would "seem like something out of a novel." But the plot was one that they were determined to construct for themselves, in a perpetual process of self-invention and renewal aimed at showing everyone what Marie described simply as "the truth in its own light." ✳

# NOTES

All translations of original material into English are by the author unless otherwise indicated.

## HISTORICAL PROLOGUE

1. www.nationalarchives.gov.uk/education/civilwar/g5/cs1/s5.

2. Philippe Erlanger, *The Age of Courts and Kings* (New York: Harper & Row, 1967), p. 209.

3. Joan DeJean, *The Essence of Style: How the French Invented High Fashion, Fine Food, Chic Cafés, Style, Sophistication, and Glamour* (New York: Free Press, 2005), p. 208.

4. John Lough, *France Observed in the Seventeenth Century by British Travellers* (London: Oriel Press, 1985), p. 149.

## CHAPTER 1   THE CARDINAL'S NIECES AT THE COURT OF FRANCE

1. Marie Mancini, *The Truth in Its Own Light, or: The Genuine Memoirs of M. Mancini, Constabless Colonna,* in Hortense Mancini and Marie Mancini, *Memoirs,* ed. and trans. Sarah Nelson (Chicago: University of Chicago Press, 2008), p. 85.

2. Ibid., p. 86.

3. Ibid., p. 87.

4. Ibid., p. 90.

5. Pierre Adolphe Chéruel, ed., *Mémoires de Mademoiselle de Montpensier* (Paris: Charpentier, 1859), vol. 3, p. 352.

6. Françoise Bertaut de Motteville, *Memoirs of Madame de Motteville on Anne of Austria and Her Court,* trans. Katharine Prescott Wormeley (Boston: Hardy, Pratt, and Co., 1902), vol. 3, pp. 171–172.

7. Chéruel, *Mémoires de Mademoiselle de Montpensier,* vol. 3, p. 328.

8. Mancini, *Truth in Its Own Light,* p. 95.

9. Ibid.

10. *Memoirs of Mademoiselle de Montpensier* (London: H. Colburn, 1848), vol. 2, p. 478.

11. Motteville, *Memoirs of Madame de Motteville,* vol. 3, pp. 176–177.

12. Mancini, *Truth in Its Own Light,* p. 97.

13. Lucien Perey [Clara Adèle Luce Herpin], *Le Roman du grand roi, Louis XIV et Marie Mancini d'après des lettres et documents inédits* (Paris: Calmann Lévy, 1894), p. 169.

14. Mancini, *Truth in Its Own Light,* p. 96.

15. Jules Mazarin, *Cardinal Mazarin's Letters to Lewis XI, the Present King of France, On His Love to the Cardinal's Niece* (London: Bentley, 1691), pp. 172–173.

16. Ibid., pp. 164–165.

17. Perey, *Le Roman du grand roi,* p. 253.

18. Mazarin, *Cardinal Mazarin's Letters,* p. 185.

19. Perey, *Le Roman du grand roi,* p. 236.

20. Motteville, *Memoirs of Madame de Motteville,* vol. 3, p. 179.

21. Perey, *Le Roman du grand roi,* pp. 367–369.

22. Ibid., p. 370.

23. Ibid., p. 319.

24. Ibid., p. 318–319.

25. Ibid., p. 332.

26. Mancini, *Truth in Its Own Light,* p. 98.

27. Ibid., p. 100.

28. Ibid., p. 99.

29. Ibid., p. 100.

## CHAPTER 2   THE DUCHESS MAZARIN

1. In Hortense Mancini and Marie Mancini, *Memoirs,* ed. and trans. Sarah Nelson (Chicago: University of Chicago Press, 2008), p. 34.

2. Ibid., p. 33.

3. Lucien Perey [Clara Adèle Luce Herpin], *Le Roman du grand roi, Louis XIV et Marie Mancini d'après des lettres et documents inédits* (Paris: Calmann Lévy, 1894), p. 253.

4. Ibid., p. 189.

5. Pierre Adolphe Chéruel, ed., *Mémoires de Mademoiselle de Montpensier* (Paris: Charpentier, 1859), vol. 3, p. 387.

6. Guy Patin, *Lettres*, ed. Joseph-Henri Réveillé-Parise (Paris: Baillère, 1846), vol. 2, pp. 458–459.

7. Mancini, *Memoirs*, p. 36.

8. For an explanation of the monetary systems and their rough equivalents today, see Sarah Nelson's summary note in her translation of the Mancini memoirs, pp. 35–36.

9. Mancini, *Memoirs*, pp. 36–37.

10. Ibid., p. 41.

11. Ibid., pp. 43–44.

12. Georges Mongrédien, *Une aventurière au grand siècle, la duchesse Mazarin* (Paris: Amiot-Dumont, 1952), p. 49.

13. Ibid., pp. 44–45.

14. Saint-Simon, *Memoires*, ed. Yves Coirault (Paris: Gallimard, 1985), vol. 4, p. 561.

15. François de La Rochefoucauld, Maxim 503, in *The Maxims of François de La Rochefoucauld*, trans. F. G. Stevens (Oxford: Oxford University Press, 1943), p. 154.

16. Mancini, *Memoirs*, p. 47.

17. Ibid., p. 48.

18. Ibid., p. 51.

19. Ibid.

20.     Mazarin and Courcelles
        Are in a convent
        But they are too lovely
        To remain there long;
        If they are not freed
        We'll see no more laughter
        From the ladies, most surely.

21. Mancini, *Memoirs*, p. 52.

22. Madeleine de Scudéry, *The Story of Sapho*, trans. Karen Newman (Chicago: University of Chicago Press, 2003), pp. 140–141.

23. François Poullain de la Barre, "On the Equality of the Two Sexes," in *Three Cartesian Feminist Treatises*, ed. Marcelle Maistre Welch, trans. Vivien Bosley (Chicago: University of Chicago Press, 2002), p. 77.

24. Mancini, *Memoirs*, p. 52.

25. Ibid., p. 55.

26. Ibid., p. 56.

27. Ibid.

28. Ibid.

29. Ibid., p. 57.

30. Ibid., p. 58.

**CHAPTER 3   MARIE'S ROME**

1. Lucien Perey [Clara Adèle Luce Herpin], *Le Roman du grand roi, Louis XIV et Marie Mancini d'après des lettres et documents inédits* (Paris: Calmann Lévy, 1894), pp. 379–380.

2. François Poullain de la Barre, "On the Equality of the Two Sexes," in *Three Cartesian Feminist Treatises*, ed. Marcelle Maistre Welch, trans. Vivien Bosley (Chicago: University of Chicago Press, 2002), p. 55.

3. Claude Dulong, *Marie Mancini, la première passion de Louis XIV* (Paris: Perrin, 1993), p. 134.

4. Marie Mancini, *The Truth in Its Own Light, or: The Genuine Memoirs of M. Mancini, Constabless Colonna*, in Hortense Mancini and Marie Mancini, *Memoirs*, ed. and trans. Sarah Nelson (Chicago: University of Chicago Press, 2008), p. 106.

5. Perey, *Le Roman du grand roi*, vol. 2, pp. 573–574.

6. Lucien Perey [Clara Adèle Luce Herpin], *Une princesse romaine au xvlle siècle, Marie Mancini Colonna, d'après des documents inédits* (Paris: Calmann Lévy, 1896), p. 33.

7. Mancini, *Truth in Its Own Light*, p. 107.

8. Ibid., p. 108.

9. Quoted in Dulong, *Marie Mancini*, p. 137.

10. Mancini, *Truth in Its Own Light*, p. 113.

11. Ibid., pp. 113–114.

12. Jacques de Belbeuf, cited in *Dizionario biografico dei italiani* (Rome: Instituto della Enciclopedia italiana, 1961), p. 356.

13. Valeria De Lucca, "'Pallade al valor, Venere al volto': Music, Theatricality, and Performance in Marie Mancini Colonna's Patronage," in *The Wandering Life I Led: Essays on Hortense Mancini, Duchess Mazarin and Early Modern Women's Border-Crossings*, ed. Susan Shifrin (Cambridge, UK: Cambridge Scholars Publishing, 2009), p. 126.

14. Mancini, *Truth in Its Own Light*, p. 117. Penelope is the loyal wife of Ulysses who waits patiently for his return. Phryne is a Greek courtesan as famous for her beauty and sexual power as for her conversations with philosophers.

15. Mancini, *Truth in Its Own Light*, p. 130.

16. Per Burgstom, *Feast and Theatre in Queen Christina's Rome* (Stockholm: Nationalmusei skriftserie nr. 14, 1966), p. 81.

17. For example, the *Gazette de Leyde*, December 21, 1670. Quoted in Perey, *Une princesse romaine*, p. 101.

18. Perey, *Une princesse romaine*, p. 107.

## CHAPTER 4    A RUNAWAY DUCHESS

1. In Hortense Mancini and Marie Mancini, *Memoirs*, ed. and trans. Sarah Nelson (Chicago: University of Chicago Press, 2008), p. 61.

2. Ibid.

3. Ibid., p. 65.

4. Marie Mancini, *The Truth in Its Own Light, or: The Genuine Memoirs of M. Mancini, Constabless Colonna*, in *Memoirs*, Nelson, p. 119.

5. Mancini, *Memoirs*, p. 70.

6. Claude Dulong, *Marie Mancini, la première passion de Louis XIV* (Paris: Perrin, 1993), p. 162.

7. One of these rumors was that the Duchess Mazarin had become pregnant. A French traveler to Rome in 1669 described meeting her and noting that she was "five or six months pregnant." I am unaware of mention of this or of the birth of a child in any other documents. See Lucien Perey [Clara Adèle Luce Herpin], *Une princesse romaine, au xvlle siècle, Marie Mancini Colonna, d'après des documents inédits* (Paris: Calmann Lévy, 1896), p. 90.

8. Vatican Library Manuscripts, Barberini Latini collection, 6405 (henceforth Vatican, Barb. Lat.).

9. Francesco Petrucci, "A Brief Iconography of the Duchess Mazarin: Between Portrait and Allegory in Baroque Rome," in *The Wandering Life I Led: Essays on Hortense Mancini, Duchess Mazarin and Early Modern Women's Border-Crossings*, ed. Susan Shifrin (Cambridge, UK: Cambridge Scholars Publishing, 2009), p. 112.

10. Mancini, *Memoirs*, p. 70.

11. Vatican, Barb. Lat. 6404, March 22, 1670.

12. Ibid., p. 147.

13. Charles de Marguetel de Saint-Denis, seigneur de Saint-Évremond, *Mélange curieux des meilleures pièces* (Amsterdam: Pierre Mortier, 1706), vol. 2, p. 284.

14. Mancini, *Memoirs*, p. 29.

15. "Lament of the Statues," quoted in Patrick Michel, *Mazarin, prince des collectionneurs* (Paris: Editions de la réunion des musées nationaux, 1999), pp. 570–572.

16. Roger de Rabutin, Comte de Bussy, *Correspondance* (Paris: Charpentier, 1858), vol. 1, p. 331.

17. Ibid., p. 336.

18. Georges Mongrédien, *Une aventurière au grand siècle, la duchesse Mazarin* (Paris: Amiot-Dumont, 1952), pp. 84–85.

19. Ibid., p. 86.

20. Ibid., p. 88.

21. Mancini, *Memoirs,* p. 75.

22. Ibid., p. 75.

23. Monsieur de Lauzun, in Mancini, *Memoirs,* p. 76; letter from Madame de Scudéry to Bussy-Rabutin in *Correspondance de Roger de Rabutin*, vol. 1, p. 387.

24. Mancini, *Memoirs,* p. 76.

25. Ibid., pp. 76–77.

26. Marie de Rabutin Chantal, Marquise de Sévigné, *Correspondance,* ed. Roger Duchêne (Paris: Gallimard, 1973–1976), vol. 1, p. 170; Bussy-Rabutin, *Correspondance de Roger de Rabutin,* vol. 1, p. 388.

27. Vatican, Barb. Lat. 6405, October 11, 1670.

28. Ibid. 6406, March 14, 1671.

29. Mancini, *Truth in Its Own Light,* p. 125.

30. Ibid., p. 129.

31. Mancini, *Memoirs,* p. 78.

32. Mancini, *Truth in Its Own Light,* p. 128.

33. Mancini, *Memoirs,* p. 78.

## CHAPTER 5    ON THE ROAD

1. Marie Mancini, *The Truth in Its Own Light, or: The Genuine Memoirs of M. Mancini, Constabless Colonna*, in Hortense Mancini and Marie Mancini, *Memoirs,* ed. and trans. Sarah Nelson (Chicago: University of Chicago Press, 2008), p. 130.

2. Colonna Archive, Biblioteca Statale Santa Scolastica, Subiaco, Italy. Letter dated August 1, 1672.

3. Ibid., letter dated October 14, 1672.

4. Mancini, *Truth in Its Own Light,* p. 130.

5. Ibid.

6. Ibid.

7. Ibid., p. 131.

8. Hortense Mancini, *Memoirs,* in Nelson, *Memoirs,* p. 80.

9. Claude Dulong, *Marie Mancini, la première passion de Louis XIV* (Paris: Perrin, 1993), p. 191.

10. Mancini, *Truth in Its Own Light,* p. 135.

11. Mancini, *Memoirs,* p. 80.

12. Roger de Rabutin, Comte de Bussy, *Correspondance* (Paris: Charpentier, 1858), vol. 2, pp. 127–128.

13. Colonna Archive, letter dated June 10, 1672.

14. Ibid., letter dated November 1672.

15. Ibid., letter dated January 1672. Translated by Giovanna Suhl. Published in Marie Mancini, *La Vérité dans son jour*, ed. Patricia F. Cholakian and Elizabeth C. Goldsmith (Delmar, NY: Scholars' Facsimiles and Reprints, 1998), p. 95.

16. Mancini, *Truth in Its Own Light*, p. 137.

17. Ibid.

18. Colonna Archive, letter dated June 19, 1672.

19. Ibid., letter dated July 14, 1672.

20. Dulong, *Marie Mancini*, pp. 203–204.

21. Ibid., p. 207.

22. Mancini, *Truth in Its Own Light*, p. 138.

23. Lucien Perey [Clara Adèle Luce Herpin], *Une princesse romaine, au xvlle siècle, Marie Mancini Colonna, d'après des documents inédits* (Paris: Calmann Lévy, 1896), p. 156.

24. Mancini, *Truth in Its Own Light*, p. 138.

25. Ibid., p. 139.

26. Ibid.

27. Ibid., pp. 140–141.

28. Ibid., p. 142.

29. Bussy-Rabutin, *Correspondance*, vol. 2, pp. 452–453.

30. Perey, *Une princesse romaine*, p. 180.

31. Colonna Archive, undated letter (August 1672).

32. Ibid., letter dated September 1672.

33. Mancini, *Truth in Its Own Light*, p. 144.

**CHAPTER 6   SAVOY AND BEYOND**

1. A. D. Perrero, "La Duchessa Ortensia Mazzarino e la Principessa Maria Colonna, sorelle Mancini, ed il Duca Carlo Emanuele II di Savoia," in *Curiosita e recherché di storia subalpina*, vol. 1, p. 18.

2. Georges Mongrédien, *Une aventurière au grand siècle, la duchesse Mazarin* (Paris: Amiot-Dumont, 1952), p. 107.

3. Colonna Archive, Biblioteca Statale Santa Scolastica, Subiaco, Italy. Letter dated October 14, 1672.

4. Mongrédien, *Une aventurière au grand siècle*, p. 104.

5. Marie Mancini, *The Truth in Its Own Light, or: The Genuine Memoirs of M. Mancini, Constabless Colonna*, in Hortense Mancini and

Marie Mancini, *Memoirs,* ed. and trans. Sarah Nelson (Chicago: University of Chicago Press, 2008), p. 147.

6. Letter to Duke Mazarin quoted in Mongrédien, *Une aventurière au grand siècle,* p. 111.

7. César de Saint-Réal, *Oeuvres de Mr. L'Abbé de Saint-Réal* (La Haye: Frères Vaillant et Nicolas Prévost, 1722), vol. 3, p. 322.

8. Ibid., p. 324.

9. Ibid., p. 319.

10. Hortense Mancini, *Memoirs,* in Nelson, *Memoirs,* p. 27.

11. Ibid., p. 81.

12. Mongrédien, *Une aventurière au grand siècle,* p. 121.

13. Colonna Archive, letter dated October 29, 1672.

14. Claude Dulong, *Marie Mancini, la première passion de Louis XIV* (Paris: Perrin, 1993), p. 228.

15. Colonna Archive, letter dated May 17, 1673.

16. Ibid., letter dated April 19, 1673.

17. The expression "six candelabras" indicates thirty years of age. Candelabras, or "lustres," contained five candles each.

18. Mancini, *Truth in Its Own Light,* p. 153.

19. Ibid.

20. Ibid.

21. Colonna Archive, letter incorrectly dated January 5, 1673 (correct date was 1674).

22. These letters, now housed in the Colonna Archive, may have been intercepted and delivered to Lorenzo, thus never reaching the Duke of Savoy.

23. Colonna Archive, letter dated March 17, 1674. Nicolas Fouquet was imprisoned in 1661 in a citadel off the coast of Brittany, after being convicted of abusing his position as royal treasurer to enrich himself.

24. Mancini, *Truth in Its Own Light,* p. 158.

25. Colonna Archive, letter dated March 17, 1674. "Cornettes" were the starched white hats typically worn by women in Savoy.

26. Lucien Perey [Clara Adèle Luce Herpin], *Une princesse romaine, au xvlle siècle, Marie Mancini Colonna, d'après des documents inédits* (Paris: Calmann Lévy, 1896), p. 333.


## CHAPTER 7   HORTENSE'S LONDON

1. Marie de Rabutin-Chantal, Marquise de Sévigné, *Correspondance,* ed. Roger Duchêne (Paris: Gallimard, 1973–1976), vol. 2, p. 169.

2. Marie-Sidonie de Lenoncourt, Marquise de Courcelles, *Mémoires et correspondance*, ed. Paul Pougin (Paris: P. Jannet, 1855), pp. 105–107.

3. Charles de Saint-Evremond, *Oeuvres en prose*, ed. René Ternois (Paris: Didier, 1966), vol. 4, p. 243.

4. "A Coffee-house Conversation," in *Calendar of State Papers, Domestic Series* (March 1, 1675–February 29, 1676), ed. F. H. Blackburne (London: Mackie and Co., 1907), vol. 17, p. 474.

5. Georges Mongrédien, *Une aventurière au grand siècle, la duchesse Mazarin* (Paris: Amiot-Dumont, 1952), pp. 127–128.

6. Ibid., p. 129

7. Ibid., p. 130.

8. Ibid., p. 133.

9. Ibid., p. 134.

10. Hortense Mancini, *Memoirs,* in Hortense Mancini and Marie Mancini, *Memoirs,* ed. and trans. Sarah Nelson (Chicago: Chicago University Press, 2008), p. 31.

11. Denys Potts, "The Duchess Mazarin and Saint-Évremond: The Final Journey," in *The Wandering Life I Led: Essays on Hortense Mancini, Duchess Mazarin and Early Modern Women's Border-Crossings,* ed. Susan Shifrin (Cambridge, UK: Cambridge Scholars Publishing, 2009), p. 170.

12. Marie-Catherine Le Jumel de Barneville, Comtesse d'Aulnoy, *Mémoires de la cour d'Angleterre* (Paris: Barbin, 1695), pp. 2–3.

13. Marie-Catherine Desjardins de Villedieu, *Histoire de la vie d'Henriette-Sylvie de Molière* (Paris, 1672–1674).

14. Charles de Saint-Evremond, *Oraison funèbre de Madame la Duchesse Mazarin*, in *Oeuvres choisies* (Paris: Garnier, 1867), p. 392.

15. Potts, "The Duchess Mazarin and Saint-Évremond," p. 161.

16. Anthony Hamilton, *Memoirs of Count Grammont* (Edinburgh: John Grant, 1908), vol. 1, p. 197.

17. Ibid.

18. Cited in *Dictionary of National Biography* entry on Saint-Evremond.

19. *The Works of Monsieur de Saint-Evremond* (London: J. Darby and A. Battesworth, 1728), vol. 2, pp. 207–208.

20. Charles de Saint-Evremond, *Oeuvres en prose*, ed. René Ternois (Paris: Didier, 1962), vol. 3, p. 332.

21. Courcelles, *Mémoires et correspondance*, p. 279.

22. Mongrédien, *Une aventurière au grand siècle*, p. 146.

23. Charles de Saint-Evremond, *Lettres,* ed. René Ternois (Paris: Didier, 1968), vol. 1, p. 381.

24. Ibid., p. 392.

25. Mongrédien, *Une aventurière au grand siècle,* p. 163.

26. Ibid., p. 165.

27. Marie de Rabutin-Chantal, Marquise de Sévigné, *Correspondance,* ed. Roger Duchêne (Paris: Gallimard, 1973-1978), vol. 3, p. 161.

28. John Evelyn, *Diary and Correspondence* (London: H. Colburn, 1850), vol. 2, p. 210.

**CHAPTER 8   MADRID**

1. Marie Mancini, *The Truth in Its Own Light, or: The Genuine Memoirs of M. Mancini, Constabless Colonna,* in Hortense Mancini and Marie Mancini, *Memoirs,* ed. and trans. Sarah Nelson (Chicago: University of Chicago Press, 2008), p. 161.

2. Lucien Perey [Clara Adèle Luce Herpin], *Une princesse romaine, au xvlle siècle, Marie Mancini Colonna, d'après des documents inédits* (Paris: Calmann Lévy, 1896), pp. 343–344.

3. Marie-Catherine le Jumel de Barneville, Comtesse d'Aulnoy, *Relation du voyage d'Espagne,* ed. Maria Seguin (Paris: Desjonquères, 2005), p. 233.

4. Ibid., pp. 215–216.

5. Colonna Archive, Biblioteca Statale Santa Scolastica, Subiaco, Italy. Letter dated June 26, 1675.

6. Perey, *Une princesse romaine,* pp. 350–351.

7. Mancini, *Truth in Its Own Light,* p. 162.

8. Colonna Archive, letter dated October 2, 1674.

9. Perey, *Une princesse romaine,* p. 368.

10. Mancini, *Truth in Its Own Light,* p. 162.

11. Colonna Archive, letter dated March 5, 1675.

12. Colonna Archive, letter dated March 26, 1675.

13. Colonna Archive, letter dated June 12, 1675. Translated by Giovanna Suhl and published in Marie Mancini, *La Vérité dans son jour,* ed. Patricia F. Cholakian and Elizabeth C. Goldsmith (Delmar, NY: Scholars' Facsimiles and Reprints, 1998), p. 97.

14. Ibid.

15. Colonna Archive, letter dated August 7, 1675. Translated by Giovanna Suhl and published in Mancini, *La Vérité dans son jour,* p. 100.

16. Hortense Mancini, *Memoirs,* in Nelson, *Memoirs,* p. 27.

17. Anonymous, *Mémoires de M.L.P.M.M. Colonne, G. connétable du royaume de Naples,* published as Marie Mancini, *Cendre et poussière,* ed. Maurice Lever (Paris: Le Comptoir, 1997), p. 33.

18. Ibid., pp. 33–34.

19. Ibid., p. 47.

20. Ibid., p. 49.

21. Mancini, *Truth in Its Own Light,* pp. 83–84.

22. Colonna Archive, letter dated March 4, 1677.

23. Mancini, *Truth in Its Own Light,* p. 92.

24. Ibid., p. 92.

25. Ibid., pp. 162–163.

26. Colonna Archive, letter dated September 13, 1677.

27. Ibid., letter dated March 19, 1677.

28. Ibid., letter dated August 2, 1677.

29. Ibid., letter dated March 17, 1677.

30. Claude Dulong, *Marie Mancini, la première passion de Louis XIV* (Paris: Perrin, 1993), p. 275.

## CHAPTER 9   DIVORCE

1. Toivo Rosvall, *The Mazarine Legacy: The Life of Hortense Mancini, Duchess Mazarin* (New York: Viking, 1966), p. 204.

2. Ibid., p. 205.

3. Marie de Rabutin-Chantal, Marquise de Sévigné, *Correspondance,* ed. Roger Duchêne (Paris: Gallimard, 1973–1976), vol. 3, p. 665.

4. Claude Erard, *Plaidoyé touchant la demande faite par monsieur le duc de Mazarin pour obliger madame la duchesse de Mazarin son epouse de revenir avec luy, après une longue absence, & de quitter l'Angleterre où elle est présentement* (Toulouse: J. J. Boude, 1690), pp. 7, 18.

5. Ibid., pp. 17–18.

6. Ibid., p. 19.

7. Charles de Saint-Evremond, "Factum pour Madame la Duchesse Mazarin, contre Monsieur le Duc Mazarin son mari," in *Oeuvres choisies,* ed. A. C. Gidel (Paris: Garnier, 1867), pp. 17, 20.

8. Rosvall, *The Mazarine Legacy,* p. 206.

9. Charles de Saint-Evremond, *Lettres,* ed. René Ternois (Paris: Didier, 1968), vol. 2, pp. 147–148.

10. Ibid., vol. 2, pp. 155–156.

11. Lucien Perey [Clara Adèle Luce Herpin], *Une princesse romaine, au xvlle siècle, Marie Mancini Colonna, d'après des documents inédits* (Paris: Calmann Lévy, 1896), p. 398.

12. Colonna Archive, Biblioteca Statale Santa Scolastica, Subiaco, Italy. Letter dated February 1679.

13. Ibid.

14. Ibid., letter dated January 6, 1679.

15. An "agnus dei" is a circular medal made of wax, imprinted with the figure of a lamb and blessed by the pope. Colonna Archive, letter dated March 18, 1679.

16. Ibid., letter dated January 21, 1679.

17. Madame de Villars, *Lettres de Madame la Marquise de Villars, Ambassadrice en Espagne, dans le temps du mariage de Charles II Roi d'Espagne* (Paris: Michel Lambert, 1759), p. 70.

18. Ibid., p. 67.

19. Perey, *Une princesse romaine*, p. 418.

20. Ibid., pp. 423–424.

21. Colonna Archive, letter dated November 18, 1680.

22. Ibid., letter dated December 24, 1680.

23. Ibid., letter dated December 4, 1680.

24. Marie-Catherine d'Aulnoy, *Memoirs of the Court of Spain* (London: Horn, Saunders and Bennet, 1692), vol. 2, pp. 173–174.

25. Perey, *Une princesse romaine*, p. 436.

26. Claude Dulong, *Marie Mancini, la première passion de Louis XIV* (Paris: Perrin, 1993), p. 313.

27. Ibid., pp. 317–318.

28. Perey, *Une princesse romaine*, p. 466.

29. Ibid., p. 468.

30. *Mercure historique et politique* (La Haye: Henry Van Dulderen, 1689), vol. 6, p. 609.

31. Dulong, *Marie Mancini*, p. 326.


**CHAPTER 10 "DUST AND ASHES"**

1. Charles de Saint-Evremond, *Lettres*, ed. René Ternois (Paris: Didier, 1968), vol. 2, p. 203.

2. Colonna Archive, Biblioteca Statale Santa Scolastica, Subiaco, Italy. Letter dated July 26, 1692.

3. Saint-Evremond, *Lettres*, vol. 2, pp. 235–236.

4. Ibid., p. 251.

5. Ibid., p. 281.

6. Ibid., p. 301.

7. *Mercure historique et politique*, vol. 27 (1699), p. 108.

8. Colonna Archive, letter dated March 26, 1689.

9. Ibid., letter dated August 1692.

10. Ibid., letter dated June 17, 1693.

11. Ibid., letter dated simply "Paris, 1704."

12. Lucien Perey [Clara Adèle Luce Herpin], *Une princesse romaine, au xvlle siècle, Marie Mancini Colonna, d'après des documents inédits* (Paris: Calmann Lévy, 1896),
p. 521.

13. Ibid., p. 522.

14. It is not known with certainty what became of the Marie Mancini pearl necklace. It is rumored to have been reacquired in the late twenti-eth century by the Colonna family.

15. Susan Shifrin, ed., *Re-framing Representations of Women* (Alder-shot, UK, and Burlington, VT: Ashgate, 2008), p. 200.

# INDEX

ELIZABETH C. GOLDSMITH is a professor of French at Boston University. She has written books on literature in the age of Louis XIV, focusing on women's writing and letter correspondences. She teaches courses on seventeenth-century theater and the novel, travel writing, and historical fiction.

PublicAffairs is a publishing house founded in 1997. It is a tribute to the standards, values, and flair of three persons who have served as mentors to countless reporters, writers, editors, and book people of all kinds, including me.

I. F. STONE, proprietor of *I. F. Stone's Weekly*, combined a commitment to the First Amendment with entrepreneurial zeal and reporting skill and became one of the great independent journalists in American history. At the age of eighty, Izzy published *The Trial of Socrates*, which was a national bestseller. He wrote the book after he taught himself ancient Greek.

BENJAMIN C. BRADLEE was for nearly thirty years the charismatic editorial leader of *The Washington Post*. It was Ben who gave the *Post* the range and courage to pursue such historic issues as Watergate. He supported his reporters with a tenacity that made them fearless and it is no accident that so many became authors of influential, best-selling books.

ROBERT L. BERNSTEIN, the chief executive of Random House for more than a quarter century, guided one of the nation's premier publishing houses. Bob was personally responsible for many books of political dissent and argument that challenged tyranny around the globe. He is also the founder and longtime chair of Human Rights Watch, one of the most respected human rights organizations in the world.

·　　·　　·

For fifty years, the banner of Public Affairs Press was carried by its owner Morris B. Schnapper, who published Gandhi, Nasser, Toynbee, Truman, and about 1,500 other authors. In 1983, Schnapper was described by *The Washington Post* as "a redoubtable gadfly." His legacy will endure in the books to come.

Peter Osnos, *Founder and Editor-at-Large*